Endorsements for
The Last Romantic War

"Less and more than a memoir, *The Last Romantic War*'s collection of fifty-plus vignettes, jetsam and flotsam, profiles, and WWII memorabilia is a treasure trove of the 'good' war. It restores an ambiance that is missing elsewhere. His colorful prose dramatizes those memorable moments as if you might have been there too. I was his shipmate and even more, his friend."

—Edward Anthony Green, C M, 3/C, Designer of Mitchell Field Museum, Milwaukee and Great Lakes Naval Air Museum

"*The Last Romantic War* is a book the author said 'had to be written,' and I say it ought to be read. It should surprise and touch you as it did me."

—Lt.(jg) Hudson Deming, Communications Officer

"If you want a readable piece of WWII nostalgia, you will enjoy the fifty-plus vignettes. I did, and was there with him in his 'mainly true' tales."

—Lt.(jg) Jim McNelis, Deck Officer

"*The Last Romantic War* warmed my military memory and heart. The stories and memorabilia will please anyone interested in WWII ambiance."

—*Lt. Lloyd Logan, Anti-submarine War Officer*

"True, I stopped the eleven-ship convoy when I 'fell' overboard north of New Guinea, October, 1944. But I'm on board with this book. Now and then I read my gift copy and revisit those places. There was hell to pay, but we were young and came back topside. Ah, liberty! Dem wuz the days, my friends."

—*Frank Trupiano, S 1/C*

The Last Romantic War

A BLIND DATE WITH HISTORY

Anthony Gianunzio

Black Lake Press
TELL YOUR STORY
BLACKLAKEPRESS.COM

Black Lake Press
TELL YOUR STORY
BLACKLAKEPRESS.COM

Cover design by Courtney Van De Burg.

Published by Black Lake Press of Holland, Michigan.
Black Lake Press is a division of Black Lake Studio, LLC.
Direct inquiries to Black Lake Press at
www.blacklakepress.com.

ISBN 978-0-9883373-7-4

Dedication

In a most personal way, my wife Carolyn has been an excellent "un-silent," "in-house partner" who offered creative criticism graciously, persistently supported me, and was that one good reader E.E. Cummings wanted.

I dedicate *The Last Romantic War* to you, *Carolina mia.*

Table of Contents

Acknowledgements

When one is past eighty, experience, intelligence, and imagination should finally be finding their roles. I credit all three with realizing that this first attempt belongs mainly to my parents, who enjoyed a fulfilling life in these promising states of America. Nunzio and Isabella (d'Alphonso) Gianunzio raised eleven children, I being their seventh son. America offered the promise of a dream and freedom of opportunity.

I wish to thank, posthumously, military brothers Rudolph, John, and Fiore, each of whom served with distinction in the U.S. Army. Their service certainly made this book possible, as did my shipmates, a ready, sturdy, and varied bunch of 242 men, with their contributions at reunions (1989-2000). Some vignettes originated via conversations (on tape); many more remain "out of reach."

From its unlikely start, *The Last Romantic War* seemed destined. Several of my shipmates merely suggested that I write "our" book. It barely survived its birth but quickly found maturity in its romantic view of WWII. And then, by the strangest story of chance, it reached the right and "perfect" publisher/editor/writer, Greg Smith, and editor Jami VanderKooi of Black Lake Studio & Press. Artist/designer Sarah Brummels' historical perspective is just right. "Our" book quickly evolved into "my (romantic view)" book and then into an American microcosm. I must thank Richard Crispo, who directed me their way.

Preface

There was a war, a real war, but dressed in romantic clothing. I remember its ambiance and not just the logistics that often pass as history. Facts are but the residue of truth: the romantic spirit can't be contained within the deadly corridors of mere fact. These cameos of unforgettable times, people, and places are meant for the heart, not the head.

When I reminisce of my youthful Iron Mountain days, the usual landmarks dot the memory maps in my mind. But I soon switch to people. Then, swiftly, the nicknames pour over the dam of time. Who in Iron Mountain can forget "Hutsa" Soderberg, "Fungo" Tedeschi, "Web" Jacobson, "Rube" Caruso, "Frosty" Ferzacca, "Trotsky" Lindholm, "Bunzie" Rahoi, "Mudchuck" Manko, "Swamp" Tomassoni, "Yutch" Belhumeur, "Scrap Iron" Benda, "Smiley" O'Neil, "Ceedy" Richardson, "Abba" Bartolameoli, "Totters" Echolm, "Tape" Eugizzi, and a hundred or more.

Those nicknames, artistically corny as they were, brought us together, softened the cultural differences among us. We became WWII men after a dozen years of depression. It disciplined us, and coming together softened the stress. Small wonder that baseball became our national game, a super blend of the individual playing within the group and respecting the rules of the game.

WWII was a righteous war, but to me, even more than this. Its shadowy charm lingered, unforgettably, setting the stage for surprising appearances. Perhaps I can save something of those

Anthony Gianunzio

days when everything was clear and marvelous and personal and then suddenly muddied. The camaraderie of ship's company, the charm of exotic places, and the upbeat music of the Big Bands. We had heroes and the spirit of a growing-up country, of men and women. All of these and much more remain firm in my memory. Here is how I, "Buzz," recall it.

Blind Date

The summer of '42 had promised me the best of days. Then, suddenly, my world turns upside down. Tojo's rape-date of Pearl on December seven turns my halcyon world into "a date which will live in infamy..."

Youth had seemed a forever gift, and now all of it was being taken away. I have some weeks to savor and adjust my fantasy-dream of big league baseball. I am still nineteen, and it was only a few days after being chosen by the Chicago Cubs at a tryout camp in Janesville, Wisconsin, that their letter turned my world upside down. It read, "Because of the lowering of the draft age to nineteen..."

Uncle Sam's letter followed soon after. The summer of '42 would be played as an Iron Mountain Ranger rather than as a try-out rookie at Wrigley Field. Gone are my thirty days to make good. In just sixty days it is enlist or answer to the Draft Board.

The firm successes of Midway and Guadalcanal are hopeful, and I sometimes daydream of those places while tossing a stone into the outfield from my position at the keystone sack. But I squeeze something of adulthood into that period of grace, tasting my first beer and enjoying the last joyful song of the summer, "The Beer Barrel Polka." Other songs are tender and I feel indestructible, but the summer is bittersweet and already nostalgic.

Much like hundreds of young men from my home town and neighboring small towns who are first generational, I see little wrong with America, even if the country is in a disastrous depression. My childhood is memorable. Being the seventh son and tenth child in a family of eleven offers me countless experiences. Going to war like millions of others are doing seems the right thing, almost the good thing. "All's Quiet On The Western Front" and "Peg-leg Pete" are enough for me to know that this war will not be child's play. I am idealistic, patriotic, and my sense of duty somehow numbs my exciting ambition to pitch for the Chicago Cubs.

The love of my boyhood life—baseball and star players like Bullet Bob Feller, Dizzy Dean, Gabby Hartnett, Joe Di Maggio, Carl Hubbel, Prince Hal Schumaker and so many others—I will dutifully put on hold. Love of any hometown girl will also have to wait. All's fair in war will be load enough. To add the arrow of love would hardly be fair for either of us.

Tomorrow, my dreams could sink into a nightmare of who knows what. And before that gigantic step, I must find a way to say goodbye. Life so far has been a perpetual "so long and take it easy." I am surprised when after dinner my sister Mary and my father approach me with purpose written all over their faces.

"Son," he says as solemnly as his priesthood training and education at San Giovanni Seminary in Italy have prepared him, "this is for you."

Mary then says, "It's a prayer in Latin. I sewed this cloth around it to protect it, and you shouldn't open it until after the war and you're home. He wrote the same prayer for Fiore, too." My dad, who's never at a loss for words, waits for mine.

"Pa, paper doesn't cover bullets; it covers rocks." I am referring to the childhood game of scissors, rocks, and paper, trying to take the edge off what I know is a subtle act of love. He is quick to respond.

"Never mind, son. You keep this with you, and you will always be safe." It is more than fatherly advice. I know better than to disobey his offer. Sleep is a stranger that night.

In the early afternoon of October 26, 1942, when I am sure that none of the family other than my mother will be around for that "temporary goodbye," I finally say ciao to my mother, who had sat quietly, too quietly, with me for many minutes. She has dreaded this day, I know, dreaded sending a fourth son into a far-off war, dutifully disappearing. She too had done as much, leaving bella Italia behind, never to return. She had borne eleven children, and now they were swiftly scattering as if a magician were pulling some unseeable strings.

At the kitchen table I can sense her wondering if she has done enough for me as a mother, but she will not show any sign of emotional pain, lest it affect me. I try to avoid showing my mother my deeper feelings and even kid her about "being home for Christmas." Nothing can be harder than worrying that she would worry too much about me since I am her youngest son. Her blue eyes, still young, are moist. My tears are somewhere near my heart. She has loved me from the start, for she named me Idolo, probably after the figures that embellish cathedrals and churches of renaissance Italy.

"Retorno. Fa presto," she says.

Carrying a small duffel bag, I walk down the smooth path where the old train tracks lead to highway US 2, Iron Mountain's main drag. I cross the two flooded mine pits via a wooden walk and then walk seven blocks through downtown to the railroad station, where I will board the Chippewa train. I'm as alone as I have ever been.

The next day, October 27, 1942, I march miles on Chicago's State Street to celebrate Navy Day. Three years or the duration plus six months—my blind date with history!

Boots, Spuds, and... Reveille!

I am a nameless "boot," 609766, seaman second class, USCGR, October 27, 1942. The action is everywhere else. The Marines are hanging in there, semper fi, on Guadalcanal, and the army is learning desert warfare in Africa against the Desert Fox, General Rommel. Everything from here on in will be brand new to me. I'm as ready as anyone my age, also as alone, even with a couple dozen enlistees on the train, bus, and finally an open stake truck into western Michigan.

A chilling truck ride confirms my notion of the military life: expect every expectation. We empty the truck, our youthful legs half numb as we hit the dirt. The sight is a panorama of nature. I'm not too surprised to find a mansion on the hillside overlooking a vigorous lake, its steep shores clothed in color.

"Alright you boots, line up. Answer with 'aye, sir.'" The squat, big-shouldered petty officer even pronounces my name right! We march in double column down to the lake, to the boat house. It's my first sense of belonging, and it's a good feeling. I'm finally in it, the war to stop the maniacs who threaten our freedom.

Our temporary haven, the W.K. Kellogg manor at Gull Lake, is just 12 miles from Kalamazoo, Michigan. It's on loan from the cereal magnate as an induction center, but corn flakes aren't on the menu. Our boat-house quarters suggests a modern day first-class serfdom, but the grounds and lake are idyllic. Road marches, hitting the ditch sans weapons, are mere time killers. Even our drill instructor, CPO Perelli, is O.K.

The Last Romantic War

This beginning is too good to be true. In just two weeks, it's smack into boot camp, a dozen cabins on the shore of Pine Lake, 25 miles north of Kalamazoo. Gone are the last few days of a golden autumn. Here the word is *Semper Paratus*. The Coast Guard says so.

It's a brand-new world, and it begins ugly: reveille! Now, this is more like it. I do have a name, or rather a nickname, but names hardly matter here except at mail call. If something's important, it's "Hey you, Mac." I've asked the six other enlistees in our cabin to call me "Buzz." That's a lot better than having them butcher *Idolo,* which transforms into something that sounds like *Etelo*. It's what one wears on his sleeve that counts here, not what's in a name.

There's no gold braid around, just those chevrons on the arm. One stripe will do. No hash marks in sight, either. These one-, two-, three-stripers are in the deck force; they are ship's company, and they act like know-it-all demigods during exercises, obstacle course work-outs, swimming, and maintaining discipline. I suspect they like the authority, and with no commissioned officers around, they are at least semi-gods. Luckily, we outnumber them fifty to one, as if it matters.

We're full of shots. Almost recklessly, I've been stabbed in the right shoulder, and my innocent arteries now contain twentieth-century guardians against typhoid, tetanus, and who-knows-what-else. They must think this a way of asserting their authority. The pain and soreness are plenty convincing. After this military needling, a bastardly, recorded bugler pierces our dream bubbles with reveille the next morning. Time moves like lightning when duty calls. In less than moments, a burly bosun breaks into our cabin quarters, shouting his own uncensored verbal reveille. We scramble to wash at the head, the toilet facility.

Then, after surviving a chow line a block long in the cold early November air, we are face-to-face with what passes for chow. Most of the stuff is recognizable, but beans on large slices of toast seems wrong. A chow line watch dog says, "That shit on a shingle is good for ya. Lots of protein." I don't like the look of it, and I don't like the naval nomenclature. Besides, beans give me gas, but I take a slice just to stay on the safe side. No sooner than our plates are cleared, the noncoms are after us again.

"Company C, report to the lake for pulling oars. On the double!"

My right shoulder, something I've always taken great care of as a pitcher, is throbbing. Just what I need. This exercise I don't need, and I know we're not going to win the war in long rowboats. After half an hour I wish that I'd enlisted in the air corps, but I'm not too comfortable with heights, either. In the long, crocodile-shaped boats we try to catch the coxswain's rhythmic count, and sometimes we succeed. Our accidental synchronization with his command seems to justify our being on water. We know better. It's an ultimate relief to boat oars, and we say nothing when our little Napoleon says, "You boots getting' the hang o' it? Fall out." Maybe handling the heavy oars did hurry up the absorbing of the inoculations and speed the return to normalcy, but this is a heavy-handed way to go about it. I'm not looking forward to any more of this superman stuff. Morning calisthenics and running is a snap, but 16-foot oars?

There's a lot of motion at camp, and most of it is physical. After all, most of us are still in our teens. Learning to tie different knots requires some swift dexterity. Moving from one class to another every half hour keeps us stimulated and unthreatened. Even mail call has its moments of theater.

Our theater is the drill ground where we spend an hour, maybe more if our ineptness demands it. Then a strange shout.

The Last Romantic War

"Mail call!" Will that girlfriend, sweetheart, mom, or buddy back home drop a line, or even a letter? Maybe a fruitcake, even? I expect very little; my older sister had kept the family informed about my three brothers in service. Besides, I'm only 500 miles from home, and the story is that we get a ten day leave after boot camp.

A petty officer second class with a booming voice calls out the mail winners. A catalog of names begins as the mail-caller sings out and hands fly up. Sometimes it borders on poetry, sometimes comedy. Sometimes it's even pathetic when the letter doesn't come. Our mail-caller knows phonics, and his diction is stage-worthy, "Allemotta, Amalfitano, Anstottler, Achstoitler." The hands go up, but where in heaven do these names come from! America, I'm sure, is a land of variety. My own moniker fits right in. Familiar names ring out. "Buballa, Bubinski, Buttenfeld." I know he won't mispronounce my name. Gianunzio, that's easy. Easy as DiMaggio. Yeah, sure. Pity the axis mail-caller who runs into a variety like this! We are a mongrel nation, Adolph Hitler says. *Says who?* I say. Well, we're the nation of Lindberg, Ruth, Crosetti, Foxx, Louis, Greenberg, Feller—and that's just a few of the greats in our "lesser world." Ford, Edison, Firestone, Rockerfeller, Carnegie, Vanderbilt, in our recent past; Franklin, Jefferson, Washington, Lincoln, Adams (John and Samuel), D. Scott. Literature, law, architecture, artists. These United States are loaded with great achievers, and all in a mere two hundred or so years.

After three weeks and no good military news other than our Marines holding Henderson Airfield on Guadalcanal with a brand-new and undersized navy, we hear some good news: we get our first liberty. So long, days of equality in bootdom; liberty at last! My GI dress blues are in my sea bag, and they need airing. Their mothball aroma leaps at me when I unroll and press them. We're headed for Kalamazoo. "I've got a gal in Kalamazoo... Don't wanna boast, but I know she's the toast of Kalamazoo." Tex Bennecke sings it as it ought to be sung. I'm not looking for a gal in Kalamazoo, at least not one that will stick to my ribs, so to speak. Entering the Club Hollywood, the local night spot, I see a swarm of army GIs from Fort Custer who overwhelm the place. I elbow my way to the bar and finally get a Miller High Life without showing any I.D. Every booth is fully commandeered and the dance floor packed. The music is swinging and the only rotten thing is the ratio of servicemen to women, something like thirty to one. I can't even get to a booth, let alone a gal. There's nothing but army brass and a handful of blue jackets. But even if it's only the illusion of liberty, it feels good. Just hearing the hit songs is heartwarming; the band is well-stocked with a piano, a couple of saxes, a clarinet, a trombone, and a drum. They've done String of Pearls, In the Mood, and all the favorites.

I decide to take in a movie at the Michigan Theater on the main drag. The movie is mediocre, but there's a good song in it: "White Christmas." It goes like this: "I'm dreaming of a white Christmas... Just like the ones I used to know." For awhile, I recognize a feeling I've never felt before: a touch of homesickness. It had never occurred to me that there would be reason to look back. Being young and outgoing, you look ahead, not behind. Action is in the now and the future, not in the past. I've lost track of baseball. My friends and almost everyone I know are in the service. It's where we ought to be, so what's the use of longing for a semi-deserted place?

I've also had enough of "fall in," "cadence count," "on the double," and the phantom bugler. It comes as no surprise when we find out it's a recording played over the P.A. System. I have to admit it's effective and even well-played. Further, his taps is an even better piece of music, but not to my ears. Autumn is faithful to us, and the leaves hang on in the sunlit skies. It's early November and escape from boot camp finally comes.

"THE FOLLOWING MEN PACK YOUR SEA BAGS." My name is actually a sign that something knows that I exist. Boot camp didn't get me in shape; it actually eased me down into mediocrity. I helped more than one guy keep from falling. Baseball had fine-tuned me.

By mid-afternoon we're at St. Mary's Lake near Battle Creek, only 30 miles or so away. We soon find out why we've been sent to this idyllic lake and its hillside cabin quarters: the Coast Guard needs gunnery officers! Our Atlantic shipping is being sunk left and right, and their Coast Guard gun crews are going down with them. Seems that because I had taken algebra, solid geometry, and physics, I might be trainable. Nobody asked me, of course, whether I wanted the job—or would it be a *position?* Hah! *C'est le guerre,* maybe. Well, at least I'm now out of boot camp, even if I'm only a seaman second class. There is no seaman third class rating.

St. Mary's Lake snugs into a hilly, forested shore, and a dozen cabins house us escaped recruits. A tan, two-story brick building shelters ship's company. This is a return not to paradise but to civilization, at least. Noon day chow confirms my hunch. My temporary ecstasy is shattered by the bulletin board, where my name appears again, this time in small letters, perhaps signifying that this publicity is being grudgingly granted. I'm still a nobody, but the "body" part of me is wanted. "THE FOLLOWING REPORT FOR KP DUTY AT 19:00." Seven p.m. On the dot, it implied.

This definitely isn't boot camp. Although I had escaped the terror of kitchen police duty over at Pine Lake, tonight there will be potato peelings galore. KP duty has a bad reputation. Visions of huge spuds dance around my head sprouting "eye" sores. I have a machete and keep hacking away at them, but they keep swirling around me. Everything I've eaten at chow has lost its homey taste.

Even the title KP is a misnomer. We soon find out that we are the police-ees, not -ers. A cook-like creature flaunts a smirking smile and hands us large paring knives, leads us to three million-gallon galvanized tubs which are about five feet deep and four feet in diameter. We don't need math for this; we need fortitude and dexterity of digits.

"Get these spuds peeled by eight bells. D' ya hear me, Mac? He addresses us as if we are a collection, an entity, and he doesn't want to personalize it lest, perhaps, we remember him on liberty. From hopefuls we fall into the hopeless category in just one short day! There must be a thousand spuds in these vats. All four of us look at each other, and silence breaks out. There's nothing to do now but plow on, or rather, peel it off. But this monstrous chore is not appealing, a pun I keep to myself for fear that it won't be swallowed. We settle into a routine, hoping our efficiency will shorten this eternal hell, and trade off tubs—anything to ease the monotony. I come very near to developing a mild case of spudophobia. I've always enjoyed fried potatoes for breakfast, but now I even feel a bit mad at the Irish. If the cook's Irish, we'll make stew of him. Well, maybe.

We're working our butts off, our buts, too. Cookie listens not. It's eight bells, or twenty-four hundred in naval gobbledegook, but we haven't yet conquered the tubs. One hour from midnight! We're getting slap-happy and throw a few dizzy puns at cookie like, "We're cooking up some practical yolks for you, cookie." He's Ship's Cook 1/C but doesn't look like he means it. Nor is he physically menacing; anything but that. Suddenly, close to midnight, he walks into the galley and, hands on fat hips, declares, "O.K. Mac. You done enough. We don't need no more spuds." Just like that! We damn near fall off our stools.

Before hitting the sack, we check the bulletin board for impossible good news. We find it. GUNNERY MATH CLASS TOMORROW 08:00

My name is on the list. So they really are raking the rubble to find a few good or potential gunnery officers. I'm not too happy about this turn of events, but ever since joining up, this thing called fate is getting the better of my destiny. Who knows where I'll get shipped to if I don't shut up and go to class. Besides, I like math, and it's bound to be collecting some intelligent ex-boots.

Our class is in a 30x30-foot room almost filled with guys in undress blues, not dungarees. We are quiet, maybe expecting the unexpected, and we get exactly that. In spades. A red-haired Chief Petty Officer makes a late operatic entrance, flips his backside on a fragile desk, and pours out more profanity in his first few sentences than I've heard since our potato-fest of last night. His first outburst would have stunned us had we not been exposed to the quaint military jargon at boot camp. The redhead looks about, tosses his hat onto a chair, and hits the class smack in our collective faces with his macho, "Well, what the f--- do you think you're doin' here."

It's not a question the way he puts it. He looks down at his dangling feet. "God damned if I know if you don't," he says. I think it's a fair enough assumption. But his admission hits home, and I think he's won the guys over right away. We already have more than an inkling that nobody knows anything until after it happens. So far, things just seem to happen in the service.

The language of math as I'd known it takes a back seat to

our professor's profanity. Math quickly becomes, like Latin, a dead language as he spews a back-street profanity mingled with math terms fit for doctoral candidates, not nineteen-year-old graduated boots. But he enjoys peppering us with a novel military phrase. This spices the course for a couple of weeks, although the relationship of math to our gunnery purposes still isn't too clear. We figure out velocities, trajectories, ballistics on small scales now and then. Deep down, I believe we're more concerned about the volume of North Atlantic waves and how long we can survive in cold seas.

If nothing else, my classmates learn more of the infinite boundaries of math via a whiz ex-boot from Marquette University. He sometimes holds the redhead at bay as they exchange mathematical "secrets." We are as knowledgeable about their ideas as a typical high school sophomore is about relativity, or anything for that matter. More than once their little flights of fancy remind us that we've been grounded for a few minutes.

Finally, there's news. Class dismissed! The program is finit, canceled, scratched. Even the redhead knows not why. He exits gracefully and, we suspect, without regret. This has not been a bad experience; I hate to see him go. He renews my hope that a man can retain some of his personality in this semi-sane venture called war.

The bulletin board rescues us. Christmas and New Years leaves are posted! I'm lucky. I'll be home for Christmas, 1942! Just like I told my mother.

Gimme All Ya Got

In the waning weeks of winter '43, Great Lakes Naval Training Station is my new notion of Siberia. Not only are the shores of Lake Michigan ringed with ice, but mini icebergs float by with seeming impunity. The five-inch, thirty-eight surface guns common to destroyers slam their shells into them as if the navy were trying to demolish winter itself. My eardrums take a cruel pounding. Becoming a gunner's mate was never my dream: baseball still is.

These morning gunnery practice sessions are bitter cold. Target sleeves towed by slow, low-flying aircraft also seem to taunt the 20-millimeter anti-craft gunners. The targets are there, sure enough, but seem like slow, indestructible rabbits at a county fair shooting gallery. Yet it all seems real enough; the ammunition is real, the commands are real, the frigid weather is more than real. It has a sort of numbing effect. But we're convinced that this is a necessary, deadly business, and we're sure that gunnery is our duty.

The Great Lakes naval complex itself seems to be an unsolvable puzzle, a military maze. Hundreds of barracks spew thousand of boots into block-long chow lines three times daily, and were it not for my separate Coast Guard status, those lines might well have strangled the last ounce of independence from me. It feels good to know that I'm not a part of this mass movement, for there are movements galore here. Groups of forty or so are constantly being led from somewhere to somewhere. I almost feel privileged. In short, it's one hell of an existence, but closer to purgatory.

Other things are to be learned here besides gunnery. True, it's my choice to be here. The CPO at Jackson Park, Chicago, offered it to make up for a "misjudgment." "I know I've been rough on you, but Sampson just admitted he doctored the on-watch clock. So I'm gonna do ya a favor. What service school do you want to go to? Think it over. Let me know in five minutes."

It doesn't take me long to make my choice. I'd been in Chicago a few months. First at Randolph Street just across from Navy Pier, where the Chicago River meets Lake Michigan. The navy has a school for aviation mechanics here and a "practice" carrier nearby where rookie pilots qualify. German subs have made our coastlines more than vulnerable, and this allows for protection. The've been sinking our shipping since 1939, and both shorelines are still deadly places. Navy Pier is a life saver for our budding carrier fleet. I am in service to win this war for freedom against those controlling, phony, dangerous dictators. "Gunners Mate school," I say.

I still have a fair share in my choice. There ought to be a "Choices" class in the schools. We ought to keep our own school and call it our School of Choices. At any rate, seeing the nondescript multitudes of men seemingly led by their collective noses reminds me that I'm far stronger for destiny than for fate. I'd like to laugh in the face of fate for as long as I can. Here at Great Lakes, fate seems omnipresent, omnipotent, and downright ominous.

But the coming of spring, even at Great Lakes, blossoms into a beautiful renewal of hope. Here, one better have a dream, because the grim realities pose more fears than hopes. And my hope—even more than hope—is still to climb as high up in the world of professional baseball as possible. I'd like to pitch to guys like Mel Ott, "Ducky" Medwick, Paul Waner, Johnny Mize,

The Last Romantic War

Bill Terry, Ernie Lombardi, Joe DiMaggio, Charley Gehringer, Hank Greenberg, Mickey Cochrane, Ted Williams... All the greats and the near-greats. And I'd like to pitch for the Cubs with "Gabby" Hartnett behind the plate. I'd join Lon Warneke, Big Bill Lee, Larry French, and Charley Root on their pitching staff. They need help, plenty of it.

Was it impossible? Nello "Fungo" Tedeschi, who lived just two blocks away, had done it. He played some of '28 with the White Sox after Babe Ruth had recommended him. Fungo had fanned the famed Sultan of Swat three straight times with a four-foot sinker before Ruth got miffed and Fungo got careless. The Babe parked a 500-footer in dead right field over the 12-foot concrete wall and across West B Street. Fungo was going good with the Sox, but his rookie cockiness was unbearable. He was shipped out to the Three I League, and Fungo couldn't take the bushes. Well, if Fungo could make it, so could I. Not only this, but eighteen-year-old Phil Cavaretta had joined the Cubs while still in high school, and Bob Feller from Van Meter, Iowa, fanned eighteen at eighteen his first time out for Cleveland. My time is out of joint, maybe always out of joint. How many other young guys who want to play professionally are temporarily cut out of it like I am? I keep quiet about it even though some high school pals have said that I'd wind up in the big leagues before 1944.

Fortunately, spring comes swiftly, surprisingly, and just in time. With the warming, everyone walks lively. Even the Navy brass. After the usual Saturday morning inspection, I grab my Bob Feller glove and spikes and head for the baseball field near our barracks. I don't notice the collection of commissioned officers who are seated in the baseball stands. It feels good to have the spikes on and my Ranger baseball cap. My Sears Roebuck glove is in good shape, too. We play some "pepper," and then I throw to one of the guys with a catcher's mitt. We are just practicing with strangers in rag-tag clothes.

I'm a Coast Guardsman, but nobody cares. When a strapping six-footer taps me on the shoulder as I warm-up on the mound, I'm not surprised.

"Throw some to me," he says matter-of-factly. It isn't a question.

"Okay," I say, almost as matter-of-factly.

This big guy with football shoulders digs in at home plate, his spikes firmly settling into the dirt. He looks like he has certain intentions, selfish ones.

"How much do ya want?" I ask, modestly.

"GIMME ALL YA GOT."

This is just what I want to hear. It would be a good workout.

"Want me to let you know?"

"No!" It is a firm, impatient "no!" He's digging in deep in the batter's box. I'm smiling inside because he'll be fair game. I figure him to be a pull hitter like most big guys who aim for the fences. His batting stance is almost a dead giveaway. Because of it, he wouldn't be hitting the ball where it's pitched; that is, to all fields. Throw him outside and curve him to death. Keep him from the plate, of course. I'm giving this guy more than an even break. This is going to be fun. He doesn't know I'm well-armed.

In batting practice, you let a guy know what the pitch will be if it's other than a 60 m.p.h. fast ball. I throw a half-dozen different pitches: a breaking ball overhand, sidearm, and three-quarter, and at varying speeds and different sizes of breaks. I like my fingertip floater and a two-seam high hard one. The control's there, too. I throw pitches where I'd practiced them, not worrying about the hitter's strengths. It's always my strengths against theirs. Nearly every pitch would be a strike. That fingertip floater would be thrown outside just to wreck the hitter's timing or his confidence.

It's as simple as that, except for my reading the hitter's body language. There would be a good deal of poetry in the sequences, too. Old number two could translate into five or six deliveries. My "out-pitch" starts like a fast ball about a foot inside at the waist or a bit lower, then breaks to the outside corner at the knee. Nobody's ever hit it or done much with it, even when they know it's coming. It's a nifty pitch. It's held loosely and the spin is more from the fingers than the wrist, guided by the index finger. This will be pitching, not throwing.

He fouls off a grounder past first base on a sweeping curve, outside corner by the knee. Then I throw an overhand sinker that gets his attention. Now he's expecting my fast ball, so I flaunt my fingertip floater at him, tauntingly. He's either gonna get mad at me for toying with him or start respecting me. His bat is behind the pitch, blooping it into short right field. I've screwed up his timing.

This will be fun, maybe more than fun, I think. This is not batting practice throwing at one p.m. before the game starts. Hitters want you to groove 60 m.p.h. fast balls just to get muscles loosened and make good contact.

I don't know this guy; he doesn't know me. I can tell he's formidable. We're like a couple of gunfighters, and he's called me. He settles in deliberately, smoothly. He's been around. Looks like he's challenging me to bring my fastball. That's okey-doke with me. Moment of truth. It won't be my hummer; it'll be something better. It's going to start about a foot inside just beneath the waist and hit the outside corner around the knees. He hits a roller to second base. I know that I've really gotten his attention.

He's taking his time digging in as if nothing's gone wrong as I pause on the mound. My fastball's sure to be coming now, he probably thinks. I know he's drawing plenty of air, and I deliberately act like I'm mustering every ounce of strength. I wiggle my fist with arm extended, showing him the typical fast ball grip as if to tease him. It's actually a release of joy, as if my arm can't wait to throw that horsehide. As I bring the ball back, covering it with my glove, I pivot and dip my hips into a cocked position. It's all in slow motion and gives me time to reset my grip. The index finger presses into the curved seam for that spin.

This whole routine makes a sort of slingshot of me. I like to dip, keeping my left leg high, then striding to the extent that my body can follow through and be in fielding position. Well, all this rhythmic motion gets the maximum out of my five-foot ten-and-a-half inches and 165 pounds. I release a straight overhand fingertip floater. The pitch doesn't turn. It as much as stares at the hitter. But I keep it outside, way outside. Once again, it's only meant to throw his timing off.

I feel like I'm king-of-the-hill. My stuff is as good as when I'd stifled the Janesville Cubs the year before at Eddie Stumpf and Earl Whitehill's Chicago Cubs tryout camp. Pitches, control, stamina—it's all working. The big guy is grounding my best pitch, the three-quarter-arm, index-finger curve thrown as if it's a fast ball. He dribbles it to the right side of the infield a half-dozen times. Of my sixty or so pitches, maybe four or five are line-drive singles to center, some soft fly balls, and plenty of foul balls. But he rarely misses a pitch, and I'm around the corners all the time. I give him the opposite pitch that he might expect from the sequence, deliberately setting him up. After a while he looks anxious, tense. We skirmish for about forty-five minutes, just taking three or four breathers.

Finally, it's over. The big-shouldered guy walks out toward me, and while at least a dozen feet away, extends his hand. I'm surprised, and I offer mine as if no hard feelings, for it was a good workout.

"You got a damn good curve ball," he says, almost in appreciation and with a shadow of a smile lingering around his friendly-hostile eyes.

I nod and think nothing of it, though I might have given him a faint smile as a token of appreciation for his having the guts to stay in the box as well as he did and not bailing out.

I walk off the mound toward third base, but before I even reach the foul line, a scrambled-eggs Navy officer gets in my way. He leans his gold-braid hat and face smack into my second class seaman's face and in a tone that sounds more like a reprimand than a question, demands, "Do you know who you were throwing to?"

The tall officer's gold braid has already been enough to stop me cold. Before I can muster any word at all, the gold braid answers his own question.

"That's Glennn McQuillen... St. Louis Browns. Know that?"

He seems to be waiting for my reaction. I know of McQuillen alright. I kept track of batting averages and all the stats since I was twelve. The Browns' right fielder had hit a pile of homers in '41, battered around .286 and had driven in about 50 runs at the clean-up spot.

My head and heart are in sync, electrified by the blazing reality of it. I knew I could do it! I could pitch to a big leaguer, any of them. My heart smiles as I look away, shutting out the indifferent military world that surrounds me.

Later, I think that maybe I should have run madly after the big-leaguer, ask him if there's a Great Lakes team here needing a batting practice pitcher. I'd get to know the players, maybe even get transferred into the Navy. I couldn't imagine big leaguers actually being at Great Lakes. It was just a wisp of a thought, a tenth of a second flash of a wish. After all, this isn't a tryout camp; this is a war camp, not a spring training camp like the one at Janesville, Wisconsin. This is no dream-dream; there's a war going on. We're all in it for the duration plus six months.

I squeeze my $6.75 Bob Feller glove. I'll be at least twenty-three and maybe still have my arm by the time this war's over. Maybe it's a crazy dream. But it's a damn good one.

Mississippi Umbilical

There was a fighting ship, an almost forgotten ship, that helped America into its independence. Now there is another of her class, serving an equally important cause, and just as dauntingly romantic. Perhaps that's why it's called a frigate. She was launched only two months ago by the Froemming Brothers in a Milwaukee shipyard, where she was christened the USS *Machias*. Her equally modest beginning did not prevent me from admiring her the moment I saw her.

But who can recognize a true beginning and, tougher still, conjure where that beginning will lead? At Mack's Oyster Bar on Canal Street, New Orleans, no one much cared about tomorrow —today must do and speak for itself. Still, the creation of the USS *Machias* must have been something special, for after a solid month of tune-ups by our pre-commissioning crew, she looks every bit the frigate of our time.

Back to the beginning. Time and place are givens. Beyond the when and where, things get complicated. I knew little of the why and how of the *Machias*, but with a touch of imagination I saw the winding cord of the Mississippi as its "umbilical," attaching it to "mother" Milwaukee, U.S.A. She had been towed downriver, a helpless developing embryo without mast and minus the hardware of survival. She was docked some few miles north of New Orleans, where two dozen of us attended to her natal needs. Her circuitry was checked, guns greased and aligned, and her vital systems attended to.

Like most Februarys, this one of '44 is damp and cold on the mile-wide Mississippi. As the month struggles into March, the ship's remaining crew gathers at Algiers Navy Base across the river from New Orleans. Jean Lafitte prison had housed the earlier commissioning crew. The old French Quarter provides more than enough adventure and entertainment. On a modest subsistence, commissioned officers live in rented rooms and meet at a Canal Street drugstore for breakfast. I and others rediscover interesting passageways to escape the port-starboard liberty schedule at our "prison." It's a continuous breaking out of jail and heading for the promised land of the French Quarter. There is no way of keeping us from tasting what New Orleans has to offer.

The darkened Quarter defies the ominous declaration that Mardi Gras has been canceled. The Gulf and the eastern shore of the Atlantic are still infected with U-boats. Soon the *Machias'* cord will be cut, but not until the newly-born ship can safely pass from the uteral gulf and into the open waters of the Atlantic.

Down-river gin mills are magnets after our ship-shaping the *Machias*. This is not the sort of liberty Huck Finn found on his Mississippi; we're trying to assure liberty for future generations. "Down the hatch, mate" spoke for itself. Then, far too soon, we see the inevitable invitation to a SHIP'S PARTY AND DANCE at the NEW ORLEANS ATHLETIC CLUB, March 24, 1944, at 20:00. Ah, a civilized get-together at last. "You are cordially invited," it read. It seems too tame to attend.

The raucous, organized confusion of the French Quarter might soon just become a memory. Our days are numbered for sure. No more of Drinking Rum and Coca Cola or, getting In The Mood. A change of the guard is bound to happen. The gals, the gin mills—all of New Orleans has taken us for a surreal ride with little or no damage. Now this official "shore party" might settle things down.

Fine too was the party, all things considered, Stuart Whitehead tells me. "You shoulda' been there. Almost like a cotillion ball," he says. I wasn't there, thankfully. Formality would undo my urge for adventure. Junior prom stuff was fine in its time, but my appetite for the Quarter is too strong. You could feel the enormous energies among the men who crowded the bars. That energy very soon would be directed at other men. Less than two years ago, my liveliest Saturday night was across the river in Aurora, Wisconsin, where the law was almost invisible. Every Saturday night in the summer of '42 was a sort of last hurrah. It was beer, polkas, brass bands, and loud talk spiced by a strange nostalgia for what we would soon be missing. It paled in comparison with the daring Quarter.

The Athletic Club party had been utterly peaceful and damn-well chaperoned. Meanwhile, at the Roosevelt Hotel, another "ship's party" convened. The swank Roosevelt presented another side of the military coin. The tail side, to be almost exact. Reported facts and figures were enlarged somewhat, as expected, but all in harmless hyperbole. A tad of exaggeration in such matters was a military obligation, just as was a decent swearing jargon.

"Did'ja see what Toby done to that Navy swabbie?" It was damned-near a rhetorical question. It was almost expected of Toby; our reputation as a fighting man's ship depended a lot on his fisticuffing feats. Toby wasn't on our boxing team; he wasn't needed there. Besides, his were street skills. We had three guys who were undefeated, and two of them, welterweight John Cason and lightweight Joe Contini, KO'd everybody in sight.

"Did he kill him?" Larry Lorentz asked almost seriously. Toby was all-everything except on that boxing team, where he could have put away an opponent by simply going into clinches and delivering a bear hug.

"Nah, he just grabbed this guy and tossed him over the balcony rail. Lucky he landed on a table below. Called him a hooligan and Toby got mad." Jim Grabb was on Toby's deck crew, and he lavished more frosting on Toby's already legendary cake of physical exploits. Nice to have him on our side for such occasions. Toby was modest, too.

Nothing too wrong about little skirmishes within the big, universal one. This one, however, seemed to define the Coast Guard/Navy relationship for months to come: a hostile peace. Back at Great Lakes Naval Training Station, Barney and I rounded up a bunch of Marines, and we "orphans" challenged the entire block of Navy guys to a football skirmish. Barney was at halfback and I played quarter. We practiced passing routes for a week and felt ready. We could have used Toby. He played single wing blocking back at Hardin Simmons with Ray "Bulldog" Turner, an All-American center. The Marines were both offensive and defensive, and us "damn yankees" won the Civil War all over again, twenty-seven to six. Our barracks buddies hailed from Dixie, obnoxiously. But we got along just fine with the Marines. Our guys had gotten them ashore in landing barges at Guadalcanal a year ago.

We're still singing Toby's praises when Whitey delivers a copy of the next big invitation. A commissioning party! I almost ask him for it, as I have a built-in touch of sentimentality, you see. It was far more polite than Uncle Sam's call-to-arms.

"The Commanding Officer, Officers, and Crew request the honor of your presence at the Commissioning of the U.S.S. *MACHIAS* at New Orleans, Louisiana, on the afternoon of March 29, 1944, at 15:00."

One of these days the river umbilical will unwind and release us from the Gulf of Mexico womb. If we make it past the

The Last Romantic War

U-boat gauntlet to Bermuda, the shake-down training cruise will at least get us past our adolescence. There must be 242 men aboard subconsciously wondering about tomorrows. But nobody ever talks about that certain tussle between fate and destiny. Those are ridiculous ideas when you're in the state of semi-euphoria down here in jazz country. And there is Rosa H., eighteen, as fine a gal as one can be.

But this historic date with fate has stepped in. I have a hunch this won't be its last interruption.

A Little Bit of Huck

The Mississippi is cold. Bone cold. I still imagine the river as our umbilical cord. Even though the slim commissioning crew are feeling the heat of the swelling Mardi Gras spirit, the river breezes numb us to the bone. An upriver jaunt in a fifty-foot powerboat is a far cry from the charming Mark Twain paddle-wheelers of the mid-nineteenth century that cruised the unpredictable and mighty Mississippi. It's been a relief to board our unfinished ship and get her guns, depth charges, and hedgehog battery ready. Every piece of metal I touch chills my fingers. The 20mms look like robotic jack-hammers, frozen horizontally, and a wet film on the barrel is cold to the touch. Their magazine drums must be loaded and greased. The fantail clip shack at least keeps the cold at bay, and maybe a little wool gathering there might warm my memory and link the present to the past.

My constant companion has been the river, but I hardly feel like Mark Twain's Huckleberry. He hasn't entered my mind 'til now. Maybe the cold froze him out. That's ridiculous of course; Huck is unforgettable.

But the book I read in the ninth grade has changed! I got a kick out of his adventures, his tricks, his narrow escapes, his language, his boyish curiosities, and his grasp of some truths. Huck never went further than Cairo, where the Ohio joins the Big Muddy. Maybe Cairo, Egypt, and the enslaved Israelites have rubbed off in my imagination as I'm trying to keep warm. I know that Huck gave Mr. Mark Twain credit for "telling the truth, mainly." It hits me right now that he was talking about freedom, liberty with a touch of equality thrown in. Maybe I need a little "escape" of my own.

Huck was a darn good teller of yarns, and he helped runaway slave Jim to escape. But it was a freedom of a different sort. A running away kind of freedom.

Huck's trip down the river and the fakes that he out-maneuvers obscure the real issue in the story: a person's right to liberty and the pursuit of happiness. Jim was running from slavery. Here and now, I'm not running from anything. I and millions of others are fighting for the freedom to be. But it's nice to reach for those halcyon days when the problems always seemed to be someone else's. So why not think of Huck and those black-and-white days? After all, whose river is this?

I enjoy staging within myself a half-awake dream, especially its dialogue. Everybody knows that Mark Twain dished out the truest dialogue and made it stick. But you don't talk about Mister Mark Twain's masterpiece aboard a frigate. On a raft, maybe. O.K., Huck, she's all yours. I'm all yours, I mean. Sometimes it takes a war to understand something. Right now, I'm tired of greasing these 20mms. A little daydreaming will break the monotony.

I'm feeling a momentary kinship, a seeing of the world with clear, forever young, romantic eyes. Lumping people into categories makes it easy to control them. Makes thinking easy, too. Right, Adolph? This little dream is getting deep.

Huck's words on the raucous Mississippi will never be silent. Hitler should have read it before scribbling Mein Kampf. He might have learned that the greed for power is like that of a cat chasing its tail: futile. But should it succeed by some crazy accident, the end result would be far worse.

A dream is a dream is a stream. That old stream of

consciousness couldn't be dammed now. Dam as in river. A 20mm clip shack is a helluva place to be thinking about Huckleberry Finn. Wonder what he'd 'a said about the would-be kings raising hell in Europe. Maybe they think they're aces trumping kings and queens. Ole Huck would have exposed 'em like he did the Duke and the Dauphin. He and Jim knew what freedom was all about. Never mind making the world safe for democracy or from any ism. Make it safe for the wild cards of freedom and liberty! That would be the ultimate new deal. It's in the cards for sure. Play with a full deck and call a spade a spade. In the beginning was the Word, but who would have the last word? We could use a Twain now. I sure can't get the word out.

This is one helluva dream. I'm one blink away from wakefulness. Also have one foot into tomorrow. When the lights go on again all over the world, it'll be everybody's world. There's world enough. Freedom to, not freedom from. Slavery is no more. I'm rambling, but it all connects. "To be or not to be... That is the question." I like that infinite infinitive "to be." Maybe the word will beat the sword.

Kind of ironic that our ship has no library. A few Reader's Digests, that's all. But it's gonna have some negro steward mates who'll serve the commissioned officers more dutifully than "civilized" slaves. They'll bunk near them and eat near them, but in segregated quarters. They'll be mostly free, but out of sight. Yup, Huck, we've come quite a ways since that raft. All the way down here to me in New Orleans. You know, Huck, that raft was your island, a kinda Eden-island of Freedom, Liberty, Equality, and Fraternity. You were one-up on the French. Now if we can think of planet Earth as our island... Well, maybe that's too big a dream.

Somewhere in the distance sitting on the river in a rocking chair, I see a likeness of Sam Clemens, and I can almost come near enough to hail him. Guess I feel a bit too young to engage him in conversation. Maybe my dreams are getting better all the time. There's plenty to ask him. I know he was born at just the right time, when America tried to find itself, and he defined it with his big book, Huckleberry Finn. America needs defining again, more fleshing out of its profile. Picture Mark Twain swinging America around by its umbilical, the mighty Mississippi. I almost feel that we've got the polecats by the tail and now we can't let 'em go 'til it's over. Funny, I never saw it this way when I first read Twain. Maybe it takes some daydreaming.

This is New Orleans, one of the great liberty towns, I tell myself. Forget the river; think of the French Quarter. Who says the twain shall never meet? For the first time ever, Mardi Gras is canceled. No parade or celebration. Still, this does not shut down the town. If anything, the darkened French Quarter is more charming this way. Inside the bars and dives the lights glow dimly, the guys are ten deep, and the gals everywhere. Every branch of service is here, sometimes mingling, sometimes looking for a scrap. A serviceman's buck doesn't last long here; in fact, nothing seems to have permanence. It's a perfectly unreal world. All we can do is spend what we have. We have a lot of ammo to spend too before we return. Be the sailor with a gal in more than a few ports.

My privacy is gone. Yup, here comes my pal Barney. "Blarney" Barney, I sometimes call him. "Hey Barney, let's make it to the Quarter tonight. This every-other-night liberty stuff can't keep us cooped up in pirate Jean Lafitte's prison, right? I know a passageway the other guys are taking. O.K.?"

"Damn right," he says. "Chrissakes, this is New Orleans and they're cooping us up. Not me. Let's hit Mack's Oyster Bar on Canal Street first."

Getting out of the old prison takes some fast athletic moves, plus cooperative guards, plus a seldom-used passageway. We climb the wire mesh fence easily enough and make it to Mack's in less than a half hour. The place, as usual, is packed. The Oyster Bar is doing wholesale business. I try a couple and they taste too fishy until I irrigate them with a draft, but Barney is gulping them down as if this is his daily bread. Bo LaBeau is there with a beer and a pile of empty oyster shells.

"Watch it you guys," he warns. "The SPs are on the prowl. Threw Toby in the brig to cool off. Took the Moose to get him out. Came close to putting him in, too." The "Moose" is Lt. Henry Hanna, and we already know he won't take any crap, not even from the Navy. Not even from those veteran submariners lying in wait. Very few of us have sea duty under our belt, but we're well trained in our specialties. We're grassy green, and staying alive from New Orleans to Bermuda will take some doing, plus a little bit of luck. We are just as ready as Toby is to take on anything our size and bigger.

Bo goes on nonchalantly as if this were routine stuff. "Toby flattened a half-dozen sailors and a marine. One of them called him a hooligan. Toby asked him how he spelled it and then threw a right before the sailor got the 'h' out. He swept the bar stools clear, but a shore patrol cold-cocked him from behind. Took him ten minutes to wake up."

This night is starry enough for anything. I mean, everything.

A Havana for Hanna

"You know, Buzz, I can't even spell Ski's name, but thought I could read him like a book. It's the in-between-the-lines that got me. Ski's the youngest sailor aboard. Told me he's sixteen. Shows you right away he's foolish. Got caught up in joining up. Could'a made ten times the money workin' in a shipyard in Milwaukee. He must'a joined just to get in on the 'big show.'"

"Ski's just sixteen? Zed just made him gunner on my fantail 20mm's. Yeah, go on."

"Cripes, he's got a baby face and a kid smile. Skinnier than a rail with corn-silk hair and dead-blue eyes. Looks damned innocent. He ain't suave, but he ain't innocent neither. A practical joker. Thinks he's a pugilist, but his buddies keep bailing him out, and they wind up with Shore Patrol on their backs. He's slippery. Lousy deckhand, too. Can't do nuthin' right.

"Always calls me Bo LaBeau. Likes rhyming the O. Thinks he's clever, using my full name. Shouldn't let him get away with it. Anyways, he's goldbricking as usual, and I don't find him until about eight bells. Sent him on a little paint detail which I thought would keep him busy all morning. I suspect something ain't right when I see him half an hour later putting the paint away. Ensign Barstad looks into the compartment, just pokes his nose through the hatch, and says O.K., good job.

"Me, I know better. I wasn't born yesterday, Buzz. Been bosun-second a year now and I know the goldbricking tricks better'n anybody. I seen 'em first-hand. Done 'em, too. So I get on my knees and look into this storage compartment. More'n half of the bulkheads ain't done.

"Trouble is, you can't get pissed off at this crazy kid. Can't take it personal. But I'm tired'a houndin' him. I'm workin' harder at keepin' tabs on him than he's at workin'. So I get a brainstorm. I'll take him with me on liberty. This here New Orleans is a damn good liberty town, 'specially the French Quarter. Me'n Toby usually hit the bars together, and it's pretty safe with him. He played football at Hardin Simmons and Drake. Was a blocking back. Him and Bulldog Turner was a two-man wrecking crew. Turner was All-American. Anyways, I figure if I show Ski a good time, maybe he'll show me some respect. Shoulda' took Toby instead.

"It's one helluva liberty. Makes up for no Mardi Gras this year. We're having a pretty good fling. After the second rum and Coca-Cola, I finesse a brawl with five, six dog-faces. Ski takes a sloppy overhand right swing and I rescue him. But it's no fun unless you finish it. Toby could start and finish it. I'm on his clean-up committee.

"I steer him out into a narrow Quarter street. There's lots of balcony babes up there, and his language wouldn't pass inspection in a sailors' crap game. He thinks he's havin' a good time. 'Bo,' he says, 'you're pretty shitty aboard ship, but you're a good liberty buddy. Hey, there's the Blue Rooster joint. Let's go pull some feathers.'

"Course, this doin' the town ain't the story, but I'm getting' to it. Even though we're navigatin' by the skin of our teeth, it's not goin' bad. Maybe now I can get some decent work outta him. Then Ski pulls out a good-lookin' cigar and I ask him if he's celebratin' somethin'.

"'Nah,' he says. 'This here Havana is too good for smokin.'

"My mind is none too good at the moment, either, so this

goes in one ear and out the other. Also, I don't want to trigger his imagination if I linger on it.

"Well, Ski is keepin' unduly quiet, and my curiosity is getting' aroused. He's nursing the cigar like it was a pet or somethin'. I figure I'd better let unlit cigars stay unlit. I'm steering him shipboard and he doesn't object. This is puzzling. I don't think he wants to call it a night. True, we grabbed a few wildcats by the tail, but we let go in time.

"'There's the ship, Ski.'

"'Friggin' *Machias*,' he says.

"'Hey, don't knock it,' I say. 'It's a damn good ship. Made in your hometown, ya know.' He's not listening.

"'Gonna give it to that friggin' Hanna.'

"'Give what?' I say. 'You crazy bastard. He'll stick you on permanent K.P. just for looking cross-eyed at him.'

"It's then I suspect Ski's got a plan. But if there's anyone with a plan aboard the ship, it's Hanna. He's saltier than our whole crew put together. Right, Buzz?" There's some maudlin in his voice.

I can't do more than nod. But I want to find out about the cigar.

"He can be mean. One or two ensigns already been known to feel his wrath. He's running this ship god-like, and not even the skipper is calling his moves. He's holding a royal flush, *carte blanche*. He's not unfair, but he's judge and jury.

"I know Ski ain't gonna politely offer him a cigar. He's got something more creative in mind. I don't wanna be around him because Hanna's been riding me ever since commissioning. I'm thinking we're both headed for the shittiest of shit lists. Maybe back to seaman first for me.

"At least we're coming in under our own power. Barney's at the gangway, petty officer of the watch. He knows me and Ski are maybe snockered. Ski comes alive and asks a question as if it's not a question. 'Barney, where's Hanna,' he sez. Barney just looks at him with one eye. 'Where's Hanna?' This time it's a question.

"'In the wardroom. Watch it, he's got a bug up his ass,' Barney says, looking serious.

"Ski is all goofy grin. He goes that way and I head for the head. I've got to go. I wake up too late. He's already lurching through the hatch, and I see he's running a smoking cigar into a snoozing Hanna's mid-section.

" 'Ceegar fer ya Hanna,' he yells. I freeze, damn near pass out.

"Ole' Moose Hanna's wearing his natural scowl, you know, like when 'the Moose is on the loose'. He knocks the cigar out of Ski's hand, straightens up to six foot, thirteen inches, and sizes up Ski from top to bottom.

"'You friggin' lout, get outta here. You're on report,' he sez. He spins Ski around and dumps him on the deck, just like when he's playin' defensive end for Southern Cal Trojans in the Rose Bowl.

"Hanna don't see me. I move fast, about four knots. Sonofabitch, I'm in hot water now. He's gonna think I had something to do with it since he saw us sign out together. I shoulder my way down the passageway. I'm goin' to the head and his voice over the conn catches me. Must have seen me staggering down the passageway. 'LaBeau, report to the wardroom on the double,' he sez. It ain't what he sez but how. I'll be swabbing a deck tomorrow for sure. Maybe it's irons for Ski, but curtains for me.

"I'm seeing Hanna's mug before me: leathery, weathery, with 50,000 sea-duty miles on it. Never can tell what color his eyes are; couldn't look him in the eye. Anyway, I'm sporting the best poker face I can muster. But I suspect I'm going to acquire some knowledge in a hurry.

"'Drag this drunken shit outta here!' he sez. He doesn't accuse me, but he stares and looks like he's finding me guilty. I must'a said 'aye, sir' three times. I grab Ski under the armpits and head for his sack above the engine room. Ski don't weigh over 140, but I'm already over-loaded, so the dragging is as tough on him as it is for me. Every few feet there's some puke, but he's grinning through it all. 'I done it!' he must be thinkin'. Right then and there I resolve to terminate all brotherly love, dependin' how merciful Hanna is.

"Bo, I saw Ski in the galley this morning helping Steed and Schirtz bake. Want another Miller?" Had to show appreciation for his story.

"Jeez, he's baking? Now I can't eat bread, even if it ain't soggy! Was hoping he'd be peeling spuds. Anyway, he's outta my hair for awhile, bread or no bread. Might even celebrate and light up a Havana at chow in Ski's face. But not in front of Hanna. Hell no! I ain't made second class bosun fer nuthin."

I had to agree with him. Especially over a beer.

The Gulf Womb

"Cast off the bow line."

That short, declarative sentence carried the finality of an obituary sentence when pronounced by Executive Officer Lt. Henry "Moose" Hanna. There's no turning back now. The United States Ship *Machias* and its crew of 232 plus twelve commissioned officers are in the war for keeps, for better or for worse. She let go her leash at last.

There's no fanfare, no waving of goodbyes. Our graceful *Machias* obeys Hanna's commands as if they are old friends. The river pilot stands idly by, yielding to a "salt," but standing in full readiness with his wisdom of the Mississippi delta. The "Big Muddy" is fully a mile wide here, but the thinning will come swiftly as the delta approaches. A strange hush, a solemn quiet deepens as deck hands meander about, some standing by the port railing and looking shoreward at nondescript shacks.

"Set condition, Baker. The smoking lamp is out."

Gunner's mates first class Zed Zaunere and Johnny Votava arm the more than thirty depth charges with red, cylindrical detonators with a swift efficiency. But this is an artificial readiness, for of the men aboard, only a dozen or so have been to sea, and of these only a handful are "shellbacks." We are a "pollywog" crew if ever there was one. Or to put it in Oliver Hardy's lingo, "this is a fine kettle of fish" we've gotten ourselves into.

The famed crescent has now long faded away, and the unpredictable twists and turns downstream seem to foreshadow an ominous future. And the men topside seem to sense it. The noose of inevitability, like a wayward umbilical, is drawing tighter.

These newly-armed depth charges don't have a depth setting yet. We're like an unborn infant, no more than a developing embryo in this gulf womb. We'll soon be in that formative gulf, too, and still attached to the Mississippi umbilical. My metaphor goes beyond my acute sense of reality as I picture myself cut adrift in that gulf/womb, and I turn it off quickly.

Right now I can use a laugh, any kind. It's good security medicine. I catch seaman Hank Hauck throwing a fast line at Toby Switzer.

"Hey, Toby. Heard you pitched another swabbie overboard off the dock last night. Hanna bailed you out, huh?" A glowing grin decorates Toby's blonde face, a face far too small for his massive shoulders.

"Ya. Bastard tried to give me some urine in a Coke bottle, but I wuz wise to him. Friggin' MPs ganged up on me. Put two of 'em in the drink."

"What'd Hanna tell ya, Toby?"

"Said if I let them Navy guys pull that crap on me he'd throw me inta the brig hisself. Hanna's a good ole boy."

"You ain't just akiddin', Toby. We shore need him to keep the Navy off'n our backs. Us 'n the Marines is in the same boat. Got two wars to fight: thim and the Japs." Toby squinted at Hauck, a Georgia reb who almost included "damn yankees" on the list of potential enemies.

"How ya know we gonna fight the Japs, Hank? Hear somethin'?"

"Nothin' but scuttlebutt. The Atlantic's full of Navy. We'd only git in their way over here." Hauck looks like he's said something thoughtful and seems pleased that Toby respects his reply.

I agree, but for a different reason. The Pacific calls for pure anti-sub ships like the *Machias*. Besides, the Navy wouldn't build about eighty of them to dump them into the Atlantic. That's Navy destroyer escort country. We Coast Guardsmen are more companionable with the Marines who are taking islands right and left in the Pacific. Maybe it's just wishful thinking on my part. Big as the Pacific looks on maps, I'd rather see the island sights there than buck the risky Atlantic weather. The Pacific ought to be pacific, period.

Drill exercises—gunnery, fire, general quarters—having been done, the pilot gone ashore at U.S. Naval Frontier Base, Burwood, Louisiana, and the war cruising watch set, there is nothing, nothing but sea duty dead ahead. The day previous, twelve sleep-inners were hoisted before the Captain's Mast, a sort of quick trial to mete out fit punishment. Standard punishment: "turn-to one hour before reveille and one hour before sea watches." The skipper declares the doses lickety-split. Hanna executes them.

And suddenly, the purple gulf is there and here and everywhere. On the bridge, quartermaster striker Bill King is given the first bearing.

"Steer course 165, true. Standard speed, two-thirds."

It's April 18, 1944, and the hour is 07:40.

The *Machias*, ship of the United States Coast Guard, is now presumed to be ready. In a pig's eye, it is. At least that's what Moose Hanna thinks and knows for damn sure. What he knows is no more than what most of us know: this is a bunch of young Americans from east of the Mississippi capable of becoming a fighting crew. And we will be if the *Machias* can run the gauntlet from New Orleans to Bermuda where our shake-down "cruise" awaits us. But there are lots of ifs between Louisiana and Bermuda. Plenty of drills, too.

As bad timing would have it, GM I/C Zed Zaunere crosses my path. In just twenty minutes I'm due on watch.

"Buzz, give the first three-inch gun some graphite. That salt spray might get to it." It would be a test alright. We've already begun to pitch as the Mississippi meets the gulf. A spray is already coming over our bow. It's a sea legs test; maybe a seasick test, as the pitch is worsening. The whole world seems like it's going topsy-turvy. I'm hurriedly shooting graphite grease into every zerk fitting in sight.

Now the gulf looks purple. My stomach feels like it's purple, too. I hoist myself into the trainer's seat to settle myself down a bit. Our bow rail is skimming the gulf and my stomach is doing chin-ups. This is not good at all. The salty spray is not cooling my hot face, and my hands are sweaty. I've never had this feeling before. Am I getting seasick? Am I imagining all of this? I've seen shipmates toss their cookies after boozing it up, staggering to the ship's head, looking dizzy and helpless, just the way I'm starting to feel. The delta looks greenish; the bow sinks and rises rhythmically, defying my attempt to keep my artificial balance. If this is just the gulf, what must the oceans be like?

Reality is getting the better of me even though logic tries to discipline my imagination. The world has suddenly become a voluptuous gulf, a moveable sky and a salty mist. My chow is getting rebellious, and I make a staggered run for the rail, foolishly not caring if I fall. I've never puked before. It seems like a waterfall is coming out of me. God, do I have to live with this? Then, almost as suddenly as the swift swelling of the sea, the wind slackens and the gulf's fury subsides. My stomach subsides, too. I gratefully manage to reach my watch at the depth charge racks 300 feet astern on time.

I'm not looking forward to another baptism in the gulf. Thankfully, the next couple of hours are as placid as the Mississippi, and I recover my confidence. Topside is active again. Maybe other guys hit the sack when the ship pitched. Wonder what it would be like in a rolling sea.

A serene sea, I'm about to learn, can be trouble. Fate knows no boundaries. U-boats know no boundaries.

"Conn, sonar contact five miles at 095 true."

Within seconds our *Machias* is bearing down cautiously on the suspicious object via a 50 degree zigzag course. General quarters alarm is on. Ping, ping, ping... Pinging away. The conn blares, "All hands man your battle stations. Man your battle stations!"

I sense that the next minutes won't be the best of times. Maneuvering through the moderate swells brings water up to the gunwales. In under three minutes, the crew have manned their battle stations. We seem to be chasing a phantom enemy below. Water washes under and through the fantail depth-charge racks, but fortunately no setting is ordered. On the next zig our stern falls into a deep trough and, upon lifting, a torrent of water forces Buchanan and me to jump on the racks to keep from being washed overboard.

Just the thought of meeting a sub in the gulf to begin with is hardly funny. To chase it while zig-zagging isn't a child's game of hop-scotch. My fear evolves into a hot anger. I wave my depth-charge setting wrench and throw a challenge spiced with an expletive or two. Suddenly, sonar loses contact and we get back on course. Nice war so far, I'm thinking. What's next?

The Florida Keys are a welcome sight. Our *Machias* is emerging, at last, right into the ocean of salt water reality, finally thrown out of her gulf womb.

We're born; now we've got to live.

Triangulation

Two hundred forty-four men are berthed within some 307 feet by 42 feet by 25 approximate feet and, except for chow, their daily disappearance becomes a strange routine. Perhaps our immersion into the great gulf womb has lulled us into a desire for motherly security. The shock of leaving our tethering Mississippi River might figure in it subconsciously, perhaps instinctively. Maybe symbolic images impress us more than we know.

Short-lived as it was, the sub chase is indelibly implanted in my mind. A baptism by saltwater rushing over the fantail was real enough. In the two days since the immersion, I'm almost accepting the unpredictable at sea, both at the hands of our enemies and nature herself.

This same mid-April night, we near-innocents aboard cut through a slot in the Florida Keys. I find the Big Dipper and its anchoring North Star and from it conclude that the swing to north by northeast means that the Atlantic stage of our voyage has begun. Nearing the middle of the eight-to-twelve watch, an odd realization startles me: our *Machias* is now in the infested Atlantic and alone. Alone! I ponder how inexperienced, unproven we are. A scan of our service records would show us to be practically a virgin crew manning a brand-new ship. And even though we have pursued what might have been a sub, the stand-off is hardly reassuring. The Gulf of Mexico hardly put us to the test. That was like playing against the neighborhood kids on a sandlot diamond. This ocean is a big league ballpark. Wow!

We're in it up to our necks and deeper!

The hours bring more troubling news. Where is the *Machias*? Her position is in doubt. Ensign Logan declares in a manner worthy of any upstart junior officer, "That island out there about 285 degrees is about 40 miles dead east of Miami. I grew up in Miami." Radioman second class Gillam pipes in quickly, "Yeah, we're off Miami. I forget the name, but that's where we are."

But on the bridge and near the helm, that certainty is missing. The skipper is looking for hard facts and asking hard questions. When he inquires of his executive officer, a former department store owner from the Midwest, what is the *Machias'* position, no assurance is given.

"We've got navigating instruments aboard. Aren't you using them?" The reply is slow. "No sir, they're locked up below decks. No one has been trained to use them."

"Damn. You're charged with navigating this ship, Hampton." The skipper, barely five-foot seven, brushes past his navigation officer, scowling. This turns into a slow head-shake as he leaves the bridge, a ship's captain who doesn't know where his ship is.

Truth turns into rumor within minutes. No one has been trained to use the navigating instruments! Our position is only approximate. That insignificant duty has been left up to the stars. Very dead-reckoning! There's Shakespeare again with his romantic wisdom: "The fault, dear Mercutio, lies not with the stars, but with us." Or something like it. So we're alone in the Atlantic and presumably headed for the Navy's shake-down base in Bermuda. And to complicate matters, there are rumors leaking everywhere that something is smelly in the Bermuda area. Something about ships lost at sea, and aircraft that fail to return to Florida flight-training fields.

The Last Romantic War

A warming spring sun does nothing to ease the top-side tension. Bermuda can't be that hard to find. After all, a good part of the Navy is already there. If we have to lower ourselves, we'll ask any ship passing by.

Evening watch begins uneventfully. Flying fish launch from the moderate swells and land on the fantail deck. They don't know where they're going, either. Their florescence is strange and their aim almost deliberate. Aesthetic torpedoes, I muse. Wonder why I've got torpedoes on my mind. I toss them back into the dark waters. Our cooks wouldn't be interested in them. Chow, that isn't a pleasant thought, either. It's been less difficult keeping food down, thanks to the calm waters around the Florida peninsula. Seasickness is even more threatening than the dreaded U-boats that still invade American waters like a creeping cancer. Maybe we're not big enough game for them. They hunt in packs now.

If there's a secret for neutralizing seasickness, I haven't learned it. I'm guessing that it's a problem of attitude: going along with, instead of struggling against, an overpowering Mother Nature might be the solution. If a truce could be worked out then the sea and I would both be at peace. As for the lurking subs in the Gulf of Mexico, well, that was a different game. Maybe the U-boats are ambushing big convoys more than catching stragglers. Why else had we used a 45-degree zig-zag course and occasionally a 50-degree pattern? Maybe they pick on a loner more than convoys, which are guarded by destroyers and destroyer escorts. On the other hand, sinking a frigate isn't nearly the prize that a loaded freighter or tanker is. Being at the depth charges makes me feel all the more in a deadly cauldron for survival.

Darkness falls early tonight. At 20:00 only a sprinkling of stars shine through. Over our sound-powered phones I hear that a surface craft blip is on the radar screen, the size and movement of which would qualify it to be a submarine. A request for a recognition signal attracts the wrong code response. This object is on the surface. The vessel closes its range as if to intercept us. Leave the depth charges and captain the port quad-forty, I'm ordered. I'm joined by a skeleton gun crew.

"Half-load. Load!" My gun is ready. The distance between us narrows quickly to a mile, then to a thousand yards. Somebody has to make a move, a serious move. Our distance shrinks to little more than two hundred yards.

"Stand by to fire!" This command is the epitome of what I imagine "action" would be like. This is life and death in a second or two. In a moment I'd deliver the command to my gun crew to "commence firing." Damn it, I've never captained a quad forty!

At first, the searchlight beam seems surreal as it's lost in the sea. Then it finds the super-structure of a smallish surface craft. A patrol craft reveals its friendly identity as PC 1167. In another second the bridge of the *Machias* might have been be no more, or the Patrol Craft, an 83-footer, would be no more. Our floodlight flicks off.

I wonder about the searchlight. It's a magnet that would attract a direct hit on itself, there on the bridge. Yes, it helps the gunners to zero-in on their target, but it makes itself a target. Thank God it's over, and now perhaps the two skippers will check the daily codes by which recognition is determined. It would be a more decent war if it were played by actors who know their lines even if they don't fully understand their roles.

Bermuda attracts our attention, but not before possible submarine contacts, one across our bow within five miles. From a bearing of 071 True, almost due east, to a bearing of 295 T and then to 320 T and again to 245 T, is hardly a traditional zigzag course, but one which would help evade ambushing submarines. The swing from ENE to WSW, almost 180 degrees, however it is determined, brings Bermuda into reality. She's no longer a ghost island that an occasional rumor pictures her to be. But we stumble upon our Camelot by ear. It's dawn and the rumble is not quite thunder. Finally, to avoid gunfire from ships undergoing training, our *Machias* skirts the scores of escort ships and requests an anchoring berth. Before us lies the grand, pastel-dotted island; it is the morning of April 21, 1944. Tomorrow will be our first day at kindergarten.

A collective sense of "at ease" pervades the *Machias* as she slices through the changing, exotic shades of green and searches for her new quarters. We'll receive training like a baby learning to walk, and hopefully every crew member will also learn how to walk aboard ship. Birth through adolescence would be its agenda. Our *Machias* will flex her talents for a few short weeks and then play her role, somewhere.

The words "triangle" and "triangulation" disappear. Azimuth, dead-reckoning, plotting, true north, gyro are also destined to become silent echoes of the *Machias'* innocent dash through the "Triangle" in search of Britain's elegant Atlantic island on loan to us. But now rumors will give way to hard facts, facts which will indicate the readiness of the frigate *Machias*.

It's time to play the war game for keeps. We will become the best offensive defense against the submarine anywhere in the world. After we get our sea legs.

Sea Legs

If an army marches on its stomach, as the saying goes, the Coast Guard depends on its "sea legs." I've heard it referred to, obliquely, as "getting your sea legs," whatever that means. It sounds like learning to walk on decks awash, not losing your balance or footing by keeping your walking stance with legs wide open. Rarely do any of the crew talk about it for two reasons: first, only a handful of the crew has experienced sea duty; and second, since this is true, it remains a fearful prospect. Also, I don't know that a relationship between sea legs and seasickness exists. This is not a humorously illogical connection. Nausea anytime, let alone at sea, is hardly a laughing matter. It's rumored that the skipper, serving on a Coast Guard cutter in the North Atlantic, suffered it constantly and still does.

No research by the medical or maritime gods explains it, nor has anything been touted as a sure-fire help more than plain, unsalted soda crackers. But as the *Machias* wended its way downstream past New Orleans, there already were the first pathetic incidents of it. The Mississippi, wide and long as it is, has no reputation as being a bearer of the malady, so the sight of a strapping petty officer vomiting into the long urinal makes its point: *mal de mer* is everywhere on water, unpredictable and no joke.

Maybe it's all psychological, I think. A sort of phobia or inexplicable fear. Maybe it has something to do with a person's relationship to the ship. Come to think of it, the last four letters —"ship"—itself is a spooky connection.

The Last Romantic War

I remember, or think I remember, how things were when this seasickness nonsense first entered my life. It is just about six days ago, when we were nearing the Gulf of Mexico at the delta where the Mississippi green turns to deep gulf purple, that I had a ghastly visit. I don't want to think about it, but I remember that I was pumping purple graphite grease into the zerk fittings on the bow three-inch fifty gun when I'm engulfed with a queasy feeling. Looking out into the great gulf and seeing the horizon behave strangely, my stomach and forehead also behave strangely or, rather, weirdly. I close my eyes while in the pointer's seat, but it does no good, as my imagination is also out of control. My forehead is moist, but not only from the gulf spray. I'm being possessed by something that I don't understand. Damn it! It's no fun dredging this up. It's too fresh in my experience. Maybe if I think openly about it, I can find some angle. Maybe if I just use some common sense logic, something will turn up. I'll give it one more try.

I hang on, but the ship and the horizon don't agree, despite my desperate attempt to fuse them. The Gulf of Mexico's purple-blue waters form a liquid continent. Has the earth abandoned me for good? My grease gun is puking a wormy, purple grease, and I lean back as if to correct the plunge into the waters of the gulf. Then the bane of every sailor—seasickness—grabs me. I have a feeling of fullness and grab the pointer's gunsight to steady myself. Like a bronc-busting rider I lean back, thinking I can balance things out as the *Machias* pitches even deeper.

Instead, it pours things out. Tasting the bitter beginnings of an outflow, I swing ever so carefully out of the pointer's "saddle seat" and stagger to the bow railing just in time to release what has been a perfectly decent breakfast by ship cooks' standards. I'm forced to let it go. The temporary relief is ecstatic. *OK, logic, get to work.*

So much for my memory and logic. Every time I recall it the pain is slightly worse. But now I need a halfway optimistic explanation leading to a solution or I'm doomed. Sure, the river flowing into the Gulf of Mexico is like what a salmon has to put up with swimming upstream. Yes, I was on that number one three-inch fifty no more than 30 feet from the tip of the bow. Was it the pitching that brings it on or how I reacted to it? Birds can handle the vertical stuff. Why not us? They do not only fly parallel to mother earth. Then I'm struck down with dilemma two: are we headed for North Atlantic duty? God, no. I hope not. I don't mind tossing my cookies so long as my stomach stays in one place. Fortunately, the great Gulf settled down as if to apologize for its rude upheaval. Hugging the coastline north of the Florida Keys, the *Machias* sailed smoothly and the waters were glassy. An armada of cumulus sunbathed on the north horizon, and we navigated by stars. No lurking U-boats as yet.

But now the shallow waters near Bermuda will have their say. They are more vulnerable to wind and turn choppy easily. The ocean, like time, is no gossip; it keeps its secrets well. Water and wind is a troublesome combination, so I keep plenty of soda crackers on and in hand.

"Shakedown cruise" is a big misnomer. Shakedown, yes; cruise, hardly. Bermuda's waters are unfriendly: they are choppy and snarling with whitecaps or quarreling with swells and troughs. The island, at least, doesn't move. Everything else does.

Almost dead in the water and caught in deep troughs, our *Machias* rolls enough to fling a bowl of soup down the mess table. An experienced bosun, Ed Doaks, holds on to his tomato soup while I turn slightly pale. Others at chow hold on to the anchored tables as if expecting our ship to capsize. Master-at-Arms Eric Stromsta, guardian of the mess hall, smiles feebly as if he were duty-bound to do so. His fair toughness is respected. He's hiding a jittery stomach and, like many of us, just doing his duty.

But the leering bosun seems to be enjoying the swinging hammock, our ship, which is in an ugly, persistent trough. Doaks smiles as he slurps the blood-red soup, knowing full well the rest of us can barely look at it. I'd like to heave my tray's meager scraps of food at him.

Luckily, the pitching and rolling subsides during our sub-chasing practices. But then something fortunate happens: the crew is given liberty at Hamilton, the island's capitol city. The shake-down cruise is going great; our *Machias* excels in all functions, except it's average in seasickness. Going ashore will be an adventure. Leaving the liberty whaleboat is like setting foot on American soil again. Sighs of relief come from my shipmates as well.

We are granted an afternoon liberty ashore. These ocean shore waters are a rainbow of greens, finally blending into dark ocean blue. A tram ride around the island reminds me that I am a land creature only temporarily displaced into sea duty. The honeymooners know the right place to romance their marriage. Something tells me I'll profit from this island visit, but differently.

Hard to believe that perhaps twenty miles from Bermuda's shores, subs are prowling. The swirling shades of green near the island, however, are Edenesque. This panorama of watercolor greens, their many shades, also help me to feel "at home." But the ride on land does something else: it teaches me the difference between being on land and being at sea! How could this simple, logical truth have escaped me?

Bermuda is indeed a beautiful island like the graceful and seaworthy *Machias* is an island. Each is a home. But each is a different kind of home requiring a different means of navigation. Holy cow! There's the answer: go along with the ship as if you are part of it, literally. Don't try to correct it. Lean with it naturally; do not try to "right it." Just go with it, harmoniously, acceptingly. There will be no struggle, no overworked nerves.

"Got your sea legs yet?" I'd been asked more than once before ever being on a ship. It's like learning how to "swing it" to a song like *In The Mood*. You simply get inside the music, become one with it, a partner of it. You don't force anything; you go along with it. Don't try to control it or compete with it. It's like going down the aisle of a fast-moving passenger train. You roll with it. You let it roll. You do not try to straighten it out. It's that easy!

Yes, it's the mind that decides, not the legs. And it isn't the legs that boil over into a state of nausea. If a person tries to keep his body on a level with something other than the ship, the nerves ignite. Let the sea be; it takes care of itself. And since the stomach is lined with the stuff that nerves are made of, well, that's it. Voila! Overworked nerves rebel. You could stuff your stomach with soda crackers, but that would only soak up some of the acidity. If I were to tell some shipmates my remedy, they'd call it wishful thinking or voodoo. Well, time will do the telling.

Another hunch. Because every ship rides differently, you must adjust to its rhythms and mannerisms. Maybe a carrier or troop transport will be easy on sea legs, but a "tin can" or a DE or a PT boat is a ship of another shape. You have to submit to your ship and be a part of the whole. My surrendering to the ship and the sea is like time accepting a junior partnership with space. Three years or the duration plus six months of a partnership with Uncle Sam...better join the *Machias* and the Atlantic, too. Hopefully the Pacific.

The Last Romantic War

Right now I haven't got anything more than a hypothetical analogical leg to stand on. But back on the "Mighty Mac," maybe I'll have two sea legs to stand on!

Ah, Romance!

The stars are dancing tonight, and an almost full moon is darting among the racing clouds. And I am alone on the fantail, the stern of the ship, sitting wakefully on the depth-charge racks. It's a good night for gray and any matter. The air is warming and the soft swells and engine screws can barely be heard. Perhaps one of the best things about sea duty is the solitude. This despite the heavy population aboard. Almost no one sallies forth to the fantail after dark. I'm wearing sound-powered phones and only occasionally do sonar sounds and voices break this immaculate silence.

Without knowing it, or rather without identifying it, I suspect that I see the world through different eyes, my own eyes. Different, in the sense that I see and appreciate so many things that seem to be passed over by my shipmates. It seems that this was true of my childhood as well. I was fascinated by ancient history and geography as early as grade four. I knew every state and every capitol and proved it, on demand, in Miss Matteson's fourth grade class. The same was true on the playground. At eleven, I filled in at left field for a grown-ups' softball league game and got three for five, all liners down the left field line. It must have helped, being caught between two cultures plus nine older siblings. It was a childhood that money could not buy. I grew up in splendid poverty, you might say. We had an abundance of nature: the piney Pewabic, Pine Mountain, and Millie Hills were like background music that replaced the grating racket of the iron ore conveyers that poured ore into industry. Nature held sway over the man-made streams of ore no less than it served my youthful imagination.

Not that my mind's eye was brighter or better; I was simply interested in everything. I loved the songs of the late twenties and early thirties and knew many of their lyrics. I enjoyed ski-jumping on the small hills behind B Shaft, a mine entrance. We used rubber bands scissored from inner tubes of Model A cars to keep our feet in the skis. Flying in the air for about fifty feet was fun for a ten-year-old. Life was loaded with outdoor experiences. I could never get enough and often invented new ones, some via the Arthurian tales written by a writer less formal than Alfred, Lord Tennyson. At age eleven, I carved my Excalibur out of wood lath and hacked down a few rows of autumn-brown corn with it. Our neighborhood was filled with kids, both boys and "tom girls," whose intentions were to have as much fun as possible by our own making. It was an excellent melting pot of imagination too.

I'm saying all of this as a way of partly accounting for my romantic view of life. I'm sure the presence of a friendly nature contributed. The pine-covered hills of the Iron Mountain country are picturesque. So are the lakes and streams and their seasonal changes which continually make the familiar strange. And one cannot help but stretch the imagination, since the Menominee Range in the Upper Peninsula of Michigan is unlike any other place in our country, or so I've heard.

So when Bermuda's flying fish skimmed the swells and landed aboard the fantail of the *Machias*, I think it more than curious. On watch, there's time to think about that particular fish that I had read about. I pick it up gently, looking for its "wings" before sliding it back into the sea. Perhaps it's only a touch of empathy. But I did ask of it, "Don't you know you've sailed onto an American warship, you fool?" I can ask myself that same question and be none the wiser for it. The reasons do not seem to matter; how it travels, does. The "how" always seems central, for how something is done tends to define the "whatness" of it. For example, Babe Ruth looks better striking out than most hitters do getting a home run. There is art, joy, and passion in his every swing. It's the romance of style.

Yet there is a war on. And it promises plenty of dangerous experience. If the occasion demands it, maybe I'll go beyond simply doing my duty. Honor doesn't come easily; heroes are made, not born. I learned that in sports. Books are stuffed with heroes, more than enough to go around, and just about all of them are forgotten, too. While a fourth grader, I read about the early wars of conquest, about Roland and Charlemagne and the battles that supposedly had changed the course of history. My older brother, now in France with Patton's forces, would tell me much of the history that he had learned before sleep overtook us both. And now we are both making history, my brother more directly than I. Fiore will someday be telling me about the defeat of Hitler and how his setting up communications played an unsung but vital role.

So, when I climbed Hulst School hill which overlooks the crescent city of Iron Mountain, I saw far more than the city and 20 miles of scenery. I tried to see my future. What would the woman I'd some day marry look and be like? How would it feel to be pitching in the ninth inning of a shut-out for "my" Chicago Cubs at Wrigley Field? What could college be like? Even if I had no starting money, I knew there would be a way. There was too much to know and do, and college was the best place to find out and prepare. From this, my favorite hill, the scenery was more than exotic, especially in the full regalia of autumn. And more, it seemed like a magical window to the whole world, a world that demands both contemplation and meditation and accomplishment.

I have faith in God and in man, too, for that matter. But it is up to man to do the dirty work, so to speak. Equality of opportunity fits into my "profile of man," and this is all encompassed by the idea of liberty. America always moves so slowly but in a good direction, mankind's direction. We're on the exciting path of destiny.

This colossal war seems predicated on the idea of liberty, freeing our spirit and energy, and assuring all people of the "right to become." We finally got the Declaration of Independence right. There are duties and responsibilities, of course, but it is both honors and fulfillment that really matter. Living each moment, creating an identity, learning how to live is what counts. It isn't the goal or the ends that are supreme: it's how you travel.

It's easy to be an amateur philosopher aboard ship, privately, I remind myself. It would be jake if we'd get in touch with nature and learn how to enjoy things. Right now the soft sea doesn't give a hoot that we're trespassing on it almost recklessly.

In my classical high school, I read some Twain, Thoreau, Fitzgerald, Hemingway, and even the easier stuff of Shakespeare. But aboard ship, we are too busy and mentally preoccupied to even notice the absence of reading material. Maybe these or any authors might be too distracting to our purpose of chasing submarines and looking out for enemy aircraft. Just survive the war, I tell myself; the rest will take care of itself in due time. Easier said than done, my imagination tells me.

I'm all for experience, even if it "keeps a dear school," as Franklin said. "Book larnin'" has its place, but when you're nineteen, experience can be the best teacher, the final teacher.

Anthony Gianunzio

I've learned plenty since enlisting in October of '42. The ideals are still in place, but they're tempered by that experience. Idealism often gets out of control in people with vicious ambitions. Stalin is a prime example. Communism fairly reeks with good intentions, just like the road to hell is paved with them. Idealism is a tempting bait. Is there even an ideal idealist? The means always seems to get in their way. Hitler is no more than a perverted example of an idealist. One part idealism blended with four parts pragmatism and one part expediency might be a workable formula. I like what Honest Abe said: "You can fool all of the people some of the time, some of the people all of the time, but you can't fool all of the people all of the time." The "what" of idealism is fine; how we get there is the stumbling block. How I'm getting through this war right now is worth a few minutes of thought. Anything can happen and it probably will. Even now.

There's little room for cynicism in my life. The freedom to play as a child has taught me to love, to adventure and discover. I learned how to throw a curve on my own. It started at twelve with a sweeping roundhouse which I later honed into a sharp-breaking fast ball. Sort of an index finger curve that looks like an inside fast ball but drops from the inside waist to the outside corner at the knees. It's fun to throw and it doesn't require an unnatural snap of any joint. I throw it with everything behind it. That curve has a personality of its own, a one-of-a-kind.

Baseball is loaded with romance; it's open-ended, unlike the limiting conditions of football, basketball, hockey, and it depends on how you, individually, play the game. It's the perfect relationship of the individual to the group. In many ways it's like what living in America is. And deep down I know that's what we are fighting for. Maybe it's a questionable idealism to think so. It's simply the freedom to create one's identity, to become a person, to live a special and unique life, to get a lot of things done, to leave the world a bit better.

I wonder if my shipmates have come to the same conclusions on some playing field. It's sort of funny that of all places to be ruminating over such thoughts, and sitting on deadly depth charges to boot, I'm at a place with a scary reputation: the Bermuda Triangle. Were it not for the presence of roving subs, I'd direct my fears to the triangle instead of those dreaded U-boats.

Tonight's watch is an unusual one. I feel thoroughly alone. I hope we don't encounter another American patrol ship that offers no recognition signal like we did north of the Bahamas. We were just one command away from gunfire. A moment of truth like that defines romance to a "t." I was never more alive.

Romance can color any activity, any idea, even love. Now, about women: not that I'm a saint or even want to be, but the talk I'd heard about women by servicemen is often none too flattering. Maybe it's only the bad guys who talk about their so-called exploits with women. Getting bragging rights, you know. Maybe it's the war itself that threw home-town values out the window in favor of devil-may-care, away-from-home behavior. Things are topsy-turvy alright, as in "It was the best of times, it was the worst of times" of Dickens. I'd had the best case of first love with an unforgettable, ideal girl. A sophomore boy is surely no match for a senior girl, yet it lasted two months: from the Sadie Hawkins dance to her graduation in January. Although she had left to go to nursing school right after graduation, no one could take her place in my heart while in high school. The romantic truism, "absence makes the heart grow fonder," easily out-distances the classic cliché, "out of sight is out of mind."

With the coming of war the playing field is expanded, but the rules of romance haven't changed. Desire for experience hasn't affected how I treat my date. There are no regrets; the memories are O.K. A well-lived present makes for a perfect past.

I'd heard that romance is unrealistic, that a romantic couldn't understand what is real. "Incurable romantic" is a phrase that annoys me, young as I am. You can be an incurable anything, an incurable cynic, for example. It's like begging the question. One can be an incurable saint. However, a person sees the world, and if the world is fully available, I see that as a healthy relationship. I simply see life itself as a romance.

The realm of love doesn't have a monopoly on romance. A doctorate is always stated as the philosophy of medicine, the philosophy of this or that. The same goes for romance: the romance of the high seas or whatever. I have a strong feeling that this war, bloody as it has been, has more romance in it than all previous wars together. I believe this even knowing that our Civil War contained much romance on both sides. Margaret Mitchell recently wrote a book that could live as long as Tolstoy's *War and Peace*: *GONE WITH THE WIND*. The passing on of the mellow, classic South into the vigorous energies of a newer America reveals what we have become and always were: a romantic nation.

What romance itself is changes. Once upon a time, a picket fence symbolized the ideal, the classic. But now a picket fence has the flavor of romance: the distance of time brings an added dimension. Days of yore, the imagined halcyon days, have that romantic charm about them. It's probably why our parents are always harking back to their youth or the good old days. Anyways, romance is just as bona fide as reality for its ability to change. Somebody, probably an ancient, said that things must change in order to stay the same. For me, romance is my reality. Just hope there isn't any sub lurking between us and Bermuda.

Sometimes on this unforgettable depth charge rack during

the dark hours on my eight-to-twelve watch, I can foresee an enlightened world, a world still a long way off. At least my life is centered on fulfillment, and once this duration plus six months is served, I'll go flank speed ahead.

Quality of life, I believe, is equal to the quality of one's thoughts. I've made the most, or tried to, of what there is. Sitting on this depth charge rack is a once-in-a-lifetime experience, and few people get to do it. Who knows how many months, how many close calls? The excitement of being blown sky high wouldn't be fun since there'd be no earth to come down to. I don't mean to digress. What I mean to say is that how you look at life determines what it will be. I remember this saying: "Be careful how you see the world: it is just so." The people I have known all have something to offer; their good stuff easily overriding their shortcomings. Even when there is a Mordred there has been a Gareth or a Galahad.

I wrote a short story when a high school junior, and its last line summed up my boyhood dream: "It was great to be young and to be a Yankee." This world war will probably take that opportunity away from me, but only if I choose another course. I'm sitting on this depth charge rack because I know doing this will allow me to choose another course.

How I'd gotten bitten by this incurable bug, romance, still puzzles me. It can be explained logically, unromantically, of course. Anyway, I'll see this war through the mind's eye of a romantic. And that shall be more than real enough for me. If this war is worth fighting for, it at least owes us the privilege of living life via the spirit of romance.

Our *Machias* is a brand-new ship, both in design and age, just like America. Both have much of the familiar, but both flaunt a strange design. Our flair is in the graceful, seaworthy sweep of the bow that slices water in a most natural way, but

America's design has a far greater reach. She dares put more trust in and offers more opportunities to its people. The old, rigid hierarchies are melting away, giving ground to the energies of individual men and women. Both America and the *Machias* are sailing into fairly uncharted waters , but with a forward look to the future. Now, that's romance for you: dangerous, beckoning, and passionate. As with the romantic music of the thirties which I took for granted, so do I expect the same of America. The melody of our great American experiment has always been our yearning. Now the lyrics need just a little polishing, and certainly not an ism-atic mutation!

Viva America! Viva Romance! I have to admit that sitting on my puffy, kapok life-jacket which I've placed on the last depth charge with legs dangling over the side, hardly seems a romantic experience. But the wake glitters and the moon is on a roll. You can bet I'll turn this into "my" romantic war.

Chippewa Run

One of the sweetest, most heartwarming words in my lexicon—Chippewa—has nothing at all to do with that Indian tribe in the Upper Peninsula of Michigan. It's heartwarming because it was the way you got home on a swift and reliable train out of Chicago that arrived in Iron Mountain at 7:15 p.m. daily. It traveled "The Milwaukee Road" straight north through Milwaukee, Green Bay, Iron Mountain, and a couple of stops further north.

It was a godsend. With gas rationed, no flights, and thousands of servicemen anxious to get back home on furlough or leave, it was a perfect fit. Had it not existed prior to our big war, some venturing railroaders would have created it. The Northwestern 400, its companion and competitor, stopped at Powers, some thirty miles shy of Iron Mountain.

But it was far more than a matter of convenience for me and the thousands who packed its comfortable cars. You see, the Upper Peninsula country is a country of its own, ever different from Chicago, Milwaukee, and even northern Wisconsin's small towns. You were entering a unique land when the Chippewa crossed the Menominee River bridge and into the U.P. of Michigan. The land itself is different; the bluffs and hills rise almost instantly, separating from the soil-rich but flat Wisconsin terrain. A colorful combination of hardwoods and pines decorate the autumn and spring seasons. The pines of winter offer a pleasant eeriness as they shelter dry white snows. It's as if no one lives here, but in truth a comfortable ambiance rules. At least that is my impression of "God's Country."

And more, it exemplifies our melting pot land, made so by two generations of Europeans who came to work in the mines, sawmills, and the like. They grew up together, went to classical schools where the main function was college preparation. They sensed the American Dream, and the Great Depression, fortunately, was withering away.

Life was chock-full of stern lessons for us all, but it was also filled with the joy of being in a country where freedom was more than a word or a promise. You could complete high school, steal third base, even join a union. You devoured a "cousin Jack" pasty, forked genuine Italian spaghetti, and explored plenty of ethnic foods a la carte. And there was the American Dream childhood, too, for it was filled with a variety of experiences that seemed perfectly natural.

Therefore, a "yooper" (a native of Michigan's upper peninsula, or U.P.) was accustomed to this built-in variety, and it was easy to be friendly. And it was easy on the magnificent Chippewa to be friendly. Conversation almost seemed a duty. Everyone seemed to have earned a natural togetherness on the war trains.

I'm on the home-bound Chippewa and look around to see if a familiar face is there. Uniforms of the army are everywhere, but the blue sea-going garb stands out. Somehow, sailors always look like they're having a good time. Our tailor-mades are swanky in comparison with the GI olive-drabs. The white-striped collars, the kerchief, the bell-bottoms and the snug fitting pants contribute a lot. All of this is topped off by a white cap resting jauntily on the back of the head. What gal could ask for more?

All the boisterous gab, the glasses clinking in the club car, and I, I want to be on my last Chippewa Run back home. That's it in a nutshell.

To hell with it. Might as well, as the saying goes, "eat, drink and be merry, for tomorrow...?" It would be damned good to hear the conductor sing out the familiar names.

"Pembine, next stop."

My heart always raced a bit when I heard the name. I remember my second baseball game in the Interstate League. Had a single, double, and a triple. The triple started low over second and kept low just over the center-fielder's head. Felt like I could hit anybody's pitching. That was the America I loved, even if it happened in Pembine. At least I was eighteen; all of life was still ahead.

A bunch of GIs are starting to sing. A corporal with a row of ribbons and a guitar starts up. He is trying to keep up with the *Beer Barrel Polka*. None of them know the words, but it doesn't matter.

"Next stop, Iron Mountain... Iron Mountain, next stop."

Now this is real music to the ear. "Pembine... Iron Mountain," is a helluva one-two punch. By now the friendlies aboard almost sound rowdy. More than a few look more than friendly. Everybody is on your side here. Civilians even offer their seats to servicemen. They rarely accept, except when it could improve their nearness to some interesting and interested gal.

"Gonna take a sentimental journey. Gonna put my heart at ease..." Everybody's singing it now. Wishful thinking. "Seven, that's the time we'll meet, at seven... This railroad track that takes me back..." It IS seven and the Chippewa is roaring over Horse Race Rapids on the Menominee River. In just another seven minutes I'll be home again. I can almost see the crowd at the station.

There would be no one for me at the station. No gal I'd left behind. No tears of joy. Oh, my heart was there, alright. I simply hadn't wanted a sweetheart who'd worry about me. Being out there is tough enough. That homecoming crowd looks just fine, too. Plenty of sweethearts in it. Parents and family, too. It's America a la carte and America, for better or worse, is my sweetheart.

The Readiness is All

It's mid-May and the shake-down cruise has gone admirably. Our three-inch fifties have scored well on surface targets and the anti-sub drills went well. We've been dueling a captured Italian sub, and gunnery officer Hanna seems to have learned tactics and strategy on that California University football field. Setting pattern Able and Baker and a deep 500-foot Charlie setting come easy enough. What it would be like on a dark night might be another matter.

Our massive Atlantic convoys with heavy DD, DE, and air escorts are controlling the supply situation. General Rommel's army is kaput, and there's little doubt that we'll win this war. All that seems questionable is the cost and the time. My brother Johnny is there in charge of army motor transport. My sister Mary is sending me the news.

Now that the terror of chronic sea sickness has subsided, I almost feel like a genuine sailor. Feels good to be in summer whites. The Gunner's Mate third class chevron looks good on the right arm, too. The Bermuda breeze is even better. No more in the deep troughs and swells that rolled my stomach into an inferno of nausea. What a relief! We're about done here, and no doubt we need more guns and other work at a shipyard, probably in Philly.

ANCHORS AWEIGH!

So long, Great Sound Anchorage, Bermuda. Not a bad honeymoon here. Maybe in ten years?

So long destroyers 339 and 582 and a fleet of other

destroyer escorts. So Long DD U.S. Porter. Maybe we'll meet again. Welcome Norwegian freighter Braga. Let's do the zig-zag dance back to the states.

Saturday, May 20, 1944, 16:09 (4:09 pm). Pilot boat alongside. Lt. Comdr E. Reid, USCGR, came aboard as pilot.

Maneuvering...into Philadelphia.

The veterans aboard–guys twenty-four plus–are making ready for a cinch liberty. They are scrambling furiously. I'm barely twenty with only limited big town experience. These are hungry seadogs. Nothing, not even the skipper will keep 'em aboard.

• • •

You don't need keen ears to catch the hell-raising postmortems. Seems like they painted the town red, white, and blue. Can't wait. I'll go it alone. Maybe Ed Green from Milwaukee will join me. Philly is crammed with blue uniforms. Plenty of ships being outfitted, some in dry-dock, nothing but sailors spending dough and plenty of gals on the enjoying end. Thought Milwaukee was hot; Philly is right there, too. Plenty of memory material. Seems like this war is made to order for the music. The Brass Rail nightclub is just right for a break. You wouldn't guess there's a war on. Not that we forgot. This is as sweet as it gets for someone ready to spend a little of his youth. But, of course, romantically and innocently. There was Marie and...

Half of the *Machias'* crew is gone on ten days leave less than twenty-four hours after docking at Pier B Navy Yard for alterations and repairs. The rest of us are barracked nearby and report to dry-dock at dawn.

There's a different war going on aboard the high and dry

The Last Romantic War

Mighty Mac. Riveters are rattling our eardrums. Welders'
smoke-screens are stinking our nasal passages. Dense cloudlets
hang head-high in the 90 percent humidity in what must be
more like a July heat wave. River dampness compounds the
sweltering heat. The debris is ugly, the noise deafening. There is
no relief except the assurance that in about ten days it'll be our
turn for a leave. Nothing could be better than to spend the time
in Iron Mountain, where June really busts out all over.

The shipyard guys have fortified us with another five 20mm
anti-aircraft guns, three of them on the fantail to keep me
company. They're bound to come in handy. Being harnessed to a
20mm is something like riding a runaway horse. Trouble is, I'm
both mechanic and their gun captain. I went to gunner's mate
school naively believing that I'd be firing one. In self-defense, of
course.

I feel like a bona fide *semper paratus* sailor now. We've run
the New Orleans to Bermuda gauntlet alone, passed the shake-
down training easily, and have escorted a freighter without
incident across torpedo alley to the states. And now the *Machias*
is headed for real duty, the big show at last. But where?

This leave is going to be my last remembrance of the
disappearing days of teen life. I board the Milwaukee Road
Chippewa for the 320 miles into the Upper Peninsula of
Michigan. It will be a nostalgic run: Chicago, Milwaukee, Green
Bay, into the iron-ore mining Menominee Range. Only this time
who knows which friends I've lost and how the war has affected
my mother and father? My brother Fiore, twenty-three, awaits
the invasion of the continent. He also carries our father's prayer.
Johnny, twenty-seven, in charge of motor pool, has been
through the African campaign. It's the quiet before the final
storm. Like an indestructible optimist, I'm certain that even a
war can't bring us down.

Anthony Gianunzio

The conductor's, "Next stop, Iron Mountain!" electrifies my heart and nerves. There isn't anything now that can stop me from reaching home. Nothing. I promised my mother that nothing would harm me, that I'd be home again. Just a matter of minutes now. A matter of arriving back to the old world which I knew wouldn't be there. Well, I'm different, too. But I'm still that youngest seventh son. Not wearing tailor-mades and no big head, either.

My parents, especially my mother, show aging. Nothing can spoil the first week of June. Yet I am reminded of my last week of school in 1940. It was wonderful, the class picnic at Fortune Lake near Iron River. The caravan smash-up climbing Crystal Falls hill is already a forgotten matter; no one was hurt, just fenders. Would this leave resemble that senior week, which sent me off into a world promising nothing except obstacles?

Iron Mountain and sister city Kingsford, with more than twenty thousand people before the war, now seem deserted. Gas rationing, no doubt. They are skeleton cities short of about three thousand young men. My adventures are accidental, lonely yet unforgettable. I decide to climb the fire tower on Pewabic Hill overlooking the city. I'm going alone and maybe to prove I can scale it just to shut down my fear of high places. Maybe it's to test my ability to take on any fear that comes along. The tower rises forever and I dare not remove my hands. It's windy, and the tower sways. I reach the platform cabin. I am truly alone.

Climbing the tower was on my Ben Franklin list of things to overcome. My eleventh grade English teacher would be proud. Must be 150 feet above ground. I feel a complete stopping of everything. I'm on top of a precarious world, figuratively and literally. It's like the romantic cliché: time stood still. I'm frozen in space, and fear hasn't quite melted.

Church bells gong furiously. Something's off kilter here. Oh so carefully I retreat to the pines and hike the mile down to my boyhood home on Quinnesec Street. The Ford Plant whistle, the reliable timekeeper, is sending a new message of some kind. A cacophony of bells persists. Descending hurriedly, I head for home a mile downhill.

"They're landing in France!" Mrs. Larsen intercepts me and tells me. "It's on the radio." She looks at me with thoughtful eyes.

"My brother Fiore is there."

I picture the armada a thousand times bigger than the Spanish one plus the LSTs and landing barges. Our air power will be the umbrella covering it. I tell my parents that he wouldn't get ashore until the way is cleared. This is of little comfort to them. They know that now the real testing of our strength has just begun. There's no joy at home. My oldest sister Mary, whose husband is a Tenth Mountain Division soldier, looks after our parents and keeps the V-Mail coming. This will be a tough goodbye. There will be no "see you when" date.

The last four days of my leave disappear into an attempt to preserve my notion of indestructibility. Somehow that paper prayer is a given. But I have only a vague notion of what it'll take to destroy Japan's army and how long. They've got total control of the western Pacific. Island hopping will help. There's going to be hell to pay from now on.

I'm almost anxious to get back to the USS *Machias* and am totally surprised to learn that about thirty shipmates out of 232 ship's company are AWOL. War demands love of country, a certain amount of faith, courage, and a fair amount of ignorance. Those escapees are gonna return, I think.

Our *Machias* leaves dry-dock in mid-August, and the D Day invasion has gained solid ground. We've got new muscles. Some new crew. New York and a convoy awaits us, scuttlebutt says.

Anthony Gianunzio

We swing around the Chesapeake Bay and head north. The lady statue almost waves, and we dock up the river.

Manhattan is gleaming and tall. It is tempting and overwhelming. I dash across Central Park. Fifth Avenue is dazzling. I escape in time, but the memory is indelible. I'll be back, whenever...

It's August 28, and as Captain Alexander solemnly warns us at quarters, we are in for a lifetime of at least two years of duty somewhere and everywhere in the Pacific. The climate will be O.K., even if the hospitality will be lousy. We'll have miles to go as we escort seven British troopships overloaded with American G.I.s and others to somewhere. Their names are impressive, if not memorable: HMS *EMPIRE BATTLEAXE*, HMS *EMPIRE MACE*, HMS *EMPIRE SPEARHEAD*, HMS *LOTHIAN*, HMS *EMPIRE ARQUEBUS*, HMS *LAMONT*, and HMS *GLENEARN*. *Empire* doesn't look too American, but they've done plenty for the cause of liberty.

Three other frigates join us: the Allentown (PF 52), Sandusky (PF 54), and the Charlottesville (PF 55). Skipper's ten minute speech gets plenty of attention. The reality of WWII is etched on our faces.

Next stop, Norfolk, the Navy's "sailors and dogs keep off the lawn" town. At least we come first. The AWOLs (absent without leave guys) come next. The skipper is interrogated: Why so many going over the hill? He's not quite Captain Bly of the Bounty. A congressman conducts the hearing; it's a murky muddle, but they are replaceable. We dodge a hurricane and pull into Charleston. No stateside last liberty except for commissioned officers. Ed Green is transferred to the USS *Gordan*, a troopship making the Atlantic convoys. Brrrrrr. I've lost my best buddy.

In a couple of days we pass by Cuba's eastern shore.

The Last Romantic War

America seems remote and the sea already endless. The skipper's mutt-like dog dies. He's been seasick and totally maladjusted. He's a dead seadog. Skipper captained a cutter in the rough North Atlantic for a year or so and suffered sea sickness all the time. Yet he wanted this assignment. Patriotism and ambition might be a good combination. I'm getting the impression that he's a go-by-the-book officer. I hope he can read between the lines.

My sea legs are holding up fine, but no real test as yet. Plenty of shipmates are gulping soda crackers. Felix Magrone is woozy even in calm weather. I'm lending him a psychological hand. But he doesn't get this "go with the ship" stuff.

The bridge lookout has discovered a thin line of land. Radar picked it up an hour ago. This convoy is slower than molasses. I don't think that U-boats give a hoot about stuff going to the Pacific. They've got their hands full with the Atlantic shipping.

Colon is more than rum and Coca-Cola. It is wild. We'll wade into it. Better keep our heads above water. Me, I'll probably pull shore patrol duty. That will not be fun this being the last chance for some of our hell-raisers to booze it up. At least I'll carry a forty-five. And the gunner's mate stripe will let 'em know I can use it. My stick is a mini baseball bat. I think the GIs aboard won't be allowed ashore. Who's going to police 'em? Shore patrol duty is new to me.

What a hell of a war, and it's only just begun.

Coming of Age

Dead ahead is the Panama Canal. It brought us into the twentieth century and is now transporting us into our war zone of choice. New Orleans, Bermuda and its triangle, Philadelphia, New York, the Atlantic/Caribbean, and Limon Bay of the Canal Zone are behind us. We've run a full route: the conception and christening in Milwaukee, the Mississippi umbilical, the Gulf uterus, the weaning and training in Bermuda, the outfitting and dressing-up in Philadelphia, and now the USS *Machias* and crew are old enough to chaperone four British troopships packed with American GIs headed for somewhere in the Pacific. A ten-day leave is under our belt. We are five months old to the day. We have run our second gauntlet: New York to the canal. This troop convoy has a few thousand miles to go.

Painstakingly, the USS *Machias* needles her way through the lakes and locks of the Isthmus of Panama. Our crew is baptized by soaking monsoon rains that pin us down under the gun canvasses. Canal passages are often hidden by the tropical terrain which rims its lakes and channels. This is civilized jungle; camouflaged gun sites wink at us as we hurriedly make our way through narrow passages.

An absorbing mood of awe settles on us, topside, as our uninitiated frigate is sucked through the waterways. The air is heavy with moisture, and now and then an anti-aircraft gun undresses in drill under the cover of jungle camouflage. This South Atlantic run has been a breeze, though a hurricane diverts the eight-ship convoy into Charleston. Somehow the subs, prey-hunting as they still are, though seldom against escorted convoys, are barely a concern because our big show will be in the next theater of war. No Jap subs here.

But still the mood is ominous. We're running this carefully guarded gauntlet like a Pamplona bull tormented by picadors, and even now are being steered into that vast unknown arena of the Pacific that lies only hours ahead.

Colon and Panama City have disappeared as silently as mourners after a wake. In a brief day or so we will pass into the Pacific. It's twilight, and Balboa and the horizon dissolves and blurs into a nondescript gray line. I try to keep an image of it within me but, like most of our military past, our future has no use or need for it. I hardly remember how Captain R. T. Alexander, a wisp of a man, warned us 232 enlisted men to expect a two-year tour of duty aboard ship. His anchors aweigh speech before the mast was a sombre one. Especially after enjoying the glitter of Manhattan.

And now the rowdiness and boozing and goodbye-ing are only memorable trivia. Done. *Finit.* Kaput! Likewise the brawling and the whoring. A couple of nights ago in Balboa, armed with a service forty-five, I enter a bar in an off-limits district These scenarios are worth hanging on to. How could I forget them?

• • •

I'm on shore patrol. Five Limeys are clustered like bowling pins and are spinning their bodies towards the door and me. They're probably from the HMS *Battleaxe*, one of four troopships loaded with GIs. Very young but commanding, I know my duty. Something tactful automatically flows from my mouth like, "I know the ale's good and you're havin' a good time, mates. Drink up and out. This place is off limits, mates. Right, mates?"

I didn't expect to hear "Aye, aye" or anything cooperative. Even after pronouncing "mate" to sound like "might," which rhymes with "fight."

I'm also an American, and these grubby-looking Limeys are leaderless for the moment. Maybe my audacity, taking them on alone, stuns them. The slim, slick-haired bartender looks uneasy. I carry a nightstick and a relaxed forty-five caliber at my side. This maybe saves my neck.

"That means drink up, dammit." Damned if the Limeys don't leave peacefully. I don't turn my back on them.

• • •

Scenario two comes more easily, pleasantly.

That same evening I run into something even more risky and risqué. A sudden downpour catches me on a sidewalk. I stretch my baseball legs and cross the street in two strides, but my right foot slips on the wet sidewalk and I make a perfect split. As I'm coming up smiling and as if I'd just stolen second base, I'm looking point-blank into the face of a lady of the street. In a sure, professional way, she throws me her fastest pitch.

"Sailor, do you want some fun? Come to my place up there."

I hesitate. I'm not any more worldly here than at the bar. I blurt out, "Can't you see I'm shore patrol?"

She's quick. "That's no difference. Come on, let's go. I show you lots of love."

All I could do was walk away, flattered by a well-endowed woman of street-side manners.

• • •

I also see how the veterans of such matters are coaching the naive among us. Salty bosun "Nosey" Jones pontificates, as usual, when we hit Balboa.

"You guys ain't gonna live forever. Better get laid. There ain't no tomorrows." Another salty seaman pipes in with, "Cap'n said we'll be gone at least a couple of years. That's a lifetime, kid."

Two Years Before The Mast. I remember reading that novel in high school. Something about punishment at sea. Two years... That's ten percent of a guy's life so far.

So, like a dozen guys who refuse to call it a day, and while Balboa's horizon softly melts into the sea and the setting sun still burns the western horizon, I'm more than sure that my "old world" is left far behind, maybe forever.

The Eight-to-Twelve Watch

Radar and sonar, the eyes and ears of every military ship at sea, are the undercover and overcover agents that guarantee the crew at least five minutes of get-ready, man-your-battle-stations time. Our latest guns-ready-and-manned time has dropped to two minutes. Not bad for a five-month-old crew. Radar can pick up low-flying aircraft at 27 miles out and sonar can ping off submarines at about five or six miles. Also, the four-on, eight-off watches are manned by sailors deemed responsible enough to do the job. I mind the most powerful store aboard: the two depth charge racks on the stern of the ship.

My watch, the eight-to-twelve, is the best. It fits into the normal day: chow at seven, seeing guys around getting work done in the morning, and so on. The afternoon is open if all's well, or we do some guns care-taking. Chow is on schedule and can be eaten in the mess hall. But it's the eight-to-twelve night segment of the watch that's special.

Space and time. Not in the Einsteinian sense, but in a personal sense. Put 232 young men on a frigate at sea and these dimensions become crucial. No vessel other than the submarine carries more flesh per cubic foot than an escort ship. This packed-like-sardines situation reveals itself at every general quarters, man-your-battle-stations drill. Sardines isn't an exact enough image; ants would be more like it. But on the eight-to-midnight watch, thank heavens there's a heaven skyward rather than a crowd on your deck. Yet this kind of packed togetherness causes a unique isolation. I see the same guys each day, about 15 percent of the crew. Even general quarters makes no difference! Maybe being stationed furthest aft does.

It's not that the stars and the family constellations or the moons and sunsets are more important or even more interesting than homo sapiens. They aren't. But at sea and at war in uncertain waters, they are more inviting. It's as if they know this time is reserved for them and they mean to let us humans be more aware of our modest place in the universe. I've always suspected when on a philosophic run of thought that we are little more than magnificent specs and mighty lucky to be that. Believe me this comparison, humbling as it seems, has the foundation of sanity in it. And it has a firm place here in the time and space within me as I both contemplate and meditate on the nature of everything, including nature itself.

I know this war is robbing me of precious youth-time. When you are twenty and feel indestructible, it's an invisible wall that you can see through but can do nothing about. This watch allows you a state of mind, a chance to think and clear the decks of all that has found its way into your consciousness. It's far better than trusting that a night of good dreams will drift your way. Both the past and the future are available out there on the depth charges, and no shortage of the present tense. In fact, the present dominates my consciousness—ninety-five percent of it. But there's no short-circuiting the reminiscences and nothing to stop the scenarios of the future. What more freedom can I ask for? It reminds me of the hours spent on piney Millie Hill overlooking my home town. You could sit on a boulder and bring the past, present, and future together faster than the speed of light.

Sitting with legs dangling over the rack a dozen feet above the ship's twin-screw wake is the epitome of privacy. More than two hundred men lie asleep behind me. In front of me, the luminous wake trails into an absorbing darkness some fifty yards out into the Pacific and melts. By 22:00 the darkness is pervasive, but the Southern Cross has not forgotten me. Murky shadows of troop ships are within a mile, but no other civilized signs interrupt my watch except for an occasional indistinct word or two over the sound-powered phones. That is until someone on the starboard watch mumbles, "Captain's topside, headin' for the fantail."

The news is too late. Inches away, I feel a presence. Slowly, I turn my head to the left, and there the Captain's smallish face, dwarfed by his gold-braided hat, is transfixed, impersonally, upon me. I stare into this space, not knowing what else to do except to show a deliberate discipline, suggesting that I'm well under control. Silently, like an octopus sizing up its prey and thinking it not worth the while, the head dissolves into darkness. Whether this is my victory or his defeat, I'm not certain. Since no word is spoken and his rank is years above my rate, the stand-off is fine.

Again the word is passed. "On the alert, you guys. Captain's on the fantail. Headed for the after three-inch gun. Be alive."

Only one day past Balboa and the old man is checking the watch! You'd think he'd send the Moose out on this sort of expedition. Darkness is damned dangerous aboard ship. Maybe he's foolhardy: it's only been a couple of nights after Joey Pell's aborted drunken foray when he hunted the skipper with his knife. But there are more important things to think about than a doubting captain or even a foolhardy one. Oh yeah.

Frenchy on the port bridge watch is on the phone. He's got the best eyes, ears, and nose aboard. "You'd think the old man would stay off the deck after sundown. Heard McShane tell Barstad this morning on the bridge that he'd be goddamned if he'd make the rounds in the dark again. McShane said he heard somebody on watch say, 'Be alert, guys. Captain's on deck making the rounds.' Said he was mistaken for him. Realized they were same build, height, and looked alike. Said night time ain't the right time to be on deck looking like an unpopular captain. At least he knows the old man don't have too many friends."

Hell of a war. Isn't even safe to be captain on deck of your ship. I'm not that naive; it's a safe bet that nothin's safe, nobody's safe anywhere, anytime, even in the peaceful Pacific. Have a big hunch the eight-to-twelve will be action-time. But night time is a good time to be on watch. Plenty of quiet. Even the soft drone of the twin screws is comforting. Plenty of stars and strange constellations. That Southern Cross, for one. More dramatic than the Big Dipper of the northern hemisphere. At night the winds are soft and soothing. On the morning eight-to-twelve, the deck is scorching hot by ten. Also, it's a cinch that late dawn and evening are times of action; afternoons and past midnight are unlikely times to go looking for torpedoes. Well maybe this isn't true. It's rumored that the Jap navy has more experience at night fighting because they'd been in a state of war since using their carrier-based planes to attack Manchuria's seaports and those on the Chinese Yellow Sea starting way back in 1931.

Worse still, about the morning eight-to-twelve, the black gang running the engine room seems to pour out more smoke. Avoiding the steady stream of smoke streaming from the *Machias'* single stack means a constant walk. Not even the black gang who generally came topside at the stern would do so when they blew the stacks. To complicate matters while convoying, the *Machias'* zigzag course forces me to constantly move to avoid the puke-inducing smoke. After the four-hour stint, I'd join one or two shipmates on the flying bridge where we'd

Anthony Gianunzio

breathe perfect Pacific air to our lungs' content. After half an hour I'd feel cleansed once again.

This midnight stint has other bonuses. It allows for peaceful post-chow relaxation. Our fantail follies and frivolities usually cease by 21:00, when the deck is deserted except for a few privacy seekers. Seaman Blasco Capitani would hold comedy court; the guys would laugh it up and sometimes croon. Sinatra must have been their mentor, for they have plenty of songs to sing. Now and then they'd go on a jitterbug fling for laughs. Depression kids know how to create cheap, innocent fun and think nothing of it. Often we're playing pinochle for two-bits a game before going on watch. These preliminaries help us to accept the four-hour duty in good spirits. No booze or spirits included. Maybe I'm naive about this. The crap shooters operate on the fantail after the monthly "war zone" pay.

But brimming with stars, the heavens can't be beat for company. They're bound to stir your imagination, make you feel insignificant or even indestructible. Their constancy is comforting. I can imagine a Michelangelo painting showing God and Man on a canvas decked out with stars. And—if you have a touch of Huck Finn within—you might substitute his raft for this island-planet we're on, or even this ship-raft, and wonder about how the universe got started. Even why it got started. Nothing boring about it.

This watch is a perfect paradox: it calls for instant action, yet it's the ideal philosopher's place. Sometimes I'm blinking while the stars are winking, and I think they know more than I do. I ask, is the universe growing? And if so, growing into what? Is there an ultimate form, just as a room fits into a building, an ocean into a planet, and a star itself into space? Certainly there has to be some sort of containment. If only we could get out there and take a better look. A Flash Gordon space ship can't be too far off. Is there an ultimate form, or is it, finally, formless?

The sparkling sequins above seem to be giggling and to have a mind of their own about it. They know who fired first. America has always been out for stars. Our flag has forty-eight; Japan has a rising sun...and one that sets.

The Cutting Edge

The locks and lakes of the Panama Canal are already a far-off, strange memory for the USS *Machias* crew and the crews of her sister frigates the Allentown, the Sandusky, and the Charlottesville. Colon, Panama City, and Balboa accommodated our sailors, who think these are their last call liberties and that they'd better go all out. They're easy prey for enterprising women and wicked whiskey. I know... I did some Shore Patrol duty... "Eat, drink and be merry for tomorrow..." was a dangerous *modus operandi* there.

It seems that we're just out of our own end zone and on the two-yard line. We lose one guy from another frigate via rot-gut whiskey. And there's a well-founded rumor that a coxswain aboard another frigate has been battered and left unconscious to die. According to this rumor, several of his shipmates had ganged-up on him in the head. The head is a toilet area located in the ship's bow, and no one lingers there for other than constitutional needs. An inquiry yields no suspects, for no shipmate is willing to talk. It's about as sickening as a rumor can get.

The booze victim was transported ashore a few hours underway in the Pacific when he seemed desperately ill. Our ship's captain, Lieutenant Commander R. T. Alexander, says nothing about either fatality. It is strange indeed that once we plunge into the Pacific, presto! Two lives are gone without a shot being fired. A third was only a minute short of termination.

"You guys hear about 'Joey Pal'? He has a knife, a pet knife.

He's been warned about keeping it to himself more than once. Pal staggered up the gangway with 'Dixie' Towns one hour, five minutes over liberty in Balboa. On first sight they look like ordinary swabbies who painted some of Balboa-town red, plenty red. Balboa, however, is a town of a different color. Weird booze flows all over the place and is dirt cheap to boot.

"Yeoman 3/c Joe Kerber told us the story about skipper's close call. Happened after the Balboa liberty. He came in pie-eyed, and if my memory hasn't deserted me, it was like this.

"Friggin' cap'n. Where the f--- is he, no goo' sonofabitch. Gonna' slice him like a sardine. Where's cap'n. Kill 'im."

Ordinarily, even such language wouldn't excite the typical petty officer of the watch. More than one plastered sailor has talked far stronger than his do-so. It's damn easy to big-talk when a commissioned officer isn't about. No petty officer is going to say more than "knock it off, you're drunk." They've got to live with you the next dozen months. I've taken a shitty word or two from soused swabbies and not thrown them over the side or reported them. After all, a seaman doesn't have too many conversational privileges.

But this one's different. One long knife different. According to Kerber, Pal shoulders past quartermaster Levine on duty and a bunch of us telling stories around the gangway. He heads for the wardroom passageway. No matter that he's rolling sideways. "Hey, he's got a knife, grab him!" Levine yells.

Pal also has a reputation. More than one buddy has seen him fondle the long blade and heard him say, "Better not bug me, nobody's gonna bug me." He's had a deck court warning. Just a friendly scuffle, but the friend suffered minor cuts. Now he's gonna prove it; it's big game he's after. Pal is from somewhere in South Chicago where the livin' is not so easy.

Levine is shoving some late liberty hounds into the

passageway leading to the wardroom in hopes of calming the mouthy drunk. He's also muttering to himself. After all, he let Pal get past him.

"C'mon out, ya chicken-shit," Pal pounds on the wardroom hatch. Nobody answers. The captain is in his exclusive stateroom, not the wardroom. Pal is none too bright; in fact, none of the "volunteers" is too brave, either. It's a standoff. Then the hatch opens slowly. Steward's mate Reilly slips his head out. He's a Chicago negro and knows the street. He distracts Pal and grabs his wrists, and Pal drops his blade and groans under a blue pile of bodies.

Pal is subdued and placed overnight in irons for being drunk, disorderly, and with a dangerous weapon. Pal is no longer Seaman I/C and he's knife-less. He's also in the deck log for as long as there is a United States Coast Guard. And his little sortie earns him plenty of privacy down below in the hold. Pal spends the night under guard and in irons until he sobers up. His knife goes by the deep six, and his reputation with it.

Steward's Mate 3/C W. Reilley is either brave or foolhardy. He probably won't be mentioned in the deck log where Pal's name will appear. "Jes doin' mah duty," he'd say. He and I Indian wrestled a few times, all of them draws.

We've cut the final umbilical cord and thrown away the knife. We're sort of free of motherland America and the Statue of Liberty. Until we see Honolulu, if ever, we might not get another American-style liberty.

South of us lay the Galapagos Islands. We'll receive our second christening there. Because we will have crossed the equator, we get promoted from pollywogs to SHELLBACKS. We'll be the greenest shellbacks in the world.

Shell Game

September 3, 1944. Aboard the troopships are thousands of uncomfortable army GIs, packed in like sardines, headed for that mythical South Pacific paradise, one that I doubt exists. Hedy Lamar's version isn't good enough. Nor is that of *Mutiny on the Bounty*. Guadalcanal, Tarawa, Tulagi, Midway, Wake, Palau of the past few years are a far cry, too. I haven't seen them, but it's a cinch they've been battered. So far the ocean has been a watery desert. Maybe any island will look good in another week.

Our bearing is 249 degrees true, convoy speed 13 knots in a zigzag pattern, and we have begun our fifth day from the port of Balboa, Panama. Our convoy speed is about nine knots or 10 m.p.h. Less than slow motion. Two days ago a depth-charge drill blasted our fantail several feet out of the ocean. Pattern Able, the shallow 50-foot setting at a 13-knot speed, turned the noon chow into garbage, and a whole lot of the crew went into mild shock. Emergency generators turned the lights back on within five minutes. It was an indelible experience, enough to last us until the real thing, which is sure to come. At least we are not prey to the deadly doldrums as was Coleridge's ancient mariner.

It's shortly after ten hundred. Suddenly the shrill bosun's whistle piped by Toby Switzer electrifies the topside. Lt. (jg) Casey Kemper is on the speaker.

"Now hear this. Now hear this. We have just crossed the equator, you polliwogs. All hands not on watch report amidships. King Neptunus Rex will hold court. All hands not on watch report amidships. On the double!"

As soon as the dreaded order is delivered, port lookout Frenchy chimes in with his message. "Con, land bearing 240 degrees. Land off the port bow, Con."

"Con, aye. Radar picked up land thirty minutes ago. Galapagos Islands. The equator." Seaman Bill King, who mans the bridge control phone, seems to be always in the know, overhearing the news quickly, first-hand from the communication shack.

It never fails: every time things seem quiet and uneventful, the expected unexpected hell breaks loose. I know there will be more serious hells in a month or so, but this peacetime throwback ought to be thrown back to the naval academy. Rumors about the shellback initiation, the crossing-the-equator bit, are exaggerated slightly because we know who will run the show. You become suddenly "transformed" from a fresh-water sailor into a veteran "salt." But there's a price to pay. Out of a crew of 232, maybe ten guys are salts. The skipper and exec. Henry Hanna, for sure. Zed Zaunere, our gunner's mate, first class, yes. Who else?

Zed fits the picture of King Neptune perfectly, scepter and all. A youthful king, but a commanding presence. Zed has short-cropped, curly hair and a rectangular, expressionless face penetrated by a pair of steel-blue eyes. He'll be a capable king, alright. He was a New Jersey state trooper when he enlisted.

I can see my wavy hair shampooed with a rotten-egg batter after cutting it into a crew cut. Can almost smell it. Heard someone yell that there's a ten-gallon container of scrambled eggs, not the kind on a high-ranked officer's hat. We haven't seen any kind of eggs since the gulf. Fat chance I'll escape it. Thin chance I'll avoid a scalp job. This is not a skinny operation. Glad I'm on watch. I'll size up the goings on as the guys get their hosing and paddling here on the fantail. Maybe they'll run out of water by the time I get temporarily relieved from watch. Run out of water? Must be dreaming.

The laughing and shouting is a maybe encouraging sign. There must be a touch of mercy—except that the sound of paddle slapping wet pants occasionally punctuates the infrequent spells of silence.

"Hey Frenchy, tell us what's going on below you," I implore over my sound-powered phone.

"Oh, you wait. You'll get your turn and find out soon enough. They're getting haircuts and rotten eggs. There's Barstad now. He wants the old man to excuse him from the haircutting. Ha, the captain told him let his crime fit the punishment. Yup, he's cutting what little hair he had. I don't think Argo will be ship's barber anymore. Lot's of guys are pissed-off at him. He's only doing his duty."

"Nice goin', Frenchy. Is Spinks there?"

"Ya, he's putting up a fight, too. Skipper just told him he's lousy at taking inventory and late on relieving the watch. Zed is putting it to him, too. Just told him he's guilty of tripping the hedgehogs off. Said you almost wiped out the guys on the number two, three-inch fifty. That happened, you know. Just now told him that if he contests the punishment they'll send him down into Davy Jones' locker. The old man's laughing his head off. Nobody's seen him laugh aboard ship. Gotta go. 'Spook' Gray is relieving me."

Well, the die is cast alright. Hope Argo remembers that five bucks I loaned him in Philly. Hope he remembers I always complimented him on his hair cutting. Not worried about running the gauntlet. Give 'em a fake hip here and a change of pace there and maybe I'll get home scot-free. Maybe, sure. Ya, maybe.

Anthony Gianunzio

I'm sporting a strange crew-cut. Damn, this will take at least three months to grow out. Argo at least spared me a bald pate. He knows I'll kill him first time ashore. He's kept his full head of wavy, blond hair. Son of a gun. Fortunes of war, I guess. He went light on the shampoo, thank God. They were running out of juice. At least the water tender cooked up plenty of fresh water for us. Peden has a heart. Now all we have to do is make a face and scare the Japs to death.

I'm headed for the flying bridge to get some uncontaminated, clear air free of the smoke stack.

I spot Dee D' Rosa, and he looks almost spotless. Even looks smug, somehow, a survivor of the ceremony. He's in the laundry business and in position to do a lot of quick favors for both coms and noncoms.

"What did they get you on, Dee?" I ask even knowing it's a kangaroo court.

"Oh, being out of the laundry and spending too much time on the fantail."

"Did you plead innocent?"

"Hell no. They were outta rotten eggs and Zed felt sorry for me. I done him a few favors back in the states."

"Let's hit the flying bridge. The Galapagos Islands are over there on our port beam."

The air is good and the rotten-eggs smell is a mere stinking memory. Funny thing, the islands look like jagged, deformed eggs. At ten miles they give that impression. Maybe the rotten eggs have gotten to me. Maybe it's the egg symbol, the life originator. Damn Darwin and his survival of the fittest!

We weren't too fit today. Barber Argo naturally selected the fittest, and butchered their hair. Yeah, the war is a good test of the natural selection doctrine. Survival of the fittest among the varieties within the species. Us or the Japs. We should take 'em on in baseball. We'd get it over in a week. Old Babe Ruth could take them on. Thanks to baseball, our guys are a lot better at throwing grenades. They're better freedom fighters, too. Any of us can lead if needed. There's no shortage.

These islands look ugly and foreboding from a distance. If that's what survives, heaven help us. Maybe Darwin doesn't believe in heaven.

The waters are calm and the sun is pouring fire. The fantail deck is scorching. Wonder how the GIs are faring aboard the British troopships. Bet the Limeys are starving them. One thing for sure: being a shellback means less than nothing to them. They've been at it since '39. We've got a foothold in France, but it'll take a year at least, and the Pacific will take time.

Two years! That's what the skipper said in his "Farewell, USA" soliloquy before the mast. Two years. Ten percent of a guy's life. At least we're not in the icy North Atlantic.

Veni, vidi... VICI. Easy for Caesar to say.

Squalling Around

"Water, water, everywhere and not a drop to drink." Maybe we've already had enough. Coleridge had to be alluding to the Pacific, for if there is one body of worldly water that fits his ancient mariner's lament, it's the Pacific as I now know it. We're seven days beyond the Galapagos Islands and still no sign of rain, not even clouds. There's plenty of salt, but it's good for one thing only: it makes it easier to stay afloat. Although salty showers are detestable, salt could buy more time while waiting for rescue.

I sometimes wonder what the water-tender rating is all about. Clevenger, Peden, and Hobson wear it proudly enough. Their job is to keep a decent or livable supply of fresh water available. At least one refrigerated drinking fountain is in operation. But what about showers? Shower hours are few and far between. A lot of guys avoid the primitive showering because the salt film feels sticky and unclean. This is no going-out party. But Fels-Naptha soap is more treatment than treat.

Seaman Louie Badman of Huron Indian lineage is as foreign to saltwater as the rest of us. Of course, when we were watered-down in the shellback fiasco, our taste for it hardly improved. And Louie, skinny-tall and fair with cool, blue eyes that denied his ancestry, detested saltwater showers. But under the Pacific sun for a day or two and on depth charge watch, dodging the gaseous and dirty smokestack, showering is imperative. If we had been polled, I and two hundred other guys would have thought that a fresh-water shower is a downright necessary luxury. We keep our eyes peeled for a posted notice that the fresh water spigot is turned on. But without fail, Louie and I are always on watch during the designated times.

"Badman," I say, "we got to shower or else get our watches changed."

"Don't even mention water," he says. "My skin feels itchy when you say shower. Pity those poor bastards on the troopships out there."

Finally, on the twelfth day there is a mirage, or maybe just wishful thinking. Low-hanging cumulus clouds on the horizon dead ahead, and we don't go off watch 'til noon, half an hour away. Within minutes the clouds turn dirty and touch the water itself. I hear a seaman squealing, "Hey, we got a squall!" Nobody pays attention: the dice, as usual, are running hot for Joe Contini, crap-shooter par excellence. Even I'm an interested bystander. It means nothing to the deck hands; they want to get some money back.

I grab Louie. "C'mon Lou, let's go."

Timing, it was all a matter of good timing. Just like right now. Timing makes all the difference, even dead in the water, even in a game of crap shooting, even in an honest one.

As a mildly interested spectator, you are on the alert in figuring odds. It's a form of timing. As for squalls—something I know very little about—ideally, the first time ought to be mid-afternoon of a scalding day. And if you are bored enough to submit to temptation and losing a few bucks, a heavenly downpour might cool off any hot-shot Joe. Even Joe Contini, who always adds to his winnings. Also, if a bar of pure, genuine soap like Ivory is handy, you can make a run for it to the fantail. You're then ready for a nature-sent shower. Tough luck for the guys hiding out or the goldbricks losing dough.

"Break it up, you guys. A squall's off the starboard bow."

Anthony Gianunzio

It works. Master at Arms Stromsta cannot moralize the crew without demoralizing it. So he sometimes gives a little rein, looking for positive benefits, of course. At least twenty bucks are in the pot. They get the free hint. So long, pot; hello, squall. It's like a football team breaking out of the huddle, but they're not stopping at the line of scrimmage. The game's over, we've won, crap-shooters and spectators alike, even if some guys lose a sawbuck or two. In seventy-seven seconds every last craps player, towel waist high, clutching bars of bona fide American soap, is laughing loud enough to attract a dozen unclean shipmates. They look down upon us fantail revelers, mainly with a curiosity much like that of a pup that watches a rolling ball but isn't tempted enough to go after it.

Faster than suddenly, the *Machias* slices into the squall as if she too were alive and thirsty and in need of a cool, fresh-water cleansing. Screams and mild shouts of delight chase even more shipmates out of hiding, and the audience is formidable. Formidable and envious. They ring the three-inch fifty gun shield and think they're going to be entertained. They are.

"Hey Louie, soap my back." Everybody is buddy-buddy. It all feels like a sort of salvation, maybe someone else's baptism.

A dozen of us lathered guys are out there, all in less than two minutes. That's our record time so far for manning all guns at a general quarters drill. Every head of hair is smothered into weird configurations. The gallery is cracking wise.

"Bout time you took a shower." Another joker jibes in with, "Geez, for a while I thought you wuz a steward's mate." It's a Southern voice that I hear.

Surprisingly, even more suddenly than the squall's invasion, a flooding light descends upon us. Panic! Our *Machias* has knifed through the squall! It's like coming out of a darkened cave right into daylight. Within five seconds that heavenly-pure water is no more! A swift evaporation, as if King Neptune waved his wand in punishment. Nothing but hot sun, nothing but guffaws from the circus crowd staring at our confusion and laughing at our lousy luck. Double whammy. First at craps and now this.

The ship's shower is 300 feet away, way up in the bow area. Plenty of passageway to navigate. It would be like walking another gauntlet, like the one in the Galapagos shellback ceremony, only without paddles whacking away at you. We all lost a little pride there, and rotten eggs in one's hair wasn't my idea of crossing the equator, either. Another rotten joke on us.

"Alright, you guys. I warned you about them squalls. They don't last more'n couple, three minutes out here. Need experience, huh," joshed M.A. Stromsta. "There's plenty of hard-water soap up in the head."

Rain in the Pacific is not a simple matter, I'm learning. What looks like a long, warm, and juicy downpour to a Midwesterner might not be that at all. Bet the natives wouldn't be fooled. I had to laugh; brand-new, shiny shellbacks could hardly be expected to read Pacific skies.

Down the starboard passageway we kindergarten kids go, shouldering our way side-to-side with the ship's roll. The barrage of pleasant obscenities count for nothing. Snips like, "Didn't know you finks had a club. How much for the shower orgy?" This, despite the fact that any sign of homosexuality never surfaced aboard ship. Nobody talked about it. It was their business so long as it was kept quiet or from view. And privacy aboard, or rather the lack of it, kept it on ice. Any manifestation of it and you were out, pronto, back on shore duty. So far, all hands opt to stay on this free, sight-seeing government cruise. What else can we do?

Our squall detail is a sight to see. We pass the mess-hall

chow-hounds, who are aghast at the soapy sights before their eyes. We walk with a wide stance, in unison almost, like kids who had failed to reach the urgent goal: the toilet. The mess-deck lingerers are damn near shocked out of their scuttle-butting, being unaware of the five-minute squall. One smart-ass pipes up, "You guys lucky we're not into hostile waters. Going through the mess deck nude could be hazardous to your health, Joe."

Punishment is yet to come: one dozen soapy guys cram into the small shower room, waiting for the cleanest dirty water on the planet.

Hard-water soap smells like Fels-Naptha. It's a poor-people's soap. Looks like it, too, tan and rubbery. Geez, there's something in it. Downright stinks. Whew! But even worse, a saltwater shower leaves your skin sticky-dry. Probably the Naptha "soap" did the dirty work. From Ivory to Fels-Naptha; from crap shooting to squalling. A real good fun life, and we haven't even faced the real baptism yet: bullets that won't just stick to your skin.

We should have showered in the Panama Canal rains. They were endless downpours, something like what I imagine monsoon rains to be. And now this phantom, ethereal squall. What next? Maybe a typhoon.

At least when that happens, there will be no need to shower.

Godiva of a Pagan Sea

Sometime deep in the seventh grade of Hulst Junior High, I created thirty or so salt-flour maps of North and South America. Miss Cruz and my mother both tolerated my prolific mapping; my geography teacher by posting them all around the room and resting them on the chalk runners at the base of the blackboards, and my mother by an occasional reminder that Gold Medal Flour is not inexpensive. My seventh-grade classmates probably were amazed at this mild form of insanity, but a few would produce maps not too short of being works of art. They were more interested, evidently, in letting just one speak for itself. Miss Cruz probably saw each of my accurate, well-painted efforts as motivators. I simply enjoyed this "mastery" of the world, perhaps like how the earliest cave men drew pictures of animals so as to have a power over them by the magic of art.

At any rate, that's how I first became aware of the Galapagos Islands. Now, a mere eight years later, they seem stark colossals of rock as prosaic as the dullest prose can be. I had imagined that the islands would at least offer a unique strangeness, something to rival Charles Darwin's upstart theory of evolution and natural selection. Had it not been for our crossing of the equator, these lack-luster islands might have gone unnoticed. In fact, had it not been for Darwin's fame, the *Machias* probably would have taken a more direct route to the French Society Islands. Perhaps the thousands of American GIs likewise are unimpressed by their army-eye view of these desolate-looking islands.

As if reluctant to reach their appointed destinations, our eleven-ship convoy moves like snails. Galapagos at least provided some comic relief: Lt. (jg) Spinks looks improved with his crewcut. I'm not sure why, but Galapagos seems a fitting host for the ceremonies. The sterility of both is compatible. Bet the Pacific has a lot of fitting hosts.

These are sunburned days, and the metal decks are more than unfriendly. Where 232 men almost disappear to on a ship 307 feet long is a minor mystery, but it does hint at our adaptability, a la Darwin. Hiding places like the bow paint locker, which keep tender stomachs at bay, probably house an occasional card game or a dice shoot-out. Nobody ventures there. Thankfully, the seas remain calm. Unthankfully, this calmness intensifies that ennui which leads to jangled nerves. Men turn inward, do their duties, make their appointed rounds, and that's that.

Thankfully, too, the nights are serene and provide a cooling relief from the heat-radiating decks. The last two hours of my ten to twenty-four hundred watch are especially kind, for the abandoned decks allow the sky and stars to impose their presence. Familiar constellations seem hard to find as we sail westward; even the memorable Big and Little Dippers have strayed. But if one has a shred of aesthetic taste, just looking at the heavens can generate an amateur touch of religion, philosophy, history, and new thought. And I am, as was poet Robert Frost, "out for stars."

Within our diamond formation the gigantic British transports–the HMS *Empire Battleaxe*, the HMS *Spearhead*, the HMS *Empire Mace*, and the HMS *Glenearn*–appear far smaller than their true size. They seem like invisible guests in this long, lonely journey to lands few of us have ever seen, even on maps, or even read about. Guadalcanal surfaced only because of the fighting there. I first heard of it when on the baseball field in the late summer of '42, but hardly expected to be heading toward it. It and other island places already are on my mind, and I know we'll see them.

There's a lot of time to think, maybe even meditate, while seated on a depth charge rack 307 feet from the bow and only a dozen or so feet above the Pacific. In the dark nearing midnight, no one would know if a man falls overboard. Sitting on the rack is risky; you don't fall asleep there. I wear a pneumatic air-inflating jacket around my waist. And my kapok life-preserver is beneath me. Having both assures me of seventy-two hours in the big drink, sharks excluded. But if I were the captain, I would not prowl on deck after dark.

The hours before midnight are rarely dull. These are good working hours for the imagination, whereas logic seems to be more needed during the day. Characters and dialogue can't wait to make the scene. Experiences are replayed, sometimes with different outcomes. All of the bad endings are improved, or at least polished smooth. One moment it would be the horrors of making a three minute report on some news event for Miss Baird's sixth-grade class in history. I'd die two thousands deaths before class time and another thousand before being called upon. Somehow I'd survive even though I thought it was my end. I often wondered if my internal fears were showing, but nobody said anything. They probably saw their own death warrants. I'd rather have faced any other test, hundreds of others that I thought were easy. At least now under warm skies I finally put those fears to rest.

In the center of the convoy, the troop transports with the war-like names keep a low profile. Each is packed like sardines with American GIs, perhaps four or five thousand. What's their chow like? Not that the *Machias* chow is enviable: it barely satisfies. But how do you feed such a mass of humanity? They'll be eager to spot land and feel glad to get ashore after their days at sea.

It has already been ten days and no sign of any land, no rain, no wind, not even any whitecaps or choppy water. It's a desert of an ocean, as empty of personality as a watery soup. Fresh water aboard ship is not even fresh. The "Evaporator Man" simply removes the salt from it so that we might drink it and, if our timing is right, shower in it. My timing is downright lousy. So, it's a Fels-Naptha-like kind of salt-water soap when showering maybe twice a week.

The most annoying problem is the 100-degree plus climate in the sleeping compartments. My asbestos-covered bunk, one of four high, can qualify as a mild torture chamber. Here on the high seas it's even worse. Asbestos covering is used to protect against fire, though I suspect some smart military provider has made a killing on the sale. After a few nights of unbearable heat, I carry a three-inch mattress topside and park it on a ready-service locker amidships on the starboard side. The locker is part of the gunnery division property, so it's easy to lay claim to it. It doesn't matter that a single cable separates me from the sea; the cooling night air is too refreshing to turn down. Sleeping topside is heaven, or some modified version of it.

Earth is fullest at the equator, some 25,000 miles of it. About two-thirds of the globe is covered by water. Aboard a ship such facts become more than facts. Powdered milk is a fact, too. I once loved milk. Our big Jersey cow gave us 22 cream-rich quarts of it daily. Who could stand powdered milk? The cows would be pissed-off if they knew that their cure-all product is corrupted in this way. The French would probably have the usual cliche, *c'est le guerre,* or maybe not. Maybe they'd spell it differently. Anything that resembles a fact out here is bound to be bad news.

I'm as anxious as the next enlisted man to end this strange episode of solitary confinement in the middle or thereabouts of this Sahara of the Seas. I feel frozen in time in the hottest watery real-estate on the planet. Not yet twenty-one and not even looking forward to my birthday on the morrow, I go through the daily routines as if they matter. The chief source of entertainment is watching deckhands make themselves scarce. This scarcity is in abundant supply, especially after morning chow about eight bells.

Nothing I had heard, seen or done prepared me for my first birthday aboard ship. I awake swiftly, having slept lightly on a ready-service locker starboard amidships. Topside is silent, and then Sicurella, the starboard lookout, breaks the silence.

"Con, land bearing 010."

These are the sweetest words since Panama. Big Moose Hanna, now our executive officer, brushes by me en route to the bridge ladder. He seems excited or at least relieved.

"Christ, it's about time," he says. "So this is Bora Bora. She's a beaut." He sounds like it's a matter of discovery. He has seen plenty of the ocean world, having served in the merchant marine. Right now any piece of *terra firma* will do. Hanna is near the helm and he's already got an order out.

"Steer course 160 true." Some of the crew are topside as the word of land gets out. It's barely dawn; the sun is peeking over our shoulders. Curiously, the island shapes itself into the profile of an American destroyer. Aft of its flat, bow-like southeastern tip, a modest mountain resembles the bridge structure. A second high-rise, flat projection imitates the smokestack, and now the island slopes severely, completing the likeness of the profile. My imaginary ship is more than a mirage. But in a few minutes this impression re-focuses into a strange, romantic reality of the island itself.

Only several miles from shore, the crisp lines of the two totally unlike mountains are a fitting crown for an island so generously endowed by nature. This pairing of opposites reveals itself as the pastel greens of the shallow lagoons fade into two deep blue bays parted by a thumb-like peninsula. Coconut palms fringe the bays as far as I can see, and the unseen coral reefs which ring the island are frothing as the tide rolls in rhythmically and stronger each time. It begins to look like a natural castle surrounded by an invisible reef-wall and lagoon moats. Tiny motu islets lush with greenery bookend the reef opening.

Our *Machias* skirts the island's southwest perimeter, and I feel as if we have just discovered an unknown jewel, so unlike the austere Galapagos. The view from the flying bridge is a feast as my eyes roam the full extent of Bora Bora. There seems to not be anyone at home; it is nature a la carte. And now something even more strange: the swelling tide is crashing into the entrance reef a mile away, spewing a fifty-foot rainbow spray skyward! It's not a fluke; it's as rhythmic as if it keeps the ocean's pulse. Every ten seconds or so the spray forms a rainbow curtain. It's strange, but any park fountain will project a rainbow if the sun is at your back.

Nature has played more than one trick on me. I've seen a rainbow is a rainbow is a twin rainbow. But none like this. It is Bora Bora's trademark, no doubt.

Now the *Machias* veers to the northwest and finds the narrow reef opening. The spray bathes our faces. It's like a cosmetic baptism or, maybe, a fantastic wet kiss. The pale-green lagoon is a shallow three fathoms. Now another natural miracle is awaiting. I turn to give the rainbow a last look. It is gone! The spray still shoots skyward, but its makeup is mere mist! The strange has turned into the familiar. In brief, from the romantic to the familiar. That's the key to it all, even of life itself. That will take a book to explain. Maybe some day... From ancient Galapagos to Godiva of a pagan sea, I muse.

The island of Bora Bora could not have been better named. It could not have been more beautiful. It could not have been a better birthday gift. Can't wait to go ashore.

Once Upon An Island

Some islands know instinctively where to be born, forcing their way volcanically, and then in a brief passage of time wrap themselves in a coral necklace linked by a dozen pearls of motu. Seeing her up close is like love at first sight!

Remember how as a child at a park picnic you turned on the drinking fountain and the spray turned into a panorama of color? And when you got on the other side of the spray, it lost its color? Like then, as if a baptism by nature, the spray settles upon us. Turning about to get a last view of that towering rainbow, nature throws us yet another magical curve: this marvelous, sky-high spray suddenly pales! It seems, laughingly, that my island "Godiva" beckons me, charms me with her rainbow attire and, just as soon as I am in her harbor-cocoon, she shows me her unmade, pale face, the one which I am at home with.

Musing further, I suppose that the strange beauty of her "rainbow face" represents the romantic nature of things, and the paled image the classic. After all, people spend nearly all of their time in port or harbor, at rest, in their civilized, orderly world. Familiarity and predictability refer to the classic view and the customary certainties that we live by. We see the paled tidal spray because we are usually at home. When we venture—as romantics are wont to do—we see a rainbow spray occasionally. That strange, often dangerous outer-world is in the realm of romance. The secure familiarity is the opposite side of life's coin. Of course there is much more to it than this, but it's a true clue and maybe a beginning.

Our *Machias* is gliding gracefully into the three fathoms of a clear, soft green lagoon. "Let down the anchor" brings a cluster of "sack rats" topside. From the shore just yards away now, outriggers slide into the lagoon as if racing to reach a supply freighter. Four or five outriggers with tanned Polynesian males press against the hull of our ship.

"Coloa, coloa me hair," a young Polynesian sings up to the deck railing, where curiosity is rampant.

"What t'hell is he sayin'?" Louie Badman asks of no one in particular.

"He's an albino, don'cha see. Wants his hair colored or somethin." "Spook" Gray has it right. "Needs peroxide to keep it looking freaky white. Then he don't have to take a wife. Can have all the women he wants. Free wheeler, sort of. Not a bad life, hey Columbo?." It is a good rhetorical question, for we know curly-haired Columbo has a winning way with women.

"He the only native out here getting away with it? We got peroxide in sick bay, ain't we Spook? Let's jump ship for a day or two." This brings more than one laugh Columbo's way.

A couple of the guys are digging for money and talking odds about their jumping ship. They know they're bluffing. The island is too small, only a couple of miles wide and four miles long, and almost all of it is mountain and slopes.

Larry Lawrence shoulders his way to the rail, flashing a small bottle of colored liquid. "What you give me? Albino. Good for hair," and he points to his crew-cut. The native stands up in the outrigger. "Me see," he says doubtfully. Larry has light brown hair. We and he suspect Larry is pulling a fast one. The native holds a fistful of cat's-eyes for Larry to bite on. Natives dive for them in the lagoon and polish them. They flash in the sunlight, almost translucent with their waves of swirling browns and greens. These stones are oval-shaped, half an inch thick and look like souvenir keepers.

"Good deal," Larry smiles as if it's a defacto matter. The albino smiles and pitches a small sack on deck, and Larry drops the small bottle of who knows what into the native's grasping hands.

"More albinos?" another sailor asks of the native.

"They sleep. Come later," he answers, anxious to leave with his loot.

The lagoon soon becomes a swarming traffic jam, each outrigger fighting for position. An occasional whaleboat putt-putts through them, rocking them. Voluptuous females show their brightly colored sarongs. They gesture and say, "Two dollah, two dollah. Fo cheap. Two dollah."

These women want "lop-lop," white sheets. But no sailor is crazy enough to trade bedding to these fish-market women. When the trading slows to a trickle, the natives pull out, mumbling something that sounds like Frenchifried English. They do not seem pleased; white sheets must rank high for their marital beds.

More boats swing around the bow, but these are grown boys. They point to the lagoon bottom and show coins. A shower of pennies greet them.

"You cheap," the biggest boy says quietly and grins. They know the market well. Other warships have anchored here. Bora Bora is the refueling stop en route to Allied-held islands.

"Give this," he says, and holds up a half dollar. A few sailors respond, and the diving is excellent but brief. One outrigger lingers and the native in it paddles it to the Jacob's ladder amidships. His left leg is swollen and gigantic. Laboriously, he lifts it as he shifts his weight and says nothing. He looks up at the sailors leaning over the rail and appears to be begging. Now, almost every native seems suspect. His leg is the size of his trunk. Some coins are dropped into his boat. His pathetic flaw makes the beauty of Bora Bora seem all the more perfect. Elephantitis is too heavy a burden to carry, but he seems not in pain.

Helmsman Bill King gives us the hoped-for good news. "We're docking soon as the natives clear out. Maybe get liberty parties going, too. Heard there's mail ashore for us."

Twenty-one letters await me, and so do some not quite ripe coconuts. The letters are from friends and family and even though they're a month old, it's good to read the familiar names and places of my hometown. It takes me an hour to read them all. I sip coconut juice, testing my stomach, but the mild nausea leaves quickly. Minutes later at muster, Coxswain "Micky" Spillane and I get the same itching to explore the island. As soon as the "all present and accounted for, sir" comes, we slip into the coconut-grove palms and head for the foothills not more than ten seconds away. This little paradise now seems well within our grasp.

"Let's head for the mountain, Micky. We can see the whole island from the slope. Hey, this is better than rum and Coca Cola! C'mon Micky, let's go!"

My red-haired, freckled buddy is ready. So am I... For almost anything. The "anything" appears sooner. She is doing the local version of the hula, and a dozen sailors are pitching coins to her feet. I'm not too impressed with this scene just now. I float a noisy stage whisper his way.

"Hey Micky, these hula dancers are a dime a dozen. We'll find one on the way back. C'mon, the island's better looking." I want the big picture; the details can be filled in later. He waves me on. I'll go it alone.

There's no path, only exotic foliage. Palms are laughing in

the firm breeze, and it feels liberating. It's the cool season in Bora Bora, pleasant and dry. It could not be more perfect. I finger my way through the ferns and turn towards the mountain giant and realize that I'm alone. I want to make the most of it, but it would be better if Micky were along. Maybe he'll change his mind.

"Micky?" No answer. I wait a few seconds, thinking he's seen enough. Maybe he wants it on his list of war memories. Nice to tell the left-behinds how he saw these hula-hula dancers and how they had put the movie versions to shame. Well, Honolulu is the place for that. Maybe we'll get to Oahu in a couple of years.

This island is a foliage montage, a complete composition. The taller mountain seems like a pagan god and the flat one next to it his altar. A rippling of 500 foot peaks trail the altar, like worshipers on their knees. I'll climb to a point where I can see the lagoons, the ring of reefs and tiny motu islets on the western side of the island. One more haphazard yell for Micky and I'm off, alone and excited.

The mountain towers almost threateningly, linking clouds with its slopes no more than a few football fields below. The going is easy; the footing is firm, and suddenly a path finds my feet. If the Garden of Eden were a Polynesian place, this would be it. Maybe that's what has struck Micky. But a grass-skirted gal? Nah.

Now the pathway quickly broadens. I follow it to a large clearing with a log cabin-like structure and hear something like French drifting out the window. Curiosity sidetracks me. A rectangular cut-out section, ten by four feet–an open window– dominates the rear side. I approach it, hear a masculine voice, and... This is a strange Eden alright. At least forty children seated on benches, row upon row, boys to the right, girls to the left, turn to see me, the intruder. They giggle with a collective, gleeful laugh. I'm more pleasantly startled than they. Before them stands a huge collection of flesh, more corpulent than I've ever seen, holding a pointer delicately downward. The schoolmaster is poised and not startled by my sudden appearance.

"*Entre vous,*" he says, almost smiling.

Through the open window I pivot politely and sit on the unpainted sill. The kids are loaded with smiles; maybe this is a temporary reprieve for them. This is no island for them to be bored, I hope. The children look less than eight years old, and they can't stop giggling. My peaceful invasion is just what they need. Who cares at eight what the products of the Philippines are? The schoolmaster waves his wand-pointer and refers to a map. My high school French tells me that he's telling the children about products of the Pacific Islands. Cripes, there's a war going on!

I delight in the little drama of which I am a small part. The size and demeanor of the gargantuan schoolmaster contrasts interestingly with the children, but after ten minutes I have my fill. It's a polite "*Merci, monsieur,*" and with a smiling nod I pivot back to the ground and continue my adventure. After all, it's the island I'm after.

Soon this island paradise which I'd never heard of would be at my feet. If the rainbow reef had been wondrous, what would a full scale view of the island be? I glance to see if Micky has found the path and hear some talk, English, coming from near the schoolhouse now fifty yards behind.

"Hey Mack!" "Hey Buzz!" Hell, they're from the *Machias.*

"Buzz, Spinks sent us to bring you and Micky back. Said to do it quiet like. He knows you guys jumped muster. We found Micky with a hula-hula babe. Where ya goin'?"

My little escapade is over. Join the Navy and see the world? Sea it, for sure. Or "she" the world if you are a rummy with a gal in every port. They talk about the hootchy-kootchy hula gal all the way back to the *Machias*.

But I'm not giving up on Bora Bora. Ever.

On Deck

Midway, Wake, Coral Sea, Savo Island Sound, Tulagi, Iron Bottom Sound, Tarawa, Rabaul... They are big names, even bigger to me than those of the Yankees' "Murderers Row." About eighteen months ago, Guadalcanal was our toehold in the South Pacific, but "you're on deck, Buzz" meant I'd be kneeling in the chalked circle as the next hitter, not the deck of an American frigate. It was good to see "ducks on the pond" because I'd get my chance to drive them in. There will be ducks on the water now, sitting ducks. Almost anything can be analogized via baseball. "On deck" is a different ball game now. But yes, we are on deck now. "That's for dang sure," as Stuart Whitehead from Tennessee would say.

In '42, the music of the big bands captured the hearts of America's romantic youth. "Swing" captured us and jazz seized our slightly darker side and spruced-up the mainstream stuff. The other genres were more like dialects and belonged. But "Moonlight Serenade" to "White Cliffs of Dover" made the world seem right even if war seemed somewhat wrong. Well, the honeymoon of Bora Bora is gone, and Esprito Santos, too. We're aiming at Guadalcanal. It won't be long now and we'll be pitching in.

September is hot; the deck is even hotter. Sleeping topside is a must. My shoes are "air-conditioned" with a paper punch. Shoe laces are loose and chow is downright lousy, and this is a far different world. It's a far cry from being on deck for a month in Wrigley field. It was a dream almost come true for an nineteen-year-old, a pitcher who had handcuffed the Janesville Cubs with no hits and strikeouts before rain ended the game and the tryout camp. Eddie Stumpf, who caught for the Milwaukee Brewers of the American Association, and Earl Whitehill, Cleveland Indians and White Sox pitcher, liked what they saw. I saw the Big Leagues just around the corner. Honest, I wasn't afraid of it. When you're twenty, you think you're indestructible.

We're a thousand yards from shore and probably 20 fathoms above the bottom. We have skirted Savo Island now and are brushing by Tulagi, heading for anchor near Florida Island, just across the sound from Guadalcanal. "Iron Bottom Sound," where at least a dozen masts of ships stand at attention in water, now mere markers of a pitch-black-night naval battle. The five Sullivan brothers lay there in a cruiser. We were out-pointed in the scrap, but considering that their navy was far more experienced at night fighting, we pretty much made them pay. The masts are unidentified, but this watery cemetery screams its still raw history into my consciousness. A lot of fine kids barely out of high school are down there, and I breathe deeply, making doubly sure that I am alive.

"Let down the port anchor," Lt. Henry Moose Hanna commands. He matter-of-factly adds, "Port liberty at 15:30." This means a shore party on the thin beach of Florida Island, no doubt. Nice to go ashore where history was made. Only a mile or two away, companion island Tulogi was hell to pay, too. Not many Marines got to see their third island.

Hirohito's navy is paying double now. The Solomon and Russell Islands, Rabaul, and New Guinea are ours. Morotai in the East Indies is ours. Australia is no longer in jeopardy. The tide has clearly turned. We are island-hopping, skipping the big ones like Halmahera isolated by our rampaging navy.

Across the sound from Florida Island lay Guadalcanal. From

here, its shore rises a couple of inches on the horizon. It seems to be at rest from this distance, but if we could see it close up it would be in a "parade rest" posture. Bet there are plenty of spit and polish guys there now, unlike those precarious days in the late summer and fall of '42. The Marines invaded in landing barges, never expecting an unopposed landing. They saw the same shoreline that I'm looking at, but what a difference it must have been to them not knowing what to expect except the worst. Like the difference between throwing to a sandlotter and a pro. But I have no desire to pay the present occupants a visit. We hear that it's spit and polish already and an R and R post.

Guadalcanal has a legendary reputation. The name itself sounds ominous and proud, one that defies infamy. A couple of my classmates had slugged it out there, and a couple more are down in the Arizona. On the island, Ray Amicangelo played his accordion for Marine buddies when he had a chance. Had two accordions and he could really play. Heard about this while home on leave late December,'42. This he did in the midst of ugly jungle warfare. The fluid battle lines were bloodied and uncertain. Only the survivors can really talk about it. Wonder if he played John Phillip Sousa's *Stars and Stripes Forever*. Wonder if the Japs heard him. America should never forget what these Marines did there. The best of Japan's army, its elite troops from Manchuria, won't forget it. It was a goal line stand, like Gettysburg, "for the ages," as Secretary of War Stanton said of Lincoln.

After half an hour of gazing respectfully at our icon island and watery cemetery, I turn to the "now" island place. Florida must be correctly named, for no one's ever heard of it and it looks harmless enough. The whaleboat is ready and so are a bunch of us, and we're armed with a couple of cans of a nameless, warm beer. It's been two weeks since Bora Bora, and even if the place is flat with a thin beach, it's still *terra firma*.

About 15 feet of white, hot sand separates the Florida Island jungle from the sea. The beer is really lousy, more than warm, and could be mistaken for urine. I palm off my second can to Herrala, who thinks he owes it to himself to down a third can. This is what working in the ship's laundry does to you. Me, I'd like to explore a little. The thick green foliage looks harmless enough, so I force it apart and poke my face inside the snaggy twine. What I hear, what little I see, is a world that seems like an eighteenth century asylum for the insane. It's not an asylum; it's a madhouse.

The cacophony is deafening. It's as if a thousand bird lookouts each screeches a shrill warning. They sound confident that no human eardrum can stand this for more than ten seconds. I half expect a cobra to slither by or a monkey to leap on my head and tear my hair out. They were fighting with sound effects like this on Guadalcanal? Maybe not. Perhaps the machine guns rat-a-tatting, grenades blasting, and aircraft strafing would make any sane jungle creature head for the sea over to Florida Island for their kind of domestic tranquility. Two minutes of this jungle asylum, just poking my head into it, not even putting one foot through the entangling vines, has convinced me that I've joined the right branch of service.

Toby's bosun whistle snaps me back to ship-reality. I have a hunch that it silenced the jungle for a few seconds. Damned if I'll check it out.

"All aboard who's not stayin' ashore," the beered-up bosun bellows. This is one damn island Mother Nature can shove. I doubt if any of us has the notion of going sight-seeing here. So long, Florida Island!

Paint Detail

I reawaken to the same scene. The residue of war seems more romantic here. Word comes that our ensigns are now lieutenant junior grades. It's like going from seaman second to seaman first. Expectations are gonna jump to the nth degree with the war just around the corner. We're getting adjusted fast.

It's a relief to hear Lt. (jg) McShane summon his favorite bosun, Bo LaBeau, to the fantail. When there is a work detail for seamen, Bo is your man. Nothing sloppy, no Irish pennants on him; even when boozing he's holding his own. Goldbrickers and foul balls avoid him, but the others respect his command "let's turn to."

McShane only needs to give him the word. "Bo, we need five, six men. Big supply ship off Guadalcanal. Gotta camouflage this ship. Need lots'a paint. How much will it take to paint her fore and aft?"

"Jeez, about forty, fifty gallons. We'll get more than enough."

"O.K. Let's go, on the double." The diminutive McShane bears a strange resemblance not only to the skipper but to a certain shortish conqueror of Europe. Besides, he carries a very clean GI forty-five at his side. No mistaking that "might makes right" heads up his bill of rights.

"Right, sir. Maybe Toby oughta come along."

"Ye gods, no! We're gonna use a little finesse for a change. You remember what happened on that last commissary detail?" McShane threw his darkest frown at the bosun mate second-class.

"Yeah, Toby got too tough, but we brought home the bacon, didn't we? We damn near cleaned 'em out. Remember how they stuck up their noses at Chief Kelley? We done O.K. Can't fight a war on shit-on-a-shingle, sir. If the Navy don't think we belong out here, to hell with 'em."

"O.K. Bo. Just do as I say. No cuffing around. My forty-five will take care of things."

"Aye, sir. If you say so, sir."

Bo chooses pretty well. Four of the six are members of the undefeated *Machias'* boxing team: Trupiano, Lawrence, Contini, and Cason. A loaded deck, as it were. The latter two are not of the deck force, but for them, jaunting over to the famous island is more than motivation enough. And somehow McShane, himself a collegiate boxer, looks more comfortable about Bo's fisticuffers. I can't resist throwing my two bits into it as the whaleboat putt-putts away: "Don't throw any of the paint over the side once you take it into the whaleboat. This isn't the Boston Tea Party, you guys." Nobody hears me.

A left-behind deck-hand leans over the rail, watching the whaleboat trailing smoke. His eyes seem to be saying, "Jeez, I'd like to be in that boat, if only to be able to say that I saw Guadalcanal close up. I'd tell everybody back home about it."

McShane, armed with a requisition chit and his well-oiled forty-five, saluted the flag of the supply ship, then turned and saluted, perfunctorily, the Officer of the Deck. He followed the salutes with an equally perfunctory "Permission to come aboard, sir." He scribbled his name on the deck log and in seconds was before a Quartermaster first-class.

"You guys Coast Guards, huh."

McShane was quick on the uptake. "Yeah, Mac. How long you been wearing those stripes? You guys didn't take the

Marines ashore on the island over there, did you? Get us 50 gallons of camouflage paint like it says on this chit and shut your f-----g mouth." He took off his lieutenant's hat and put it under his left arm. Then he dropped his right hand to the forty-five below.

"Aye aye, sir. No disrespect, sir." He muttered something to a slender petty officer behind him. In minutes McShane and company are bucking the soft swells in a boat barely afloat, loaded with paint and sundry other items of cargo. It's a contented crew. Their grins say it all. It's like the kid brother making good, bringing home the bacon.

McShane, wearing a quiet grin which threatens to break out into a laugh, aims his five-foot six at lanky six-three Barstad, who had passed on the pesky detail to his junior officer, who was itching to take on the Navy. McShane never is down-at-the-mouth nor short on word power.

"What'd I tell ya. Takes a forty-five and a few well-chosen words." Barstad, for want of an excuse, offered a limp, "Gotta catch 'em with plenty of supplies aboard."

"No, just four damn-good hands like Cason, Laurence, Trupiano, and Contini here. Four in the ring and two others. Hey Joe, did you ever lose a fight?"

"Not if I could help it, sir."

"You invented that expression 'hit the deck,' I'll bet."

"Naw, not me. After Cason decks his man, the next guy's already softened up for me. I got a pretty good uppercut, both hands, but Cason there, he's a killer-diller. He's gonna turn pro when this thing's over. Maybe me too."

Barstad's there with a watery grin. Nobody comes close to his face for fear of getting sprayed, literally. His frozen grin slowly melts. It's an enigmatic grin, a perpetual, sea-drunk grin, signifying nothing, maybe nothingness itself. His facial mask suggests a perpetual drunkenness. His watery eyes and long, thin nose are alien to the rest of his clumpy face. Barstad is the perfect picture of pathos, the pathetic incarnate. His counterpart, McShane, pays him no attention.

Gallons of paint disappear quickly. They'll show up when the deck crew has nothing to do. They'll tell their grandkids how the camouflage saved our ship. S.O.S. from this paint job is really the story. All of McShane's supply-getting talent wasted! The new Lt. (jg) and his forty-five are always counted on for any supply ship foray. Before all of this shooting is done, McShane will have won plenty of skirmishes with his tongue and gun. So far he's undefeated.

But the Barstads aren't all that bad. The "regs" peace-time bureaucracy minded the store. Then this war just comes along and we reserves overwhelm them with our energies and resourcefulness. For every Barstad, thank God, there are ten McShanes. For these odds alone we'll out-point the Japs. But not if we think spit'n polish and spic'n span is a serious contributor.

I have a hunch we'll never "redecorate" the ship. Where there's a will there's no way. A paint detail over the hull... Nah. Chipping hammers? Nah. I have faith in our crew's bucket brigade. But if the water won't come to the *Machias*, the *Machias* paint will go to the water. I have another hunch, too. It's going to be easy come, easy go.

There are plenty of McShanes aboard ship.

In Deep Water

New Guinea, the master word of the South Pacific since the securing of Guadalcanal, lay dead ahead. It's October, the midsummer of the southern hemisphere. It's also Friday, 13 October and Langemak Bay is deep beneath.

Troopships swing in to shore; we stand out to sea.. Helluva welcome. Ships strewn all over the bay. Now a pilot comes aboard, and with him the latest order: they'll let us in. Come fuel up and out to sea with you! Never get ashore this way. That's Finchaven for you.

This, the welcome after carrying out the longest convoy ever, New York to Finchaven? Four British troopships, overloaded with U.S. GIs. escorted across damn near half of the world, and the shore-duty Navy boys boot the Coast Guard frigates out, treating them like wet blankets. Hell, where is the fanfare? True, three of the monstrous troopships have been deposited in the Russell Islands, others elsewhere. Only the HMS *Empire Arquebus* remains, and she's out of view. The HMS *Lothian* and the HMS *Battleaxe* and another ungodly-named British troopship jammed with a fresh replacement army are no more. At least no more with us.

Turtles of the Galapagos Islands surely swam faster than our record-mileage convoy. But records mean nothing here. Being alive does. The British troopships were laying to, outside Bora Bora's coral reef for several tedious days. Now that's a record. Rotten limey chow could not be negated by the exotic other-worldly view of the island. Could any other island compare with her profile? She is the quintessential Pacific paradise, for sure. To have turned the men loose on her shore is unthinkable; to have imprisoned them aboard is inhumane. *C'est le guerre.* Some day, perhaps, some would return.

The bridge is buzzing with activity. Exec Hanna, the O.D., and the skipper are bringing her in to roost. The former defers to the captain. Swelling with some sort of cocksureness, Lt. Commander R.T. Alexander delivers the supreme command:

"Let go the anchor!"

Lt. (jg) Barstad obeys. This is damn near fatal. Down go 90 fathoms of chain, roaring like a runaway locomotive hell-bent for Davy Jones' locker. Ninety fathoms is the entire intestinal load the *Machias* carries. Our bow jumps ten feet; the captain, one. "Alex" grabs his scrambled-eggs cap, throws it down, jumps on it as if he's doing an Irish jig, and whines, "I didn't say 'Let the anchor go.' I said, 'Let down the anchor!'"

It's too late. Ninety fathoms of chain is farther than Babe Ruth's record home run, some 500 plus feet, almost two ball fields long. Langemak Bay's depth is 42 fathoms, 292 feet, maybe more. The captain looks about and says, "Hanna, take her from here."

The skipper might never dare venture again with a berthing or anchoring detail. Nevermore need the good ship *Machias* fear a catastrophe. The grizzled Moose knows the job well: no bay bottom, no docking finds him wanting. Our *Machias* is in good hands, hands that have snagged more than one football, hands that have "salt" all over them. The skipper taught chemistry, not seamanship, at the Coast Guard Academy. The skipper also knocked over a pier piling in Charleston. That won't be in the deck log. He's fine, if he'll stay out of our way. But it's his way or the water-way. Lt. (jg) Logan begs for a transfer and finally gets it.

It will take an hour to retrieve the chain, but Moose will do it. It takes one minute for Lt. (jg) Jennings to collect a wardroom of officers and testify on the screw-up. Jennings, a good two heads taller than the skipper but three stripes leaner, can't resist mimicking the cry-baby act of our distraught skipper. And in the wardroom yet!

"You guys missed a good show," he says. He drops his cap on the wardroom floor and pulls off an effeminate "nah, nah, nah, nah" mocking jig like a ten-year-old boy bullying his nine-year-old sister. A good act.

Hand-clapping, however, as if on cue, brings another actor on the scene. Slowly, the hatch opens. Enter one Lt. Commander R.T. Alexander. Jennings, seeing frozen poker faces, freezes, stands almost at attention. Then, turning 90 degrees, he is confronted with his likely fate. The captain, perhaps incredulous that ship events travel so fast, stares, stone-faced, at newly promoted Jennings. Two frozen faces. The brand-new lieutenant junior grade retrieves his hat, strides by the captain, and exits almost as if nothing has happened. The skipper follows him out. Ten minutes later Jennings returns to the scene of the crime. "How much did the old man see?" he asks of the delighted, almost brand-new jay-gees.

"You're in deep water, Jennings," McShane tells him, tongue in cheek. "The old man's gonna lay it on you. You're no longer a shallow-water sailor, kid. At least you're getting salty." McShane chuckles his Irish chuckle. Didn't matter that the whole bunch of ensigns had just gotten their automatic elevation to lieutenant junior grade. Somehow they all feel secure.

McShane couldn't wait to tell us this little gem. We can do with some humor, and it's nice to know that the captain isn't infallible, even by his standards. He might even become more like one of us. Not me, of course.

"The smoking lamp is out. The smoking lamp is out."

Out here, the only absolute absolutes I know of are the absolute rulings of the skipper and the governing iron hand of Exec Hanna. But there are also absolutes of a lower order: the smoking lamp is out, mainly true tales told by Lt. (jg) McShane, expect the unexpected, lousy chow, month-late delivery of fruitcake, a pay-day crap shoot, slightly slanted reporting of war news via ship's newsletter, more islands than anyone can remember, a guaranteed starry-starry night every night, plenty of gold-bricking, mail chasing us and never ahead of us, things getting far worse before getting far better, the scarcity of good humor, the abundance of rumor, an ocean of ignorance, the omnipresence of nature, wet dreams, photos of Betty Grable and other *femmes,* the persistent suggestion of hidden alcoholic spirits, and dozens more which we'll soon be experiencing. Life is becoming a mere existence in an ocean of absolutes. Yep, we're in deep water now. Biak and Mios Woendi now lie in our path.

I never thought it would be a cakewalk on water.

Mars, Dead Ahead!

The convoy is let loose. That task is done, well done. The news looks good. We're making gains in France and on Italy's west coast. This looks like a positive Christmas for a change. Over here, the Marianas "turkey shoot" has just about wiped out their carrier aircraft. More than several hundred Rising Sun navy pilots have hit the ocean, leaving their carriers helpless. The Philippines seem ready for the taking.

Our ship's news letter has a lot of typos, but the statistics look fine. But as a WWI song said, "we won't come back 'til it's over over there." Ye olde reliable scuttlebutt says that we're going on a scouting mission northwest of Mindanao. Our *Machias* is the troubleshooting ship in our unit. Never at rest, always on the go. Skipper's ambition coming to the fore. Keeps things interesting. Supposed to post up at the Surigao Straits, the southern gateway to Leyte. When we see the Jap fleet, report it and scram. We're not that expendable! Our flank speed is a mere 24 knots, not to mention our lightweight surface guns. The US Navy has a stronger scouting system than this. But the rumor persists, and we actually head in that direction for a few hours before returning. Whatever is going on, it's big. It's exciting to know that we're finally close to the hot stuff at last.

There's a tense mood aboard. We're not kidding ourselves. Small as we are, we're due to get into something. At least we're ready. No doubt we lost game one. Pearl, Corregidor, and Wake were all hit hard. We were shut out. Game two barely goes our way: Midway, Savo, Guadalcanal, Tulagi come through for us in the early going. Game three is no picnic either, but it's all ours. The islands of Tarawa and Paleliu are more than tough. Taking all of New Guinea has its price. Japan is only playing not to lose; we're playing to win. We might not need to go all seven games. But we're paying prices, big and small, always. They're getting shut out and wiped out. We hear about their army's to-the-death fighting and civilian suicides.

"What's the latest scuttlebutt?" That's the way our worries are addressed.

"Ask Gillam. The radio shack has all the scoops." Gillam always has the inside dope, and he tells it straight. It's easy to lose your reputation on a 307 foot ship. Word gets around fast.

"O.K. Gillam, where we headed?"

"North, straight up. Mios Woendi. It's a PT boat hangout. They patrol and shoot up Jap rafts that hug some of the islands a little north of here. Gonna have some target practice up there. We're rusty."

October 13, 1944 is hardly a remarkable day for the anxious *Machias* crew. It's just another soft, warming afternoon when the final tune-up comes: "Man your battle stations. Man your battle stations!" Nothing like that "ping... ping... ping... ping" ringing in your ears. I'll probably hear it for as long as I live.

Our ship awakens like a monstrous machine, slowly, begrudgingly, and then furiously fast. This might be no ordinary call. The Pacific waters are getting hotter, physically and psychologically.

Ship's loudspeakers are blaring the battle stations signal: the pounding "ping, ping, ping, ping" is quickly followed by a "Man your battle stations." This does not sound like the customary drill. We are reassured with, "This is a drill. This is a drill." Fine time to be giving us the word.

The target-sleeve, a cylindrical canvas, is being towed by a slow-moving bi-plane It floats about 500 feet high about a quarter of a mile out in an inert, peaceful sky. It hardly presents a challenge. Speed perhaps 70 m.p.h. Length, about 150 feet. It's a dead duck. We'll riddle it. It's like throwing batting practice that doesn't mean a thing. The purpose is simply to let the guns and gun-crews fire; accuracy is no big deal. But you get the feel of the conditions at least. It's like shooting at a barn door. Only the 20mms and the 40mms will fire. It'll go down in our deck log as having fulfilled the required drill. Drills I know about first hand. "Set pattern Charley" at 23:00 with the screw end of the wrench in the dark, feeling the clicks like a safe cracker. Pattern Charley is a 500-foot setting; "Able" is just 50 feet. I could do it left handed and maybe in my sleep. But when all four frigates line up and the sleeve runs the gauntlet, that's a little different. Plenty of smoke to smell and ears to cover.

"Commence firing. Commence firing." That voice, the Moose Hanna voice, orders the destruction of the harmless sleeve. A cacophony of machine-guns is deafening, but the sleeve keeps rolling along. The sleeve is waving at us, waving goodbye, maybe.

"Ski" is embracing his 20mm like an octopus. He's the youngest gunner aboard and would shoot down the moon if he could. Six or seven seconds expire, and the sleeve now has moved to the starboard bow, slipping out of horizontal range. Ski is still firing the starboard 20mm, and he's right on target.

"Cease fire. Cease fire!" Hanna's growling voice commands.

Ski does not cease firing. He turns to me as if asking for a minor miracle.

I know what's wrong and point to the tail-end of the sleeve. "Keep firing. Keep firing, Ski." Ski hangs on as if he's expecting an attack on his life from the gun itself. The magazine empties and shell casings are strewn all over the place. Just as the gun dies, Hanna bellows from the bridge.

"Cease fire. Cease fire! Put that man on report. You down there on the fantail twenties. Put that man on report."

Hell, that's me. I'm the gun captain. With asbestos gloves I twist the barrel, draw it forward, and slide it out and into an upright cylinder filled with water. The hot barrel fires a stream of steam twenty feet high. A runaway gun can let off a lot of steam. But a human cannon is striding amidships, and guys are getting out of his way.

"The Moose is on the loose!"

Geez, here comes Hanna, scowling mad. Maybe he just wants to know what happened. That's easy: ole Blarney Barney's done it again. Last week he let a 20mm mainspring fly out into the Pacific. While greasing the gun, some lube got on his hands, and when he compressed the spring, it zoomed out into no-man's water. That's at least worth a deck court-martial. This time he puts the parallelogram firing mechanism in upside-down. Its four links are held together by 1/4-inch pins. Stretched out, it is approximately eight inches. When lifted with the ends touching, a flexing parallelogram is formed. When turned around and joined, the same result. It looks right either way. A novel cat's cradle. And since this isn't an everyday operation, it's easy to forget the correct way or tell the difference.

I'm in for it, I think. I see Chief Gunner's mate Zed coming down the ladder beneath the three-inch fifty gun with Hanna crowding him from behind.

"The parallelogram, huh, Buzz." It's not a question. Zed knows the gun better than his own hand. He also knows good old Barney. There's a knowing grin as if this is some kind of practical joke and he has sprung the trap. He's taking charge right in front of Hanna even if no one steals Hanna's thunder.

Zed has charisma backed by credentials. Hanna respects him. Anything Zed says goes. He cools things in a hurry.

"Barney, huh." It was little more than a rhetorical question.

"Ask him." I'm dead sure he'd worked on it, but for all his faults I like him. Besides, there's honor involved.

Zed turns to the Moose and says calmly, "Ah, just a faulty parallelogram, sir. We'll replace it." Hanna is smelling the gun as if to uncover some extraordinary evidence. There is nothing wrong with the long and lean Moose. Nobody is going to louse up our *Machias*, let alone a lousy runaway gun putting on a show before Division Commander Ryssey.

Ski is a little bit wiser, Barney more careful, and me, I'm thinking about the dead ahead. It doesn't take long for us to get the scoop. It usually comes from the ship's chief insider, RM 2/C "Goose" Gillam.

"Hey you guys, the Fifth Fleet is on the move. Going to hit the Philippines. This is a big one. That's all I got. We'll be bringing stuff up there."

Mars, dead ahead for sure.

"For dang sure," as Stuart Whitehead of Tennessee would say.

Fantail Fisticuffing

A twelve-to-four watch is a scorcher when under a relentless South Pacific sun. Our metal decks are even hotter to the touch, and the sun-god sits like an emperor on his throne. Our *Machias'* twelve knots convoy speed does little to bring the temp beneath ninety. Slivers of shade alongside the 20mm gun deck are just body-width. There is no advantage even when zigging or zagging. The fantail is a Sahara floating on water, and none of it is drinkable. Six-foot rolling swells running into our starboard create the illusion of well-being, but I almost imagine an equatorial line running like a current through the swells.

The deck, back here, is deserted. My customary company is the two depth charge racks holding Mod-12 teardrop depth charges, twenty-four in all. But not in this heat. I wonder about the two-inch red detonators which trigger them and how much heat they can stand. I visualize depth charges flying helter-skelter 100 feet above me, and the scenario ends right there. Their teardrop design is the best anti-sub weapon we have. I set the explosion depth and I, or the bridge O.D., can turn them loose. Eight "K" guns can heave their depth charges one hundred yards or more to sea. Despite its obvious power, the fantail attracts no attention except for the routine, breath-of-fresh-air visit from the black gang who keep the engines running and who, more than any others, need cooler air.

I'm not surprised to hear "Frenchy" Oullette snarl at the blonde baker following him, body-to-body, spewing out a low-down stream of profanity.

"Damn Polack. You been askin' for it."

"O.K. You come and git it." Czapiewski has more bar-room scraps under his belt and permanent scars than even Toby the Titan. And he loses most of them. He is addicted to scrapping and wrongly fancies himself as a good fisticuffer.

Our ship is rolling in the soft, deep swells. No one is topside, yet. Looks like a sure brawl on tap, and I'm right there. Sans beer, of course. They're nuts, I think. Like a referee breaking a clinch, I slip between them. Neither kid is big, about 150 and five-eight. I feel duty-bound to stop it before it gets out of hand or the heat gets them. I'm serious.

"Dammit Ski, knock it off. You guys can't fight here."

They're more serious than I am. "Ski" still isn't eighteen years old, a Milwaukee kid who thought he had to see action. Could have made nine bucks an hour in a defense plant there. He's also a 20mm gunner on my fantail's three anti-aircraft guns plus the most stubborn guy on ship, always having to prove his manhood. His bread-making leaves a hell-of-a-lot to be desired, too. Bo LaBeau liked losing him from his deck force to baking, even if he wouldn't trust his bread.

Mios Woendi is a day south of us, and we're heading into dangerous waters. It's no time for civil war. Even the swells have worsened. This is gonna take sea legs, and neither one's got'em. All of these things are zooming through my mind. They're starting to jab, so I try once more.

"Hold it, you guys. You're drawing a crowd." This goes over their heads. Almost suddenly I see gold braid and a couple of CPO's and about a dozen others by the aft three-fifty. It'll be a bare-fist orgy alright. A five-ring circus, for sure, without a tent overhead. I'm restraining them somewhat.

Chief Gunner's Mate Zed Zaunere looks down at me from the 3-50 gun shield and grins. "Let 'em scrap, Buzz. Let 'em go at it."

Frenchy launches an overhand right that should end it fast, but the ship dips into a trough and Frenchy goes face-down on the deck. A few guys are gathering and beginning to egg 'em on. Just like the schoolyard scraps between ten-year-olds after school. What the Japs wouldn't give to see this fiasco. Neither has gotten into the ship's rhythm. Most of the swings are aborted. They look like drunken sailors coming off liberty.

The crowd thickens to about fifty and it's now going from comedy to burlesque and maybe now farce.

"Had enough, Polack?" Frenchy stage-whispers. He's only nicked Ski a couple, three times.

Ski bears in like he's a boxer, but the ship refuses to stop rolling. Our crew is swarming down close in on the fantail, and a few guys are showing bills. A couple of commissioned officers are getting curious but doing nothing. Nor are Frenchy and Ski, who are both out of shape and tired from just fighting the ship's unpredictable rolls.

Our crew is relishing this stuff and it's harmlessly funny, so nobody wants to short-circuit the scrap. They're head-hunting now. Wild swings. I'm standing too close and almost take a weak, errant one. Maybe the O.D. on the bridge is steering into the troughs to heighten the comedy. Comic relief. What with Halmahera around the bend and the real war there and waiting for us to show up, that's it. Maybe Zed does have a handle on things. Enlisted out of the New Jersey state police.

Frenchy and Ski finally stop dead in their tracks, exhausted. They seem embarrassed by the crew's taunting and jeers and even the mock cheers. They didn't bargain for the free show. They had a bread dispute; nobody likes soggy bread. Ski couldn't bake beans let alone bread. The crust was crust; the middle stuff was soggy. Not like my mother's wonderful bread.

Ski's bread almost spoiled those two eggs over easy at Biak. "Good tussle, you guys. What in hell you fightin' 'bout?" Trupiano of the *Machias'* famed boxing team chides. It's a deadbeat draw, for sure. Not a solid blow is landed. Lawrence, another fine boxer, tops it off with, "Sleep it off, you guys. No harm done. Shake hands." The two impromptu pugilists grin, satisfied. I am strangely satisfied. I think it defuses a lot of built-up tension. Zed is right.

Tomorrow it's Halmahera. Borneo's oil fields not far west. We're in it now. Next stop before the Philippines!

Mercury-itis

At any time of the year, the Pacific equator is not the coolest place on earth. I rarely linger on the fantail's sun-scorched deck. Instead, I usually head for the pseudo-shade of the 20mm clip shack. There at least the sun's rays are shut out. But after running that longest, hottest of gauntlets all the way from the Galapagos Islands to Bora Bora, it's easy to see why the Mediterranean peoples assign heat to hell. Emotionally, at the moment, I'm for the cold, North Atlantic version. But hotter than hell is believable here.

Bunking quarters above the boilers are unbearable. Asbestos coverings on the hanging hammocks seem to add to the heat by reminding the enlisted sailors that the heat below their berths is a fire danger. To escape the relentless heat–and there is no cinch escape–I climb to the flying bridge after the morning eight-to-twelve watch. Come hell or high water, I must go topside. They're both on my mind.

Commissioned officers' quarters, on the other hand, do have at least mild relief. Being above the main deck and in quarters that are exposed to the cooling night breezes, their separated quarters remain livable, if not comfortable, through much of the scorching daylight. The captain's quarters gather in this air, generously, via air ducts. It's rumored that they are artificially air-conditioned. In the radio shack, radioman 2/C Gillam racks his brains figuring out ways to divert the air from the captain's stateroom into the over-heated radio shack, where he spends eight hours each day on watch.

The Last Romantic War

Our captain is heard on occasion to complain about the lack of "breathing air" in his quarters. He seems unmindful that this is a standard condition aboard. Gillam, after a surprise entrance or two by the captain into a fairly cool radio shack, would cleverly answer the skipper's observation about the radio shack's favorable climate and then at a convenient time he would divert the duct back to the captain's quarters. This clandestine diversion provides more than comic relief for communications personnel. But not for me. Still, it's a well-kept secret, better than the whereabouts of the three bilge stills, the brain-child of the black gang, the engineers who keep the below decks machines working.

In consort with the frigates Allentown, Charlottesville, and Sandusky, our *Machias* inches its way ever westward, uneventfully. It is daily-ness at its worst. The oasis that was Bora Bora brought welcome but temporary relief. The moon-lit firing on a "washing machine Charley" over Biak's airstrip was cosmetic experience. It's the beginning.

The islands have fallen into place. Espirito Santos, the Solomons, the Russells, the big island of New Guinea, Biak, Mios Woendi; Morotai of the Dutch East Indies is likely the next encounter. Exec Hanna ordered me to select a softball team for a brief outing in the Russell Islands. We win the game but I "lose" my Bob Feller glove. Maybe this is an omen. Nope, I have that built-in prayer.

Coming off watch at midnight, I'd see several deck hands rolling out their sleeping mats onto the deck near the midships smokestack. By this hour, our sleeping quarters above the boilers always break 90-95 degrees. Sometimes I'd see guys scattering when a late-night squall would soak their dreams. The sight of nearly nude men rising clumsily from the cool decks amidships is low burlesque. Still half asleep, they stumble and fumble their way to cover. At least the squalling is warm.

Usually a dozen would bunk down on the cooler windward side.

Exec Moose Hanna, old salt that he is, finds nothing wrong with the sleeping habits of the few. But with the turning northward toward the true equator, Mercury challenges Mars. Our war so far is against the natural foe of heat. I compromise and choose a ready-service locker on the starboard side, amidships. I think nothing about the single cable that separates me from the sea. It's a stable place, amidships, and protected from any torpedo entering the port side where our ship is assigned at the convoy's port quarter. Not that it would matter much. Safety is a grand illusion at sea.

On October 22 at Morotai, Halmahara of the East Indies, I declare my separate space. From now on I would risk the elements topside, squall or no squall. Soon after midnight I'd lay my mat on that ready-service locker near officers' quarters, almost under the whaleboat. I did not, surprisingly, see the boat as a rescuer. My three life jackets, yes. But a boat, hell no! With 244 men aboard, who would be in it? Nor did I ever suppose that some unlucky torpedo would hit us. Only one strand of cable and a pneumatic life jacket would be between me and the waiting, enigmatic Pacific about twelve feet below.

With one ear and half an eye open, I sleep on the bubble of readiness. "*Semper Paratus.*"

Sneak Preview

It is twilight as the *Machias* rounds the northern tip of Morotai and anchors a mile off its steep shoreline. It seems ambiguously peaceful, too serene. Hulking Halmahera lies to our starboard and west about fifteen miles. A nimble PT boat is scatting about dead ahead; she stops and peppers a hillside spot on Morotai with her single 40mm cannon. What a picturesque scene. It was Hollywood-like stuff, staged, as if a mosquito is taking on a whole island. And we are mere bystanders to boot.

A hillside battery splashes shells to her aft, then beyond her bow. This is a temptation, a sort of coming attractions to the big show! Maybe an entertaining short subject. So Pacifically clean. The PT is shooting at a continent and we are mere privileged spectators.

As more shells bracket her, the patrol craft revs her engines and takes off. Then, surprisingly, we learn "War 101." A fighter-bomber clears the hilltop, dives at the white puffs of smoke where the gun emplacement is and unloads a string of bombs. End of incident. We go to evening chow, wondering. This scenario is far too romantic, too picturesque. Pure impressionism.

But I'm not fooled by this tidy, completed action. I am right.

At dawn, fighter planes with strange-sounding engines, something akin to a Model A Ford, awaken me. When one is aroused almost anywhere on ship, boot camp or shore station, it's not a civil, natural matter: it's your neck. Athletically, I swing off the ready-service locker. A seaman is scurrying down the ladder from the bridge. It's a bogey for sure and my eyes verify it. It's a Jap army fighter, an Oscar, a mile off the starboard stern. Another fighter trails it. We're tied up to another frigate and a line of ships. It's six bells and we're caught napping!

Parallel to our starboard, the lead fighter is aiming at a massive seaplane tender filled with high octane gas. A messenger from the bridge runs past me into the main deck officers quarters. I hear the captain yelling, "Call general quarters, call G.Q." I'm 150 feet away from my guns.

All hands are at battle stations. The first fighter is greeted by twenty to thirty anti-aircraft 20mms of the big seaplane tender and is afire and cart-wheeling into the sea just yards short of the monstrous ship. Clean-cut action. No confusion. Oscar number two is but 1/4 mile off our starboard stern quarter, starting his dive at the the tender. He is easy. "All guns commence firing! Commence firing!" We pour it on.

Now a moving parabola of curving red lines formed by thousands of 20mm tracer-bullets is seeking the soft skin of the Rising Sun. With every tracer, four unseen bullets are just as deadly. Our starboard guns are pounding away, including my three 20s. And then in fewer than a handful of seconds, the smoking Oscar veers to the right towards the rocky, forested Halmahera coast. Trailing a stream of black smoke, it descends gracefully. Then the Oscar disappears and reappears as a snapping red ball. A wild, touchdown-like cheer erupts topside.

But such ecstasy dies quickly. I spot a four-engine, twin-tailed bomber following the path and direction taken by the second Oscar and recognize it right away as a B24 Liberator, ours. Then a blast of the three-inch fifty just above my head explodes into my left ear, surprising me, hurting me. When the guns are firing, you keep your mouth open to let the fierce vibrations pass on through. I yell into my head phone, "That's a

Liberator, Conn, a Liberator!"

My shout to the three-fifty gun crew above me, who's bent on shooting anything that flies, is of no use. The Liberator climbs almost suicidally. Heavy flak is powder-puffing the four-engine bomber. I see the photographic moment: the big bomber is upright, seemingly framed, its pilot looking into a sky smudged with gigantic, black images. And it begins to right itself. Again I shout into the phones, "Conn, it's a Liberator, a Liberator." No response. The Liberator slides away from the pursuing puffs of flak. Nobody gives the order to cease fire. The sky is vacant.

There's an intruding voice on my sound-powered phones. It's a rare shore-to-ship communique:

"You guys on the frigate. You damn near shot down a Liberator. If you can't recognize a Lib, get your asses outta here!" That was it, short and unsweet.

The fly-guys are pissed-off but good. Moose Hanna is too. In his own way, of course. He is discipline a la carte. The Moose bellows out on the speaker a few memorable words: "Alright you f------ heroes, get back to work!" Hells bells, we haven't had chow yet!

Couldn't fault him; some of my shipmates were over-reacting to the shooting down of one plane. There were hundreds of them that had already been sent down into the sea. But it was a bit funny, I thought, for it was only about 06:00. First chow hadn't even begun. I pick up my mat on the ready-service locker. The Moose is nearby. That same night, I "find" a new sleeping place: Chief Petty Officers' Quarters in the bow, the coolest place aboard! Courtesy Exec. Lt. Henry Hanna, I figure.

The Moose has at least six reasons for changing my bunk. Hanna had probably seen me playing baseball at Algiers Navy

Base across from New Orleans. I had hit a liner over the short right-field fence. Maybe he's trying to save a baseball career. Maybe he's tired of seeing me risk my neck sleeping on the ready-service locker with just one cable-wire between me and the sea. I think he is trying to improve my odds. Still, being bunked with Chief Petty Officers is a hell of a promotion. I think nothing of it.

I don't think any Japanese has a bullet with my name on it. And maybe that little cloth-covered prayer... Maybe. I'd feel better if God had autographed it.

Buckets by the Deep Six

The Philippine campaign is going great without us. We are in a convoying mode.

Somewhere southeast of Mindanao, the old-fashioned American trait of "freedom from" pays us an unexpected visit. In wartime, the military offers precious little "freedom to," and perhaps our little cause *celebre* was caught between the two. Our benevolent insurgency originates simply and ends equally so. It has to do with an urgency, a natural urgency, and I unexpectedly find myself a sort of silent partner in it. It might have turned into a true cause *celebre* had it happened on a battleship. And it might not have happened at all had I been a teetotaler, a non-coffee-ist.

Most men in the military have heard the old saw about an army traveling on its stomach. George Washington had saved the remnants of his Valley Forge force by swiping cattle corn from the British, who hardly suspected that Americans or any humans could eat it. But it was food, and it kept the American insurgency going.

There was the other end, or maybe side, of the story, too. What comes in must, in a manner of speaking, go out. Every sailor aboard knows this irrefutable law of nature. But as usual it's just a matter of time. It's the when-and-where that count.

Not unlike the United States Navy, the Coast Guard is ruled, not governed, by laws found in the *Blue Jackets Manual*. The Coast Guard educates and trains potential officers in such rules of behavior. Nearly all of the *Machias*'s commissioned officers are of the ninety-day wonder school. Our captain and one other had been academy trained and thus are regulars. All of this simple stuff everyone aboard knows. And it seemed reasonable enough. But of course any insightful enlisted man could have predicted Officer of the Deck Lt. (jg) Peterman's behavior on that quiet, nonthreatening morning off Mindanao's coast and just a day or so away from Leyte Gulf.

Matter of fact, I could have made such a prediction, too. Had my father not nicknamed me Garibaldi? And who was Garibaldi but the rebel who led the unification of Italy despite the resistance of the Catholic Church, which feared the encroaching nineteenth-century secularism and its accompanying nationalism. Pete was a regular academy man, newly commissioned. I knew him to be everything an officer should be. He even rescued a sailor who had become entangled in a hawser line and pulled under the keel. But Pete, an academy man, had learned things the classic, academy-academic way. Thus he was an advocate of going-by-the-book. Letter for letter, he was a letter-of-the-law man. A true hyphen-ated man. The spirit of the law was foreign to him. He was fast becoming a sea dog stuffed with dogma. He was like a puppy on a string.

Even the Marines know that spit and polish is fine on home base but that on the road nature must take its course. Every sailor worth his salt knows that when at sea, do as the sea does and you won't get seasick. Some never learn.

Nowhere in the *Blue Jackets Manual* is the right–perhaps the privilege–of taking a crap denied. All, even crap-shooting sailors, know this. To further air this smelly pun, let us say that this is his constitutional right. But these rationalizations are mere after-thoughts when I recall my buckets solution.

Before coming on the morning eight-to-twelve watch, I down a cup'a joe, something I never do. I almost dislike coffee. I do not foresee my future inner turmoil, a catharsis swift in taking command.

I call the bridge. "Con. Permission to go to the head." Nothing more.

Reaction is swift. "Permission denied."

The two seconds waiting for approval is internal eternity.

"Con. Louie Badman is standing by and will relieve me." This Freudian slip gains no sympathy, though Badman smothers a chuckle.

"Permission denied. Remain at your post."

If there is no fury like a woman scorned, the same holds true of a rejection to relieve oneself. I see a lolly-gagging seaman swabbing the deck nearby. Pure busywork stuff. There are two buckets, shiny and unemployed, nearby. In two strides and two seconds one bucket is gonna lose its sovereignty and identity. Not until it serves its humble purpose, of course. Audaciously, as if I'm breaking a naval commandment, I carefully pitch the bucket over the fantail and into our wake. A perfect burial at sea, I think. I know that the Mindanao Sea rivals any in the world for depth. Must be a thousand fathoms, hundreds of deep sixes down there, some of them buckets.

Bosun Bo LeBeau's deck crew likes my sympathy strike. They're more than pleased. They have similar problems, too. It's no fun recovering from dozens of aerial visits by Jap planes and then have to turn to and swab away. Sort of demeaning the role of us warriors.

"Damn. We got any more buckets topside, Sir Bo?" Bo knows the answer but is obligated to dodge the question.

"That's five down since yesterday, Bo. Storage ain't got none. Don't know if there's any down below." Trupiano knows all about the mystery of the mysterious disappearances of *Machias'* buckets. He tells me since I've already seen a few heaved over the side. Every port we hit, Bo has his bucket requisition. If it ever was one, swabbing decks is becoming a lost art on the *Machias*. The sight of a bucket is akin to a mirage, even anathema.

We ought to coin a new phrase that'll top Sam Clemens' "By the twain, mark." I'd make it simple: "By the deep, six."

I stop drinking coffee.

The Moose

Nobody knows anything about Henry C. Hanna, Lt., USCG(R) except, perhaps, Lieutenant Commander R.T. Alexander, captain of the 2,200-ton patrol frigate, the USS *Machias*. No doubt the skipper either approves or disapproves of officers assigned. He made a wise choice. Accepted a few lemons, also. Par for the human course.

Rumors say that Hanna has plenty of sea duty under his belt, and under his head, too. Merchant Marine gunnery officer, no doubt. Hanna's hat fits his head, about seven and three-eights, as comfortably as a well-worn shoe fits a size 14 foot. It's peaked like air force pilots peak theirs and curved at every possible conforming spot.

Looking more than his forty-plus years, Hanna still moves like the college football end he is rumored to have been. But he's no has-been. Some imply that he had Trojan Rose Bowl experience. No one has ever directly asked him. He's tall, too tall, constantly ducking his head through hatchways. Yet he's nimble enough to make it look easy. Remarkably physically fit, Hanna is wiry with strapping shoulders to match and hands that look like well-carved weapons set on the line of scrimmage.

Still, he's an enigma aboard, even a misfit. But a positive misfit. Positive because he is one-of-a-kind. But he has a crew whose petty officers are almost as tough, though not of the same kind of toughness. They simply know their job and carry it out. Hanna brings a past of experience with him, a built-in confidence factor. It rubs off on gun and anti-sub crews that out-shot comparable Navy DEs at shake-down training in Bermuda. As gunnery officer, Hanna got the job done in spades, diamonds, and clubs. You want him on your side.

If you cast the exec role, the Moose looks just right for the part. Gnarled and furrowed, his face projects a pleasant snarl, yet it's a handsome or at least distinguished face. His character is imprinted in his thoughtful blue eyes that seem not blue at all. Lincolnesque, his face is a map of experience deeply etched with survival evidence. Much like a range boss of a cattle drive looks just right in his customized hat, Hanna belongs in his "salty" hat. It seems like he doesn't belong with us, or rather we with him, and he's simply making the most of it, shutting up and being borderline tolerant. Of course, I might be entirely wrong; he could all the while be wearing a mask. Come to think of it, who ever saw him smile? Yet his expressions always suggest no panic, anxiety or anger. He's probably a good poker player. Reminds me of General George Marshall. Saw his picture in a newspaper along with Ike's.

Shortly after the Bermuda shake-down training, Hanna is promoted to Executive Officer, replacing Lt. Frank Hamton. Hamton, charged with navigation duties, could barely find Bermuda, so he was sent to school to learn the instruments of navigation. For the remaining crew, it's the school of hard knocks, for which Hanna is admirably suited. The *Machias* must become a ship, a fighting ship.

This new exec keeps a high profile and runs a tight ship. Seniority and other traditions are swept away if they get in the way. A third-class petty officer—yours truly—could select a ball team for a recreational sortie in the Russell Islands because Hanna recognized and trusted his ability to put a decent team on the field. Like Lincoln, he'd pick a General Grant if the situation demanded it. No red tape; get the job done. Just like a gunnery objective: shoot to kill the enemy.

Hanna could smoke out a goldbricking cancer among deck hands and took great satisfaction in eradicating it. Master-at-Arms Chief Specialist Eric Stromsta, backed by muscular Toby Switzer, instills a pleasantly humorous reign of terror ransacking sleeping quarters at reveille backed by his command.

But the essence of Hanna is to watch him in action. He whips through a mid-ship hatch always with a mission in mind. His *modus operandi* most often is: if you want something well done, do it yourself. He's in charge of anchoring detail. To him, "Let down the anchor" is far different from "Let go the anchor." Our captain finally gives way to the Moose's talent.

"The Moose is on the loose!" is the definitive code phrase aboard ship. Or, "All hands beware, Hanna's on a tear." If the routine life at sea hints of boredom, as it often does before the deadly shooting begins, Moose Hanna's wake re-awakens the deck force, his usual target. His growl is equal to his bite: the captain's masts attest to this. Plenty of penalties are dished out at the occasional Captain's Mast. After all, there are no defense attorneys on deck. When the Moose charges you, you just pray for a warning.

On one occasion, only a bona fide rumor of course, the skipper, the Moose, and Engineering Officer Nix are on a strange mission. They've opened the hatch of Ensign McShane's stateroom and stand there. Nix mumbles something like, "No engineering officer is gonna stand watch. They got enough to do keeping this ship steaming."

Hanna measures his words economically. "C'mon, outta the sack!"

There's a forty-five hanging at McShane's headboard. McShane has just turned in after seven straight four-hour watches. He's more than dead tired though the seas have been calm. The forty-five is loaded and in his grip.

"Hanna, I'll kill ya if ya don't let me sleep. I'll kill ya. I'll kill ya."

Probably realizing that McShane means murder or a Chapter Eight, the three abandon the room. Hanna is wise enough to withdraw. It is also rumored a year later in Seattle that McShane tells another (jg) that he, Hanna, and the captain thereafter are on a *laissez-faire* relationship. A forty-five is easy to understand. He suggests that the captain has tried to break him as he might have done with Lt. (jg) Barstad, who damn near became a mental case, and Lt. (jg) Lucret, who did.

Nonetheless, Hanna reigns supreme. Even after days of nuisance air attacks in Leyte Gulf and moving into convoy duty, where routine-itis sets in, there are minor skirmishes a la Hanna and somebody not doing his duty. The loose Moose remains the most enduring phrase aboard ship, making *Semper Paratus*, the Coast Guard's famous "always ready" slogan, seem like a Boy Scout platitude.

Hanna ties the knots that hold the *Machias* together: discipline, accountability, duty, performance. He was the ship's captain in spirit for months. One day he will captain it.

Starry, Starry Night

This November night in the South Pacific is like the previous one hundred to me, but something is strangely different. The last depth charge on which I'm seated is my director's chair and the stars an eternal audience. At least for the moment. This is the sort of fantasy, a kind of fringe benefit, that comes easily when a guy has temporarily lost control of his destiny, the romantic child of fate.

This theater transcends nature's dimensions, which in themselves seem immeasurable. Other than an occasional human sound on the sound-powered phones, the human dimension is ethereal, just an imaginary character. I have the whole world or worlds to myself. This is what the vast Pacific can do to you on a given starry night when you really do not belong there.

But for the monotonously soothing rumble of the twin screws twelve feet beneath me, our frigate *Machias* is a mere illusion. Beneath the hypnotic screws is a finite watery grave several miles deep, and above it, infinity. But the third world, the inner one, is my refuge on a starry night like this, for the imagination has no dimensions. The only sensory signpost I have is the Southern Cross, and by it we are headed due north and certainly to the Philippines.

The paradox of the time dimension finally catches me at 22:00, or ten o'clock via civilized measurement. It pretends to be an absolute. A tyrant, yes, when wants are denied by needs. For a few minutes I need to be off this iron bucket and its questionable future and back to the halcyon past. When "halcyon" flashes into my consciousness, so does William Wordsworth's "The World Is Too Much With Us" and especially his line, "little there is in nature that is ours." Often I would climb Hulst School hill and view the country south of my hometown, meditating on the eternal questions that bug teenagers. Wonderful questions that define and permit a grip on reality. Here aboard ship the questions are different; the situations are instantly dangerous and unpredictable. Depth charges which could demolish submarines are my constant companions on watch. Rarely does a shipmate venture on the fantail after dark. So, by default, right now the most private place in the entire Pacific beehive of stars is mine. Except of course should a Jap sub happen by. Maybe privacy is an illusion, too.

This tandem of opposites opposing and balancing each other keeps showing up. I'll bet that even the stars get in on the act. I'm sitting on a bunch of dynamite stars which can be set precisely in four different patterns: Able, Baker, Charley, and Dixie. My depth-setting wrench fits precisely into two recesses which engage an internal mechanism for the two shallow settings. The slender handle, about five inches long, an inch wide, and 1/4-inch thick with a screwdriver tip fits into a turnable slot for the deep 400 plus settings. In full darkness, the setting could be completed and determined by touch and the clicking of each unit. Once the teardrop is released, the action is absolute and final. A partnership of science and technology render it so. I hope that no sub interrupts this star-lit night.

Yet the other side of the coin offers far more. Stars, the unfathomable, mirage-like stars, seem indestructible. They are true companions, the perfect combination of the concrete and abstract. Pacific skies often glow with starry sequins, even without a reflective moon. It seems, sometimes, that the Southern Cross presides over them, and perhaps some unimaginable unity exists there. Dark and ominous, the convoy silhouettes reveal their frightened unity and, seeing their unity, I wonder if the idea of unity prevails any more often in the distant heavens. The constellations I see are so few and certainly are not even a measurable decimal.

"Depth charge watch."

Out of the silence of the night these words sound like a shout.

"Depth charge, aye, aye," is my quick answer.

The O.D. must be nervous. We're not far from the eastern coast of Mindanao, a Japanese-held island. Seaman Leon Baham's voice, however, is calm, as calm as the sea and night.

"Depth charge watch, aye, aye," I repeat.

"Be on the alert back there. Sonar is fixing something and will be inoperable for a few minutes."

"Aye, aye, Con." At least it isn't another one of the midnight depth-charge setting drills. I can set the patterns blindfolded. That's what it takes on some dark nights.

But tonight the stars overwhelm the resting sea. Not like Vincent Van Gogh's troubled "The Starry Night" with its geyser-like, organized confusion. These stars seem inviting, like a receptive audience. They seem to know everything, that we are only bit players playing out the last scenes in the last act of this drama we call World War II. Well then, just get us off the stage of the Pacific Theater of Operations. Sonar or no sonar, this watch couldn't be better. Whoa, Con is alive again.

"The O.D. says a depth-charge drill in one hour."

"Aye, aye." So I lose my philosophic chair again in favor of a touch of reality. In this case, reality is more like unreality. I can set the patterns in just a few seconds. But the drill must be entered into the Deck Log as *fait accompli*. And the Deck Log is the next thing to ultimate reality aboard ship.

But to the two lookouts on the bridge twenties, the stars are probably of a different order. Maybe like a million minnows in a sea of monster star-sharks. Maybe our *Machias* is a minnow, choice prey for a sub's fish. No, not our *Machias*. This is a helluva tough ship and an even tougher crew.

"Stay awake, Frenchy," I whisper over the phone. Two "Frenchies" aboard, both from Maine. Cormier is earthy, responsible, duty-minded, and likeable. He's lookout on the port bridge and is wide awake as anyone. He doesn't mind a quick hello. It breaks up the gaping silences of the midnight watch.

My padded kapok life preserver feels just soft enough on the rounded, teardrop depth charge. Legs dangling but resting over the side, I return to star-grazing. Harvesting more food for thought. Tonight's stars are like Shakespeare's constant lovers: inextinguishable. I'm perched, literally, on the brink of nature. Behind, 242 men exist on a zigzagging ship in consort with three other frigates in a diamond formation convoying perhaps a dozen Liberty ships. Our Liberty ships are traveling straight ahead at about ten knots. The convoy's diameter is no more than a mile. As the waters churn they turn into several hundred feet of foamy wake that catches traces of moon glow on the crests of gentle swells. It seems dangerously safe.

I can't help but look upstairs at the stars and wonder about beginnings. They are concrete abstractions at best and, like time, only mark reality. We're all navigators, and these beginnings give us our bearings. If we can make a mathematical picture of reality, then, like the caveman artist, we can master it. Can't deny that we aren't resourceful. Hope the Jap sub captains aren't resourceful. Here I'm thinking about a shipmate's notion of an explosive beginning of our universe while in a few minutes, or hours, a big bang could bring about our ending. Neither idea appeals to me. Both seem untimely to me.

All I know is that the night is beautiful and we're island-hopping like mad. It can't last much longer. Every island taken has a rippling effect, expanding our control in the Pacific. These ripples are becoming a tidal wave of terror and Japan itself is on the receiving end. Remember Pearl Harbor? Now you're being crushed. You know we're coming. You know you asked for it.

I remember a starry August night when a strange, overwhelming feeling crashed into my boyish consciousness. At fifteen, lying outside on warm grass on an unusually insufferably hot night, a strange awareness hit me like lightning. It seemed simple enough at first, but, putting aside a scary fear, the idea forced itself in. Is there an ultimate form? Just like that. The world, I knew, is filled with forms. Man-made forms are what constitutes civilization. Both concrete and abstract forms. That was all well and good and necessary, of course, but not an answer. And when you're fifteen, answers are highly desirable.

Maybe that's the real problem: too many forms. Not enough breathing-room. Cars, cycles, buildings too close. People too crowded. Stars can keep their distance. They don't pick fights with each other. Remarque's mountains in *All's Quiet on the Western Front* didn't insult each other, thus starting a war. Separateness, the importance of separateness. The lack of it spoils romance. Familiarity breeds contempt. When the strangeness is gone, what then? Yes, Shakespeare, the fault does not lie in the stars, but in ourselves. But if we keep the flame of romance burning, we'll always have enough fire to keep us warm.

The expanding universe thing... Beautifully strange behavior. Vincent Van Gogh's "The Starry Night" might have been his strange, expanding universe. His starry rebellion in search of sanity or maybe of identity. Always it's in the process of becoming just what a person, an individual, can be. Perfectly romantic idea. But what is this universe expanding into? What's America expanding into? We're a "becoming" nation, an always becoming nation, not a static one. Geez, the stars look so concretely abstract, so mystical. Twinkle, twinkle, little star, how I wonder. C'mon McShane, lets get this little depth-charge-setting drill over with.

The wake is livelier than ever. For a moment I wonder if my counterpart on some Jap destroyer is whiling away a four-hour watch like I am.

I hope so. I doubt it.

The Last Romantic War

Tony–1942

Nunzio–Father,
Isabella–Mother, and
Mary–Sister

Iron Mountain,
Michigan

"Buzz"—June 1943

Anthony Gianunzio

The "Black Gang"
aboard the *Machias*

Ben "Pop" Bryan,
BM I/C (left)

USS *Machias*—December
1944, San Pedro Bay, Leyte,
Philippines

MILWAUKEE, MONDAY, AUGUST 23, 1943

New Frigate Takes to Water

The Last Romantic War

Polliwog/Shellback Ceremony
Galapagos Islands—September 1944

Ship's Company - - U. S. S. MACHIAS

Commanding Officer — COMMANDER ROBERT T. ALEXANDER, USCG

LIEUTENANT FRANK R. CAMPBELL, JUNIOR, USCGR	*Executive Officer*
LIEUTENANT HENRY L. WEYRAUCH, USCG	*Disbursing Officer*
LIEUTENANT HENRY C. HANNA, JUNIOR, USCGR	*Gunnery Officer*
LIEUTENANT (J.G.) HOWARD T. HARSTAD, USCGR	*First Lieutenant*
ASSISTANT SURGEON RAYMOND N. HENCH, USPHS	*Medical Officer*
ENSIGN WILLIAM A. NIX, USCG	*Engineering Officer*
ENSIGN ROBERT M. FINK, USCGR	*Assistant Gunnery Officer*
ENSIGN LLOYD M. LOGAN, USCGR	*Anti-Submarine Warfare Officer*
ENSIGN WILLIAM R. McDOUGALL, USCGR	*Assistant Engineering Officer*
ENSIGN HUDSON E. DEMING, USCGR	*Communications Officer*
ENSIGN JAMES I. McNELIS, USCGR	*Assistant First Lieutenant*

Chief Petty Officers

William J. Hahne, CRM, USCG	Hobart C. Boughton, CRM, USCG	Donald D. Branson, CMM, USCGR	Odilion A. Levesque, CPhM, USCG
William S. Bittman, CRM, USCG	Thomas M. Palovic, CMM, USCG	James L. Law CWT, USCG	Eric J. Strom, CSp (G), USCGR
			Owen L. Kelly, CCStD, USCG

Anthony Gianunzio

U. S. S. MACHIAS — — CREW

ALBAMONTE, ANTHONY V.	Y2c	GIANNUNZIO, IDOLO A.	GM3c
ALBRITTON, JOHN A.	F2c	GRAB, JAMES C.	S2c
ARGO, ROBERT E. JR.	S2c	GRAM, SHIRLEY L.	MM2c
ATEN, HOWARD G.	GM3c	GRAY, DENVER R.	S2c
BAHAM, LEON	S2c	GRABOWIECKI, FRANK	S1c
BARANY, WILLIAM A.	S2c	GREEN, EDWARD A.	S1c
BARNEY, WILLIAM A.	GM3c	GREGORY, ALLEN W.	S2c
BEHNKE, DONALD H.	S2c	GRIMALDI, LOUIS E.	WT3c
BOWDEN, ROBERT V.	S2c	GRIFFIN, EDWARD C.	CM1c
BROTHERS, JEAROLD F.	MM2c	GROSNESS, HAROLD O.	MM1c
BRUNSON, A.	STM3c	GUTT, ANDREW	GM3c
BRUSH, EDGAR	EM1c	HALE, J. E.	MM1c
BRYAN, BENJAMIN B. JR.	BM1c	HALE, ROCKWELL F. JR.	F1c
BUCHANAN, CLARENCE E.	S1c	HANSBOROUGH, T.	STM3c
CARRELL, WILLIAM E.	S1c	HANNAH, WALTER B.,	F1c
CARR, RUSSELL O.	S2c	HANLON, WILLIAM R.	S2c
CARROLL, THEODORE R.	MM3c	HARGAT, RAYMOND L.	S1c
CASON, DORIS	MM2c	HARDIN, ORIE F.	F1c
CLEVENGER, ROBERT R.	WT1c	HAUCK, F. W.	S2c
CLOUTIER, PAUL M.	SM1c	HERRALA, WARNER A.	S2c
COBURN, ALLEN C.	S1c	HIGDON, LAWRENCE E.	S1c
COLOMBO, RAYMOND J.	S1c	HOBSON, JOHN M.	F1c
COLONE, FRANK A.	S2c	HODGE, DAVID F.	SM3c
CONTINI, JOSEPH M. JR.	S2c	HOLMES, MERLE M.	S2c
COOPER, WILLIAM W.	MM2c	HOLYOKE, DEYER J.	S2c
COURTNEY, JAMES J.	F1c	HOMER, HILTON J.	S1c
CRAWFORD, M.	STM3c	HORNYAK, S.	S2c
CROSS, RICHARD M.	S1c	HORNYAK, JOE	QM2c
CZAPIEWSKI, JEROME	S2c	HOYNIK, STEVE W.	S1c
DANEN, JAMES J.	S2c	HUDDLESTON, RALPH E.	S1c
DARRAH, ROBERT F.	EM3c	HUGHES, C. A.	S1c
DE FRANCESCO, LORENZO	S2c	HUGHES, SOLOMON P.	SC2c
DENIS, SIDNEY A.	S2c	HUNTSMAN, EMMETT P.	F1c
DE ROSA, DON F.	S2c	ISELIN, ROGER E.	S2c
DONNELLY, JOHN F.	S2c	JANDA, WILLIAM H.	QM2c
DUERR, HENRY A.	BM2c	JENKINS, D. J.	S1c
ENGLAND, S. M.	S1c	JENKINS, EMMETT A.	RM1c
ENGLISH, JOHN E.	S2c	JOHNSON, CARL R.	Y3c
FINCK, FRANK R.	S2c	JONES, ENSLEY, P.	BM2c
FLAX, JOSEPH L.	S2c	JORDAN, ALDEN M.	S1c
FOREDYCE, MYRTON E.	BM2c	KATILLO, ALBERT	S2c
FOREHAND, GLEN F.	SC1c	KERBER, JOSEPH P.	Y3c
FOSS, ELWIN R.	S2c	KIAR, KENNETH	S2c
FROST, HUBERT P.	S2c	KING, JOHN J.	S2c
FUNKHOUSER, KENT L.	MM3c	KING, WILLIAM R.	S2c
GALLAGHER, CHARLES R.	S2c	KIPPENBERGER, GEO. A.	GM2c
GILLUM, KENNETH F.	RM2c	KONCZ, STEPHEN	EM3c
		KRIEGER, GEORGE D.	EM3c

(continued on next page)

168

U. S. S. MACHIAS — — CREW

KUITERT, JACOB	S2c
KUREK, THADDEUS	S1c
LA BRECQUE, BOIVIN E.	Cox
LAMPSON, FREDERICK H.	MM2c
LANT, RICHARD S.	S1c
LANSDOWN, JOHN L.	Y2c
LARSEN, ROBERT E.	F1c
LARRY E.	STM3c
LAURENCE, LESLIE G.	S2c
LEVINSON, WILLIAM	QM3c
LEWIS, CAMERON D.	Cox
LOCKETT, ROBERT J.	S1c
LOSINIECKI, ERWIN	S2c
LYONS, GEORGE W.	WT3c
MAGRONE, FELIX	S1c
MAJEWSKI, CHESTER	S1c
MAMERTO, FRANCISCO	STlc
MARSHALL, JAMES D.	S1c
MARLIN, JOSEPH E.	S2c
MASSEY, GEORGE L.	S2c
MAY, MACK D.	S2c
McALLISTER, PATRICK	CMlc
McGRATH, FRANCIS J.	MMlc
McNABB, CHRALES J.	MOMM3c
McNULTY, DONALD J.	WT3c
MERKLE, FRANK E.	S2c
MILDNER, ROBERT F.	S2c
MILLET, JOSEPH R	FC3c
MOORHOUSE, ROBERT L.	QMlc
MOORER, JOHN C.	S1c
MOTYCKA, JERRY P.	S2c
NELSON, EMMETT	S2c
O'ROUKE, J. J.	Cox
OUELLETTE, JOS. A.	MOMM3c
PALECZNY, JOSEPH	S2c
PASTOREK, JOSEPH A.	SMlc
PEDEN, HARR M.	WT2c
PENNOCK, JESSE E.	S2c
PERRA, FANCIS J.	S1c
PETERSON, CARL W.	S1c
PRATO, NESTOR J.	S1c
PUHEK, FRANCIS R.	S2c
QUITER, LLOYD N.	S2c
RAIZ, BERNARD	S1c
REED, DAVID W.	RT2c
REILLY, THOMAS C.	S1c
RHEIN, ROBERT E.	F1c
RHEIN, EDWARD J.	S2c

RILEY, W.	STM3c
RUTKOWSKI, CHARLES	S2c
ROEDER, RICHARD S.	S2c
ROGERS, BLAKELY M.	PHM3c
RONSICK, JACK	SM2c
SCEALS, WILLIAM T.	F1c
SCHAEDER, ROBERT V.	SKlc
SCHMIDT, MICHAEL C.	SC2c
SCHERTZ, HAROLD J.	S2c
SEABROOKS, M.	STM3c
SEXTON, RAYMOND M.	S2c
SHELTON, DANIEL L.	S1c
SICURELLA, ISIADORE R.	S1c
SISSON, ROBERT L.	F1c
SKERIK, JOSEPH C.	MM2c
SLACK, CHARLES A.	SK2c
SMITH, GLEN R.	S2c
SPILLANE, HAROLD W.	Cox
STEDMAN, WILLIAM J. JR.	F1c
STOELB, NORMAN N.	S2c
STOLL, WILLIAM M.	S2c
STRUMBERG, WAYNE C.	S1c
STRAUCH, RAYMOND G.	S2c
SULESTER, DONALD	S2c
SULLIVAN, JOHN C.	S2c
SWITZER, TODD JR.	BMlc
SWIBAKER, DONALD J.	WT3c
TERMANSEN, GEORGE C.	F1c
TONE, WILLIAM A.	S2c
TONNER, RICHARD C.	FC3c
TRAVIS, MOSS	Y2c
TRUPIANO, FRANK	S2c
VAN OUDENHOVEN, E. W.	S1c
VEDRA, FRANCIS J.	RM3c
VINING, JUDSON C. JR.	S2c
VOTAVA, JOHN M. JR.	GMlc
WALTER, EMERSON M.	EM3c
WALKER, MILTON	MMlc
WARNICK, LESLIE JR.	F1c
WEIGEL, ALBERT H.	S2c
WHIDDON, OSCAR C.	S1c
WHITEHEAD, STUART	S1c
WILLIAMS, JOHN L.	S1c
WILSON, BLAKE M.	SOM2c
WILSON, WARREN B.	WT3c
WIEDER, CARTER W.	S2c
YOURD, DICKSON V.	QM3c
ZAUNERE, ROBERT L.	GMlc

169

Anthony Gianunzio

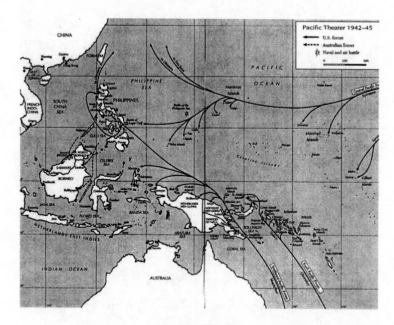

Pacific Theater
1942-1945

Steward's Mates

Edward A Green · May 1944
U.S.S. MACHIAS · PF 53
U.S. COAST GUARD ·

Painted on a 4'x 4' panel
and attached to starboard
side of wheelhouse by Ed
Green

The "author" of your Deck Log on SP-San Francisco
September 1945
Anthony Gianunzio

Richard Tonner (left) from M.I.T.
sophomore, to "boot," Fire
Controlman I/C to Triton
Missile Team.

USS *Machias* PF54
"Fantail" Spring, 1945
Puget Sound, Seattle

"Mookie" the monkey smuggled aboard the
USS *Machias*.

USS *Machias* Crew '89 Reunion

```
                        U.S.S. MACHIAS (PF-53)
                        c/o Fleet Post Office
                        San Francisco, Calif.

PF53/A4-3                                        31 March, 1943

From:          Commanding Officer, U.S.S. MACHIAS (PF-53).
To:            All Hands.

Subject:       Cruise Log of U.S.S. MACHIAS (PF-53).

        1.      The following is a cruise log of the U.S.S. MACHIAS
(PF-53) from commissioning on 29 March, 1944 to 31 March, 1945.
```

LOCATION	ARRIVED	DEPARTED
New Orleans, Louisiana (Commissioned)	3-29-44	4-16-44
Bermuda, British West Indies	4-21-44	5-18-44
Philadelphia, Pennsylvania	5-20-44	7-18-44
Norfolk, Virginia	7-21-44	7-29-44
New York, New York	7-30-44	7-31-44
Norfolk, Virginia	8-1-44	8-15-44
New York, New York	8-16-44	8-18-44
Charleston, South Carolina	8-22-44	8-23-44
Canal Zone, Panama	8-27-44	8-29-44
BoraBora, Society Islands	9-14-44	9-17-44 ✪
Espiritu, Santo, New Hebrides Islands	9-25-44	9-27-44
Guadalcanal, Solomon Islands	9-29-44	9-29-44
Russel Island Solomon Islands	9-29-44	10-2-44
Guadalcanal, Solomon Islands	10-2-44	10-3-44
Purvis Bay, Florida Islands	10-3-44	10-11-44
Finschaven, British New Guinea	10-13-44	10-17-44
Hollandia, Netherlands New Guinea	10-19-44	10-20-44
Mios Woendi, Schouten Islands	10-21-44	10-22-44
Morotai, Northern Moluccas, Netherlands East Indies	10-24-44	11-10-44
Mios Woendi, Schouten Islands	11-10-44	11-15-44
San Pedro Bay, Leyte, Philippine Islands	11-18-44	11-29-44
Hollandia, Netherlands New Guinea	12-10-44	12-12-44
San Pedro Bay, Leyte, Philippine Islands	12-16-44	12-18-44
Hollandia, Netherlands New Guinea	12-26-44	12-30-44
San Pedro Bay, Leyte, Philippine Islands	1-6-45	1-11-45
San Pedro Bay, Leyte, Philippine Islands	1-26-45	1-29-45
San Pedro Bay, Leyte, Philippine Islands	2-6-45	2-13-45
San Pedro Bay, Leyte, Philippine Islands	2-22-45	2-25-45
Lingayen Gulf, Luzon, Philippine Islands	3-1-45	3-3-45
San Pedro Bay, Leyte, Philippine Islands	3-7-45	3-9-45
Ulithi, Caroline Islands	3-12-45	3-12-45
Eniwetok, Marshall Islands	3-18-45	3-19-45
Pearl Harbor, Oahu, Territory of Hawaii	3-26-45	3-31-45
Enroute United States	3-31-45	

```
        2.      Total miles cruised since departure from Charleston, South
Carolina on 23 August, 1944 to return to United States 46,990 miles.

        3.      Copy of this letter will be inserted in service record.

   Bremerton, Wash., USA . . . . . . . . . . . . . . . 4-9-45 . . . . 6-6-45
   Kodiak, Alaska . . . . . . . . . . . . . . . . . . 6-8-45 . . . . 6-13-45
   Cold Bay, Aleutian Islands . . . . . . . . . . . . 8-15-45 . . . . 7-12-45
                                           [De-commissioned]
```

USS *Machias* Cruise Log

Milk Run

When you come down to it, if there's a problem, there must be a solution, maybe more than one. Maybe a simple antidote is the answer. Opposites by opposites are cured is the way Hippocrates put it. Everything, even every idea, has an opposite, logical or non-logical. I didn't know this, at first, that mine would be a milk problem, of all things.

Back in childhood, just a few years ago, a Jersey cow supplied our family of thirteen with 22 quarts of milk, plus cream and cheese each day. She was a super cow, the biggest of a fleet of fifteen or so that grazed on the Creek Woods hill overlooking Lake Antoine. Oftentimes this herd would wander back down into town when their shepherd, my older brother Fiore, was late in taking them back home. She softened the depression for us, providing the necessary milk and weekly milkshakes, and her milk sold for ten cents a quart. Fiore took care of these chores while I, too little to take on this gigantic animal, slipped off to the barnyard and baseball. Milk was a big word in my childhood, and I devoured plenty of it. I would invite Harold "Sody" Soderberg over for a milkshake while we listened to either Pat Flannagan or Bob Elson broadcasting the Chicago Cubs baseball game. A creamy shake more than overcame the static of our console Majestic radio. I didn't know 'til after high school that he had an ulterior but honorable interest: my sister Santina.

Anyway, the leaps from Jersey milkshakes to *The Jersey Bounce* to *The Beer Barrel Polka* to *Moonlight Serenade* is swifter than Hitler's panzer blitzkrieg. Now I hum the residues of *Missed the Saturday Dance* and think of them as days gone forever, for I'll never be that young again or young in that way again. Even in the last warm nights of the summer of '42 when I was playing with the Iron Mountain Rangers, the hot-spots were no longer the BonTon or the Igloo, but across the river at beery dance halls and bars in Aurora, Wisconsin.

I sensed like we all did that the carefree days were swiftly ending. Newspapers more than hinted that Hitler was stirring Europe's cauldron of idealized geography which the political cooks of WWI had hastily and hungrily concocted. Roosevelt told us not to worry; no American boys would serve on foreign soil. Big lies are spellbinding in their audacity, but perhaps they only work because the powerless rely so heavily on hope. So it was, bring on the *Beer Barrel Polka*, the last joyfully raucous polka. "We'll have a barrel of fun."

It was as if fate had grabbed me by the throat and chased away my sense of personal destiny. Any notion of myself soon melted into the new recipe of duty. The duration plus six months formula-contract with Uncle Sam seemed like a fair milk run to me, just as easy as delivering a dozen quarts to our neighborhood customers. But of course this is no banana boat beneath me, either.

There was a girl in every port, almost. Not love 'em and leave 'em. It was simply gathering experience, as in sight-seeing. New York's startlingly innovative skyscrapers, idyllic Bermuda, the wondrous Panama Canal, the Galapagos Islands (Charles Darwin's antithesis to the Garden of Eden), Bora Bora (my romantic garden), Florida and Tulagi Islands and their offshore, spear-like warship masts marking Iron Bottom sound–these I saw like a tourist, a traveler in a world too foreign for my brand-new eyes. Here, where travelers would be too wise to dwell, I have to rush through it all like a ninety-day wonder at the Academy training for officership. There was so much to catch up with.

Toby's bosun whistle is a case in point. Like chalk screeching on a blackboard, his high-pitched sustained piping screams through the dawn air, followed by your customary, "Alright, git outta yer sacks." A few crashing objects then punctuate his morning piss call. Trupiano has the right idea when he promotes a pleasant revolt. "Let's get that bastard one of these days. Let's rig up a line or two down low by the hatch. Like to see him hit the deck for a change." Toby is just doing his duty even if he gets a bang out of it. You could even like him if you liked the idea of a bosun mate who somehow acted and looked like a bosun mate.

Now and then there's a unanimous opinion to waylay our favorite bosun piper that nobody wants to follow, pied or not. We said the same thing, more quietly, of course, in boot camp about the bugler. We need something to bitch about. This endless con-voyage in warm waters must be the prototype milk run.

At Biak, New Guinea, at dawn, a Navy destroyer eases past into its berth. The destroyer is of the new Porter D.D. Class, sleek, swift, and powerful as a panther. Looks like it could do 45 knots, and it bristles with gunnery. "Monk" Marshall points at the sailors pouring out of the DD's midships hatches. "You seein' what I'm seein'? They got red apples for chow. Ain't had one since the states."

"Yeh, they got the chow alright. But we got the milk run." Bill Barney is half smiling.

"Barney, we ain't carryin' milk. Wish we wuz. Ain't had no milk neither since the states." Monk means what he says. He's from Duncansville, Texas.

A couple of guys nod, and I feel the urge for a cool glass of Jersey cow's milk just as I did hundreds of times ago. It's just wishful thinking, I know. Ice cream would be even better. Next thing I know I'll see a giant glass of cow juice on the horizon. We've done the Philippines to New Guinea convoy run a few times now. Sub-chasing is a helluva lot easier than charging into battleships like the destroyer USS *Johnston* did up off Leyte where it was sunk, then half its crew got chewed up by sharks, maybe red apples and all. They saved our baby flat-tops and maybe a catastrophic shelling in Leyte Gulf. Nonetheless, the Navy's getting the gravy. Red apples. Dessert with breakfast. Damn.

"What milk run?" "Troop" pounces on it, too. "Call nursing Liberty ships convoys eight days a week good duty? Must be four hundred Navy destroyers out here by now. We got the Japs on the run. All we got is the milk runs, not run. Diarrhea, I mean. Ain't funny when you're standin' watch on lookout."

"Milk? What milk? You been drinking powdered milk. Can't stand the stuff. Makes me wanna heave. Last milk I had was in Panama." "Spook" Grey tells the truth and I believe him. Powdered milk could cost us the war, maybe. Do the Japs drink milk, I wonder?

The Navy guys seem to be in an apple-eating line, as if eating "by the numbers." At least here they are topside with the small freedom of an oceanic view, cluttered, of course, by other "tin cans" and assorted escort warships. They look green as if they just came out of Great Lakes Naval Training Station. Us hooligans don't cotton to 'em. We always had a couple of years on 'em. Gunner's Mate school there was full of eighteen-year-old boots. I was truly content with being a Coast Guardsman and in a far smaller branch of the service. Seventy thousand boots and schoolees are too much humanity for anyone to bear. Any mass of humanity would be too much.

I couldn't help dragging my mind over the unpleasantries of Navy contacts. The Great Lakes chow lines were straight and long, outside, sometimes running a city block. In twenty minutes you'd make it to "shit on a shingle," browned beans on semi-toasted bread. The menu was predictable with no great expectations. Navy "boots" practiced their manly swearing, punctuating a phrase or two with clumsy sexual cliches. Three slow months of this was enough.

"Hey Barney, remember those barracks inspections? Those Navy brass think that cleanliness is godliness. Steel-wooling and polishing and all that crap. Remember when we played the Navy boots in touch football and beat the hell out of their feeling of superiority? Remember, you, me, and nine guys from the Marine barracks taking them on over at their asphalt drill field? Drubbed 'em something like twenty-six to nothin'."

"Yeh, we passed 'em dizzy."

"We invented plays on the spot, told the Marines who to block, and it worked almost every time. Sure got along with those sea-going bellhops. Yup. Took 'em into Tulagi, Guadalcanal, plenty of landings."

"Got any cigs, Buzz? My ration's all gone."

"Nope. Herrala's got mine. Likes Chesterfields. He can't stand Marvels and Lucky Strikes. I'm getting hungry. Let's see if there's anything left in the galley. Heard they're tryin' bread today. Ole dog-robber Kelley might be around. Don't ask the cooks, 'cept Schertz. He's got a heart even if the bread gets soggy." Once a week or so we get some.

Third chow section is winding down to the hangers-on begging for seconds. It's like Jap pilots tailing an incoming flight and dropping a few eggs. One can expect the unexpected in a chow line. Gotta be ready for a choice piece of jetsam or even flotsam. Months ago at Biak the Sunday menu stirred even the most serious chow hounds. Eggs, fresh eggs! Any way you want 'em: scrambled, eyes open, or over easy. No bitching. Two eggs in the middle of a war, in the middle of an ocean, a fair-to-middlin' miracle.

"Be a miracle if Cookie there'd hand over some canned peaches," chow hound Bernard Raiz lamented. Raiz is too young to be aboard. He keeps to himself, does his duty without complaint, and he's got the best appetite around. Cookie Schertz, who does the baking catastrophes, dishes him a half-hearted dirty look.

"Nothin' doin', you guys. This is officers' chow." Something funny about the cooks. None are underweight. None of the cooks look underfed. "Got some joe here if you want. Carnation milk for cream. Help yourselves."

Even a war can't stop a flash of creativity; in fact, it can help it. My brain zeroes in on the can of Carnation milk. Eureka! Milk! That's it! Mix the Carnation milk with the powdered stuff, say one part in three, and you'll be able to stomach it!

"Watcha smiling about, Buzz?"

"Ah, nothin'. Just figurin' out how to make the milk run."

Watering Holes

My fountain of youth shall never run dry. I say this somewhere in the Pacific where there's plenty of water, but of the salty sort. Salt water is one thing; the delicious spring waters of Iron Mountain and the spring-fed lakes sprinkled nearby are something else. They, literally, are true watering holes. But the metaphoric ones are even better. These will last me a lifetime even if "progress" sweeps them away one by one, which indeed it will.

One of my favorites, the little BonTon next to Khoury's Drug Store, often appears when I turn on my hometown switch that lights up my kaleidoscope of teenage memories. I'm there right now, early into age sixteen on a Saturday night. Harold "Sody" Soderberg and I are going to just hang out and Joe Sefronek's place is our first stop. He's shaking dice with a habitual customer and is probably letting him win. The BonTon is squeezed in between Khoury's Drug and Fugere's Shoe Store, but it's an oasis for us high schoolers.. The jukebox is alive with Crosby, Helen Forrest, Keely Smith, and the big bands. There must be fifty different selections at a dime apiece.

Joe makes a terrific chocolate malt. Booth intimacy is just a few steps past the counter. Booths line both sides of the rectangular, closet-like room. It's a romantic gauntlet. We'd like to spot a winsome gal to say hello to and talk to a bit. Dating takes dough and besides, baseball is still more important. An occasional familiar face stops by, and when Louie Armstrong's *Blueberry Hill* and any other hit song isn't too loud, we get a conversation going. All the while, of course, we keep our eyes peeled for you know what and who. Those were innocent days, and Benny Goodman and Glenn Miller poured out their romantic, popular songs. By 1941, the big bands swept the country. It was still good to hear *Moonlight Serenade* and even *The Beer Barrel Polka* in our speak-easy haven there on Stephenson Avenue, the main drag in Iron Mountain. It's easy for me to silently hum "Saturday night is the loneliest night of the week," and even "Missed the Saturday dance, might have gone but what for..." Granted, a chocolate malt isn't exactly great shakes, but compared with sitting on a depth charge rack somewhere in the Pacific and not knowing what might come next... Flotsam, jetsam.

When we're through with this fight, of course, it won't be the BonTon I'll head for. This great kid stuff is done with. But it's sort of like ice cream: reassuring and returning to security. A while back at Finchhaven, New Guinea, I tracked down a Red Cross hospitality station where they had ice cream, donuts, and feminine faces. Oddly, their place is high on a barren bluff overlooking the harbor. It's a hike to get there. Maybe even dangerous. Nothing like a good ice-cream cone to remind you of America and why you were there. I'll bet Kilroy was there too, though I didn't see his famous line. Japanese troops had been there a year ago, but their survivors headed into the interior where head-hunters probably finished them off.

My watering holes are strictly hometown, places I can return to and find them always warming. I have my favorite liberty towns, too. Up on the list are New Orleans, Milwaukee, and Chicago, but on the down side, the old standby, Norfolk. When the Navy and other services over-whelm a town, well, you know the locals will limit their hospitality and be impolite about it.. Milwaukee, though, enjoyed being overrun by Great Lakes boots who, like lumberjacks cooped up all winter, spent money like drunken sailors downtown and everywhere. Most young enlistees were still enough civilian to behave accordingly.

Going home on leave is surreal. Stepping off the fleet Chippewa train and into the kitchen at 203 Quinnesec Street takes me back as if I've never left. Even now, under any kind of moon or calm seas, this sentimentality always surfaces somewhere in our glittering fantail wake. My feet dangling over the depth charge racks and facing four hours of a moon-lit watch, what else is there? The smoke stack is behaving for a change. And a hop and skip of 8,000 miles and a mere two, three years is duck soup for a decent imagination. Re-reading a *Reader's Digest* two times in a week, in contrast, is nostalgic torture enough.

But just thinking of the BonTon is a morale builder. I need another twenty-second reminiscence. If proprietor Will Safronek knew how much we loved that rectangular slit in the wall, his chocolate malts would have been priced a dime higher. God, did he make a beautiful malt! You walked straight past Will, who seemed to be smiling even when he was shaking dice. At the far end, beyond the leather booths lining the walls for 20 feet, that nickelodeon was always in full swing, swing tunes, actually. It was intimate and as American as apple pie. No smoking, no monkey business. A parade of high school pals— Bob Biolo, Elton Swanson, Jack "Shoelace" Luciani, Leo "Snipe" Paoli, John "Mutt" Chiapusio, Johnny Secinaro, Jimmy Pericolose, Jack Bargo, Ted Moroni, Edmund "Hap" Rondeau, plus a hundred other guys with strange-sounding nicknames and maybe a nice-looking gal or three or more. My town was inundated with nicknames and, of course, with above-average gals.

Just around the corner and up the Hulst School Hill, the

Anthony Gianunzio

Dairy Bar could be counted on for jukebox dancing and plenty of high schoolers. Across the street, Chief of Police Al Schupp and company kept the peace in a peaceful town. The Dairy Bar offered soft drinks and it had a small dance floor and, of course, a nickelodeon and tables. The Iron Mountain News offices were next door. Perfect chaperones, but of course, none were needed. Retracing your steps and crossing the main drag, Stephenson Avenue, you'd find the Igloo. It was our hot spot. The liveliest kids in town showed up there: Goldie, who flashed the best front-teeth fillings in town; Teddie Buchman of the auburn-red hair; and lots of out-of-town gals. The Igloo's slick dance floor satisfied the smoothest swingers and the most energetic jitter-buggers. Just watching them was a show. It didn't matter that next to it an occasional freight train rolled into town. Everybody met there. It was a Braumart Theater or Capitol Theater date and then to the Igloo 'til midnight.

But nothing beat the Knights of Columbus Hall on a Saturday night. The K.C. Club, painted white, sported a fine screened-in porch, and its second floor was totally a dance floor. On any summer Friday or Saturday night, the swing bands played Glenn Miller's best stuff: *In The Mood, String of Pearls, Tuxedo Junction,* and usually closed the night playing the epitome of all those pre-war songs, *Moonlight Serenade.* The words were phantom, but oh, that melody! A bunch of us would listen to it while on the Gleason's porch across the street, and even though dancing was a bit sissyish for me, I felt its mood more deeply than that of any other song. Sitting on their porch rail with a couple of guys and gals and listening to the bands was pure pleasure. That's just how memorable Miller's stuff was. Sitting on those depth charges, I knew what a lot of other guys and I were fighting for. Funny thing, had I been dancing upstairs with the others, maybe I'd now be dreaming of the gal

I'd held in my arms.

There was no end to the watering holes, of course. Every generation has them: sentimental, favorite meeting places. The jazz age had them, too. My older sisters, Micky and Mary, raved about The Nightingale and Dreamy River, in the pines on a Menominee River bluff. On a full moon you could see clear across to Pine Mountain and its championship ski slide. They danced as late as the family curfew would allow, and even later when I would wait up and unlock the front door to let them in. They risked it all for the music of Joe Billo and Fra Corsi, whose bands drew the jazz age crowd. I often eavesdropped on their commentaries of the night's doings, though being seven was a handicap. The heavy weight of the depression couldn't stop the music. In fact, it seemed all the more needed and wanted. A dime entry fee and a three-mile ride up the Menominee river got the girls in for a full night of the Charleston and other fashionable dances. The sparkling wake of the *Machias* would have looked good on the Menominee, but had I been old enough, I would have sampled The Nightingale for sure. When the three-quarter moon peeks through a cloud opening, our ship's wake looks like champagne I've seen but still not tasted.

Those waterholes are changing, literally. BonTons are a thing of the past. Places like The Tropics, Hollywood Club, and Riverside are the new venue. A soft drink is dethroned by a rum and cola or a Southern Comfort, a draft, an Old Fashioned, or if someone is appreciative of your uniform, maybe a hard-hitting martini.

In a polite Madison cocktail lounge, I remember, I'm refused a beer. Nineteen isn't old enough. It's more than ironic because the conscription age is nineteen, just old enough to serve your country and just about the right time to begin living. And beyond this, who at age nineteen would more than merely suspect that life would be or could be far more wonderful than it is at that moment? Ken Cooper and Randy Simonson in Pearl Harbor, dead in the USS *Arizona*, would never find out. Helluva watering hole there. The time is too often out of joint, one of life's perpetual paradoxes. Being at the wrong place at the wrong time or any other case of bad timing seems typical of war. Shakespeare's "the time is out of joint" isn't just Hamlet's. Being in the right place at the right time... That's mastery of destiny. As for fate, well, let the ancient Greeks live on that. Shakespeare's romantic destiny beats Sophocles' fate by a lifetime.

Iron Mountain, like many towns brimming with first generation youth, has a variety of watering holes. Going back home on a ten-day leave quenched any thirst I might have, from walking the hill paths to meeting old friends and townspeople. My favorite path took me straight up into Creekwoods Hill and to the fire tower. I'd pause at the creek at the edge of the pine woods and, cupping my hands, drink from the cast-iron pipe projecting from the sloping hill. The hill yielded these waters, which collected underground and were filtered for at least one-half mile into the creek draw. Using my brother Joe's track shoes, I would run the mile uphill to the fire tower to get into stamina shape for baseball.

From the creek, the whole of the crescent town could be viewed. Up at the fire tower, the panoramic view was even more impressive and nostalgic. Lake Antoine and its slender, wooded island and the b/a beaches contained some pleasant and harrowing boyhood memories. In the early thirties, the Hiltonens' tin lizzie transported us like a pioneer wagon cross-country over the Creekwoods hill down to our stoney, boys-only beach. From the stoney shore to the island it's no deeper than 5 feet 9 inches, so we could walk to the island.

The Last Romantic War

Iron Mountain and Kingsford are twin cities with a population of twenty-two thousand and a European background. The cultural dimensions run deep and broad. Returning to the high school and grade schools, sometimes while in session, reawakens me to this great experiment, a republic in pursuit of democracy. Will any country ever be capable of democracy? I doubt it. Meandering the bases at Pine Mountain Ranger baseball field always reminds me that we must straighten out the world as best we can if only so that kids can play instead of serving in any youth corp under a dictator.

Newer watering holes are quickly replacing the others. Now I'll step into the Dickinson Hotel Bar or the Four Lane Bar beneath the Commercial Bank, only a block away from the train depot. There, young men, peers from all branches of the service, would congregate. With them I can find a semblance of that marvelous past. And there were women, lonesome women, eager for a good time. There were no 4-Fers and just a few of the grassy-green. "They're either too young or too old," as the song goes.

The past is marvelous—if you lived the todays well. How can it ever be forgotten? The future will be fine too, if today is taken care of. At first it's an arithmetic effect, and then when the experiences mount, the geometry kicks in. If you have that magical ingredient, the great catalyst imagination, well, you're in calculus. It's a perfect recipe for morality.

We all begin in ignorance with maybe a good dash of *apriori* knowledge embedded in our genes. With experience we wipe out ignorance and gain knowledge, the "what" of things. If the Mercury of the mind is still firing on all cylinders, then understanding kicks in. Then you must recognize quality, be able to judge and know the value of things. It's easy then, to select the right or proper gear for enjoyment, the epitome and purpose of life itself. It's in the "how" gear where the quality of life resides. A good memory simply means that one has lived fully, consciously, and enjoyably. Perhaps there'd be a Freudain block or two, but they'll dissolve through understanding. It all adds up to good watering holes. The whole world is wide open: people, ideas, places, things—it's all there for the taking and giving. The water holes I'm thinking of will last as long as my spirit and this planet lasts.

Damn, the depth charge rack is tough on the seat. Great for the mind, but hard on the seat. Maybe this deep, broad Pacific and its children islands will be as good a watering hole as any, maybe the mother of them all. That is, if I can keep dry.

This watery Sahara, with its splendid island-oases, defies description. Exotic as Bora Bora is, Chicago of America surges with far greater spirit. It reassures me that we humans give meaning to the planet; we're not just magnificent specks like mountains and islands. I feel the pulse of Carl Sandburg's Chicago, and when the Southern Cross catches more moon glow, I remember walking the long pier at Randolph Street leading to the Coast Guard station there. Across the Chicago River in Navy Pier's endless hangars, where aviation mechanics is being taught to Navy enlistees.

Jackhammers drone incessantly, as if they are the city's symbolic tool. Policemen's whistles pierce the air, inanely punctuating the cacophony. It's Sandburg's Chicago, big shoulders and all. The young, uninitiated's town. It's like the war: so many raw-boned youth thrown into the immense chasm. Behind the bluster, Michigan Avenue's fashion prevails. When I cross it, the Blackstone Hotel swallows a hundred sailors from Navy Pier. Just around the corner to the north, the Chicago Theater beckons with a movie and a second-rate Big Band that will play between the feature shows. In a second or two I'm on the mound at Wrigley field, staring down a helpless hitter with a teasing smile. This is what the vast Pacific will do to me in the middle of the darkening watch.

A midnight moon splashes on the ship's wake, illuminating the rolling swells. Each zig catches the moon; each zag, its picturesque shadow. From this watery screen any scenario is possible. Who's to give it the lie? It's like a mind's eye theater with an audience of one. The ocean, like life, is vast and almost endless. Scenarios are equally infinite. And there are days and unending nights that need to be spent. For example, this time I'd shake off Gabby Hartnett's signal and throw the index-finger curve instead. I can almost hear Gabby mutter, "Kid, you got away with that one. Don't start that shaking-me-off stuff until you learn these guys. They're laying for rookie meat."

Nights are empty pages that need filling. How do you kill an eternity? Stars don't mind if you use them for bases or spectators. You can kill time, but never kill space.

It's nice that these many watering holes fit so nicely into the big one beneath me. I'll remember all of this and perhaps a romantic book might somehow, someday become a final watering hole.

In the Dark

Homosexuality, in my small town America, is unthinkable and secretive. Like my companions, I thought of it in a simple way: a guy has gotten his sexuality confused. I never wondered about what is responsible for the assumed mix-up. I also never wondered how such a person would get along in a rugged male society where maleness is strictly defined. Anything less than toughness would be punished by ostracism. Our narrow view prescribed boxing, not ballet for a war that calls for harsh physical acts of courage. Anyone even suspected of suggestive, effeminate symptoms would soon disappear via discharge a la Section Eight.

At St. Mary's Lake, I remember a nice chap who seemed to be a mama's boy. He was shipped out fast lest he infect morale. He'd cry, softly, whispering that he wanted to go home, back to Milwaukee and his mom. The guys quickly lumped him into that vague category which we small-town guys knew little about. We were thankful that whatever it was, it wasn't us. Manliness above all meant that our sexuality be directed toward women, not men. Over the months and later on the *Machias*, I never heard any accusations. There were no hidden closets; there would have been hell to pay.

On a ship of 307 feet carrying a crew of 244, the necessary privacy, except perhaps in the officers' quarters, is non-existent. If a sailor wants a one-way ticket to home and a dishonorable discharge, sexual unorthodoxy aboard will get him there. That is, if he survives a most certain beating. I've heard that the

Marines offer them thirty days on bread and water with every fourth day some food and then a Section Eight discharge. It's a dark matter to be sure, but hardly threatening. At least not to me. For whatever reason their behavior, they've got a rough go of it. God must know, but waits. Well, hurry up.

But far more invidious and awkwardly subtle is the presence of negro steward's mates. Why do the officers need a set of domestics of another color to tend to their personal and ordinary needs? I can understand the need to separate the commissioned officers who are responsible for our welfare from the non-coms and other enlisted or drafted men. But this seems like one unnecessary segregation piled on still another.

Granted, our cultural experiences differ and the opportunities are limited, and also granted that the Navy is far more traditional than the other service branches. Traditions are far beyond my say-so or even my influence. We are satisfactorily adjusted if not fulfilled. I'm not about to start a social revolution. My contact has been typically limited: first, I saw them on the Chippewa passenger train as service people, then at carnivals and the circus, and then with the touring baseball teams. But I was curious, and it was easy to see their conditions were second-class at best. How do they think; were they really the things often said about them? I'm curious.

So, perhaps three or four times I stop amidships near the officers' wardroom hatch to talk with one of the five steward's mates who would be out for a break and some outside air. They rarely are topside; I've never seen them in dress uniform. In our brief several minutes our names were not exchanged, but my curious acquaintance said that he was from Chicago's South Side among thousands who had left the South for war factory jobs. I arm-wrestled with him, holding him to a draw in a friendly tussle. This is the extent of my socializing, and as far as

I know, it's probably more than that of any other enlisted man aboard. They are little more than domestics aboard our ship-hotel. Never have I seen any negro at general quarters or in action manning a gun. I've never given it much thought. Our segregation is both implicit and explicit.

But I sometimes wonder: just what in hell are they aboard for, anyway? When I do see them they're usually in pairs, and they seem affable and peaceful. They are quiet and seem occupied, fully occupied. Rarely seeing more than ten or so shipmates in any one day except at chow, I didn't sense this scarcity of contact to be unusual. I did hear about one incident, however; or rather, I overheard it. It was Lt. (jg) McShane's voice.

"Did you catch Spinks at coffee after dinner?"

"No. What was that about?"

"Oh, nothin'. Ole Spinks is a true gentleman of the South. Geez, did he nail Seabrooks! Seabrooks was taking his coffee cup away. It was almost empty and I guess Seabrooks wanted to clean up. Well, Spinks unloaded on him like a ton of bricks. Said something like, 'Seabrooks, I'll tell you when you can take my coffee, damn you.' Seabrooks was taken aback. In fact, he stepped backwards, probably thinking Spinks would slap him."

"Chrissake. Sounds like he's more a slave than a steward's mate, doesn't it."

"Yeah. You don't think Lincoln freed the slaves, do you?" They both chuckled in agreement.

On my way up to the flying bridge for pure Pacific air after dodging smokestack gases for about four on-watch hours, I recall a couple of eye-opening Southern encounters. The sea is calm, glittery calm. It'll be easy to reminisce, especially with likable Whitey, a good Southern boy from Tennessee. Maybe he can put a Southern accent onto it once I tell him how it was and he is.

"Whitey," I say, "give me the low-down on this." Whitey's first name is Stuart, named after a heroic Southern general of the Civil War. "I'll kinda summarize it for you. Don't say nothin' 'til I finish. O.K.?"

He gives me the slow-moving, smiley grin that he usually has for us Yankee Northerners. We, incidentally, are eighty percent of the crew, even counting the commissioned officers. I feel comfortable with his attitude. He's direct and honest and an all-around good kid. I take a couple of deep, deep breaths of that perfect air and ready myself for my tales.

"You remember Norfolk, Whitey. The place was an out-of-bounds city for us guys. Remember the signs like 'Sailors and dogs, no tresspassing' and some other signs, too, that told us that we aren't allowed? So I thought I'd go off to Suffolk for a piece of sight-seeing and some Virginian hospitality. The bus is filling fast and I take the first empty seat next to a negro sailor who is seated next to the window in the middle. I nod, casually, and sit down and make myself comfortable, I think. The bus fills, some elderly women look my way, and the driver comes aboard, looks into his rear-view mirror, and swings out of his seat. He's a big guy, maybe six-three or so. He pauses, then stares. Seems like he's going to announce the itinerary or something. Then, in a voice like LaBeau's he says, 'You there, get to the back of the bus.' He's aiming towards me, it looks like. He waits about four seconds and the bus gets very quiet, as if something's gonna happen, sudden-like.

"'You hear me? We don't leave 'til ya take a seat back there.'

"No swear words, Whitey. For a second I thought, hell, he can't mean me.

"Then a heavy-set, gray-haired negro woman way behind starts scolding the driver. 'He's good enough for that uniform, ain't he? Why he sit back here?'

"The bus driver stands up and says, 'You shut your mouth or I'll throw both of you off'n this bus. Hear me?'"

"I'm looking at the kid and he's looking wide-eyed as if he's expecting something to collapse on him. He's seaman second, probably just got in the service. He looks at me as if it's all right that a fellow sailor doesn't come to the rescue. 'It's O.K. It's O.K.,' he says. The lady on the back seat grumbles something I can't hear, and then when the sailor gets seated a few rows back, the bus takes off. Nobody says a word. Not even me. Was it right for me to shut up?"

Whitey has the warmest grin, and he holds onto it. I say, "Tell ya another one." I suspect he's got a ready answer for me, so another little tale won't matter one bit.

"Last February in New Orleans I got on a bus marked 'Desire' after being on a date with a gal named Rosa who told me that it would get me back to town. It was parked at the end of the line, just sitting there. I drag myself past the empty seats and drop onto the wall-to-wall seat at the very rear of the bus, hoping to nap after one helluva liberty. I almost fall asleep when someone shakes my shoulder and says, 'Sailor, you can't sleep back here.' I was dead tired and the long seat was perfect. I say to him, 'Why not? There's nobody in the bus.'"

"Because you're in New Orleans, sailor. This place is reserved for negro folks." It was sort of tit for tat or something . 'Desire.' Helluva name for a bus. Well, what about it, Whitey?"

"Buzz, y'all damn Yankees ain't never gonna understand us Southern folks. No use tellin' ya nothin'. Some day y'all figure it out. You was lucky cuz you had a uniform on. Down here one-to-one is O.K., but we don't do nuthin' wholesale. We don't mix it up cuz it'd get outta hand. Too much fear and no love, ah reckon."

The Last Romantic War

I understand all right. I also know that the clear, rushing air is at least good breathing. It's perfect on the flying bridge. I'm thinking, maybe I should tell him the little story my home-town buddy Joe Langlois told me. He said he got it from Will Rogers. Joe was full of ideas, sort of a philosopher. He put me on to this idea of the final form of the universe, which I guess no one can ever answer or at least be sure about. And even if we think we know the how of it, there's still the why of it and still more questions and aspects. Puts us all in our place, far beneath the creator, even if we believe that we're highest on the totem pole.

After a few minutes of doing nothing but breathing ocean air and thinking, I say to my shipmate, "Whitey, a pal from my hometown told me he heard Will Rogers tell this story. Wanna hear it?" He gives me that sure, go ahead look.

"Well, an Indian chief and a white man were on a lake shore, and the white man took a stick and scratched a little circle, maybe four, five inches in the sand, and then he drew another circle around the small one about a yard across. He pointed to the tiny circle and said, 'This much Indian knows,' and then touched the larger circle saying, 'This much white man knows.' The chief took the stick as if it were a peace pipe, pointed it to the sky and then pointed it out of the white man's circle and said, 'This, no man knows.'"

I let it sink in. Whitey seems calm enough and so I say, "I think we're all in the same boat, huh."

"No," he says. "Only on the same ship."

That really made me think.

All's Still

I was bound to find out sooner or later. It was happening right under my nose, almost under my eyes. But I don't go around like a kid turning stones over to find grass snakes, and looking for the bad isn't for me, either. Being a revenuer chasing cartoon character Snuffy Smith wouldn't do for me. So I had to learn the slow, hard, if not harmless way. My latest piece of naval education is a surprise only to me, and it's not a handout. It's from an unlikely source, gunner's mate 2/C "Kippy," formerly of the FBI.

Portly and short, and equipped with an Adolph Menjou mustache, he embraces a coffee cup like a get-out-of-my-way projectile as he climbs the gangway to the main deck. Kippy also fortifies himself with a robust cigar and exhales a formidable torrent of smoke at any too-near shipmate. This is his smoke screen, literally. He would swagger to the fantail rail and absorb himself in ten minutes of privacy. His strange accompanying stagger en route below deck, especially in a nervous sea, reminds me of Oliver Hardy. At first I think nothing of it; maybe he has a touch of *mal de mer*.

Should anyone inquire, "Kippy, you makin' coffee in your storeroom?" his reply is carefully consistent. "Still got 20 pounds of Chase & Sanborn under lock and key in the gunners' mate storeroom. Not for sale."

I think of coffee as an unnecessary addiction like whiskey is for most alcoholics. I never put one and one together. Coffee *royale* is a kingly drink, and people of and with good taste sip it slowly as if it were wine. Kippy keeps up his masquerade deep into the Pacific. Of course, the commissioned officers never fault their non-commissioned brethren, probably because their own supplies were ample and, more importantly, legal. Too much scrutiny might cause a crisis in morale. You could point to the British tars who got their daily ration of grog. This much I know. But I haven't caught on to this fringe benefit yet.

Whenever the skipper pulls an unannounced inspection, the black gang flies into action. In their daily routine they keep the engines going, and the water-tenders restore our woefully inadequate supply of fresh water. This gets done in a sort of slow motion. Lt. (jg)s Nix and MacDougall are hardly hands-on machinists, leaving the dirty nuts-and-bolts work to their chief petty officer Mike Palovic and other capable underlings. Nix rarely goes down below, and whenever Mac enters, one of the guys loosens a steam valve, which brings about a hasty retreat. The territory of the engine room is virtually uncharted and is the domain of the enlisted non-coms. And shipmates are never encouraged to see how the bottom-half lives. Temperature alone forbids it; 90s and 100s are typical readings down below. It's a perfect cover for their undercover activities.

The boiler room even influences the bunking area above it. Every two-inch mattress is encased in an asbestos covering because fire might travel swiftly there. Abundant grease on the engine and boiler room walkways further discourages visits or inspections. Below decks is pretty much off limits by unwritten law.

But occasionally word leaks out: the bilges hide plenty of booze, pure alcohol, and it's there for more than safe-keeping. The bilge rats are experts at distillation. Must have been at least five well-supervised stills. To their credit, none of it is a business interest. No profiteering. Just plain and simple imbibing. Also to their credit and perhaps their advantage, the word is mum.

During the random and seldom inspections, the CPOs carefully engage the skipper in time-consuming areas and place their personnel carefully at strategic points. So long as the black gang keep things on an even keel, all's well. This governance of the empire—some 200 feet by 35 feet—in such matters of the spirits is superb.

Storekeeper Ray Hargat, however, overcomes this alcohol "problem" with a resourceful dexterity that suits the requirements of his job. When asked by a higher authority who checks on inventory, namely, how come your supply of alcohol has diminished by fifty percent, he calmly explains with a straight-faced, "Sir, evaporation, sir."

One bubble of secrecy finally bursts at Biak, an island off the coast of northwest New Guinea. It's a PT boat haven like Mios Woendi. Here the plywood sailors are routinely shooting up the Jap barges and antagonizing shore batteries. These glamour boys live a tough life. Their main problem is water, the lack of fresh water. So they always approach us fresh-water sailors and a bosun of theirs would yell out something like, "How about a trade, ya goddam hooligans."

Now, such a salutation normally is fightin' words when exchanged between tin-can sailors and frigate sailors. Destroyer sailors look down upon their lesser colleagues, including the PT boat sailors, so we outcasts form an occasional expedient partnership.

"You guys need some fresh water?" Water Tender 1/C Harry Peden knows the right, first question. Now, any ship packed with sardined sailors always needs fresh water. Saltwater showers are anathema aboard ship. Fresh water is always in demand. But for the PTers, it's a perpetual crisis.

By some quirk of navy engineering, pure alcohol (torpedo

juice) propels the underwater missile. Valuable liquid. So far, the plywood sailors haven't done much. They laid eggs in Savo Bay mainly because their torpedoes couldn't keep a straight line. But they could harass off-shore rafts and barges, make hit-and-run raids, and do some scouting and patrol work. Their boats look like pleasure craft and add a visually romantic flair to our fleet. Anyway, Peden knows that our distilled water, ironically, is more valuable than pure alcohol.

"How's about two gallons?" The gurgling PT engines make Peden's voice sound like a stage whisper.

"A deal," the PT bosun affirms, politely. After all, a few gallons of torpedo juice can be explained away as a matter of internal evaporation, but water is a necessity of life. And from what we hear, the PT boys aren't firing too many torpedoes. But I haven't got the foggiest notion why we want or need two gallons of torpedo juice. Peden, Inc. does.

I've got survival on my mind, not booze, babes, or even baseball. So it's almost by accident that the big secret lands in my lap. A day after the PT swap, our hand-picked provisions detail returns with the spoils of war. Our raid on the usually unfriendly Navy supply ship is abundantly successful. We're fast learning the art of survival, and our guys have developed slight-of-hand tricks to sort of counteract the navy's stinginess with foodstuff. I see gallon cans making a routine flight down to after-steerage storage. Snagging footballs in mid-air is easy for me, so I intercept three of them as they fly across the passageway en route below deck. The 20:00 to 24:00 watch can use some extra nourishment.

No sooner do I wrap the three cans in my kapok life-jacket to stash them in a ready service locker by the depth charge racks, a firm hand squeezes my left shoulder.

"Whoa, Buzz," Motor Mack 1/C John Cason says in my ear.

"Take the plums and figs. We need the cherries."

This is damn near a surprise. Cason comes up for air on the fantail while I'm on watch, and we sometimes talk.

"Who's we?" I ask.

"Brush, Zaunere, Darrah, Peden, Lockett, Warnick and me." He pauses and adds, "and the dog-robber himself, Chief Kelly." Kelly is like the fox guarding the chicken coop. I'm convinced, but curious. "Why cherries, Cason?"

"Makes the best booze, Buzz. We got a still down below."

It's kinda funny. I'm out for some tasty and healthy nighttime dessert; they're out for 180 proof spirits. Mathematically, theirs is a higher purpose. Cason keeps a sharp eye for more cans of cherries.

My curiosity is increasingly whetted as the gallon cans float by our heads. I've read about hillbilly moonshiners and revenuers. I ask him, how is it done? Just curiosity, you know. He gives me a quick, bone-bare recipe.

"Take cherries, peaches, raisins... Any fruit, distilled battery water, sugar, the right amount of yeast. Let it ferment for about four weeks. Get a non-rust copper tube to let the gasses out. Gotta have a glass jar big enough. First time we done it the tube plugged up. Blew up all over Brush's electric room. Me and Ed wuz cleaning up the bulkhead and deck halfway through the night. Smelled like a saloon for awhile. Next time I set it up in that two-foot space behind the pot boiler. Skipper never looks back there. It's too hot and greasy for him."

"You guys the only ones got a still?"

" Hell no. There's four, five of 'em. Where you been, Buzz?"

I'm not exactly naïve, but I've never run into one. Maybe there's one in the bow paint locker. Nobody in his right mind goes there. About the last offense at a Captain's Mast would be for operating a still. Of course, if they were selling the stuff, that would be another story. The sea-going service can't tolerate capitalistic profiteering. Also, the gold braids have their legal supply and the gap in privilege is already pretty wide. So it's a fair standoff: legality vs. creativity. Then, too, there's that two cans of beer shore party liberty which take the measure of even the teetotalers aboard. All of this nonsense is running through my head. I'm almost willing to snag a few cans of cherries for Cason. Then I wonder out loud: "Why isn't Kelly setting aside the cans of fruit for you?" Before Cason can answer, I already know it. He's also content that I know it.

No more foolish questions. Cason is a terrific boxing champ and likeable. I want to keep it that way. Maybe my father's paper prayer can stop more than bullets.

Eleven Twenty-Four

General Douglas MacArthur and his army have gone ashore unopposed on Leyte Island! The US Navy brought them in on October 22 or so. He promised to return and did it without the help of the Marines. We didn't know it 'til days later. The Japanese were taken by surprise. Must have expected a direct hit on Luzon. Mac really outsmarted them in a purely military sense. Their surprise at Hawaii was more a political coup. We'll be convoying to it and patrolling Leyte Gulf entrance, you can bet. High time.

San Pedro Bay washes the shores of Tacloban on the western flank of Leyte Gulf. On this day, November 24, '44, heavy clouds smother the bay and occasional heavy downpours cast a false sense of serenity. Hundreds of supply and warships anchored row upon row create a sense of power, that this is the spearhead of it all. In just hours at dusk we get our second taste of gunfire. As expected, Jap planes from Luzon are going to raise hell. We have plenty of firepower company and we sure as hell are ready. There's a carrier about a mile east of us. The weather is wet; soaking rains force us under the gun canvasses.

Nuisance raids featuring "Washing-machine Charleys" make their calls at midnight simply to disturb the sleep of thousands of young sailors and coincidentally to drop a bomb or two on the Tacloban airstrip, if they can avoid being blinded by the powerful searchlights that reach a mile and beyond. Aircraft batteries pummel the skies, making for a fine show for the restless men below. Charlies do not linger because a Black

Widow or two would climb up after them. Widows are the night-fighter, radar-equipped version of the twin fuselage P38s that strike terror into the hearts of Japanese pilots. Their powerful climbing and diving ability would pincer their prey, coming from above and below. These planes seem to be assigned the task of dishing out retribution to the more conventional army aircraft of the shaky Empire of Japan. Our P38s screech out of Morotai, bound for Borneo and its vital oil refineries that keep Japan's navy fueled. They're here in full force, too.

Our ship's two-page bulletin carries its customary military items:

"UPDATED PACWAR: Leyte Island in the Philippines, as our planes for the second straight day accounted for more ships in Ormoc Bay (missed number of ships and troops aboard). This makes twenty-six thousand enemy troops who have met disaster, which the Japs have lost trying to reinforce the desperate defenders in the fringes along the coast of Leyte. MacArthur reported sinking a 9,000-ton transport and three small freighters and engulfing a 5,000-ton freighter and DD in flames. MacArthur also reported a Jap sub that was sunk in Ormoc Bay. The Navy meanwhile reporting from Washington on troop action in the Palaus, saying the 81st Army division killed 1,300 Japs and captured 142 between Oct. 20 and Nov. 22. Our losses were set at eighty-two (?) killed and 622 wounded and fifty-seven (?) missing. Main points of resistance offered by the remnants of the island garrison were from caves. The Navy also disclosed eight hundred men were rescued from the escort carrier St. Lo and six hundred from the Gambier, both sunk in naval battle for the Philippines Oct. 24."

I wonder about the completeness of the account. Of course, you couldn't tell the whole story, or even the truth for that matter. That would do the enemy a service. I also wonder why the P38s were assigned the Borneo run whereas the big B29s reportedly coming into the Pacific might easily have blown Borneo to bits and severed the vital artery of Japan's oil supply. Perhaps no air facility was near enough, except Halmahera Island, and it was loaded down with at least sixty thousand Jap troops. It would have been a tough price to pay. Maybe our subs are waylaying Jap shipping near Formosa. We never hear about their exploits. Maybe our military wants to slowly and severely punish Tojo and other worshipers of Hirohito like a heavyweight boxer who would deliberately and brutally demolish an unliked contender for a number of rounds before putting him away forever.

Our 20mm fantail battery of ten guys gratefully accept the sandwiches brought to us. Under the gun canvasses sheltering us from the sporadic rains, our crew would look out, taking turns, until a GQ is called off. This is serious business, not a picnic. It's getting more serious all the time. Japan is still a long way off. So is America. It's easy to appreciate America once away from it. It's hard when you are surrounded by it, unless your imagination and factual knowledge are in good shape. This war has to be fought if only to get more breathing room for liberty. Equality is most of the outside world's problem, far more than America's. Equality is something like a bonus by-product of liberty. There is plenty of opportunity to think about such academic matters while under gun canvas covers waiting for the enemy to show up. If both sides could send barrages of words instead of bullets... Never happen.

A heavy squall is rolling in from the gulf, and I dash for amidships and cover. I've always loved the rain, almost any of the dozens of different kinds. Pacific rains are of a different character, but I like the personality of its various kinds. Even its squalls vary. They would lie in ambush on the horizon, appearing as light gray puffs of low-hanging cumulus clouds. Ship and clouds seem to be on a collision course, neither giving way, acting as if they were drawn together magnetically. Almost suddenly, the *Machias* would slice into it, spilling its contents everywhere in a deluge. This is a God-sent natural shower, a gift for any sailor tired of salt-water showers and opportunistic enough to be ready for the heavenly downpour.

Morning has already been pierced by Jap fighters looking to drop their bombs on any available ship. Our *Machias* has peppered the sky with three hundred rounds of 40mm ammo and eighty-two rounds of 3" fifty and thousands of 20mms during a solid five minutes of misses. A P38 streaks into a high dive behind two of the Jap planes, turning both into smoking pencils. They skid into the sea, harmlessly, beyond a patrol craft.

Heavy cloud cover reaching down to 500 feet gives little time for attacking pilots to find suitable targets and even less time for ship gunners to lead their fire. Our *Machias* gun crews hang around their assigned guns in anticipation of the next GQ and are fully at the ready, gun breeches loaded, for the next ten-second hello and goodbye. It looks like it will last all day and into the night, for there are ample sitting ducks on the pond.

Several minutes after another all clear, the strange-sound of a Jap fighter about a mile off the port side alerts the men lingering topside. Soggy, darkened skies barely reveal a diving aircraft. This aircraft takes aim at a refueling ship that is nursing a patrol craft, a 165 footer. The fighter dives in from the tanker's port quarter but releases its bomb early, hitting the PC right down its smokestack. Smoke and fire spurt from its wound. Followed by a hail of fire from the stricken ship, the plane veers toward us. I see the shells dotting the water, and almost before I hit the deck, hear them rattling off the hull just feet beneath my head.

This hit-and-run is over in fewer than ten seconds. I'm numb from the close call or being a bit slow to react, but content that the 20mm PC gunner had no shells with my name on them. Maybe there was a touch of truth about your name being on a shell. Well, nobody could spell my name, anyway. And nobody knows about my close call. Once again our *Machias* ping, ping, pings into general quarters while I am rolling myself up off the deck.

I hear Lt. (jg) McShane bellowing away at Assistant Surgeon Mench Trent. I also hear loudspeakers from the PC calling for help. "We've got casualties. Send help over. Need help immediately!" The speaker's voice is almost pleading, almost as if he himself were wounded.

The rush to GQ submerges McShane's tirade at Trent. Trent is standing in the hatchway port side amidships, wearing a poker face, as if waiting for the gods to relieve him of any obligation that he is not capable of. After all, he is but an assistant surgeon with hardly any successes to his credit beyond removing an Aussie's appendix. Even if only 300 yards away, the stricken patrol craft is far beyond his modest talents.

Black smoke coils like a serpent from the small patrol craft's midsection. Our *Machias* is now at the ready two minutes after the attack. The PC is fighting small fires and detaching from the massive tanker. All eyes are on it and few, if any, hear McShane's scorching of Trent. In an ironic way there's a touch of burlesque in it. Trent surely outweighs his tormentor by 100 pounds and towers above him. But the short lieutenant's words cut him surgically, somewhere inside.

"Christ, Trent. Can't you see that PC over there needs help? Can't you hear 'em hollering? I'll get you over there in the whaleboat. C'mon, dammit!"

A confused Trent blurts out, "Skipper says I got duty here.

Wants me here. Told me I'm needed here, dammit."

Trent is still dead in the passageway, refusing to move. There's a puzzled and dazed look on his spic'n span face. He has a neatly trimmed mustache even if it is an ordinary, nondescript one. He smells good. He keeps limited sick bay hours. His dress is immaculate. He is all the things few officers aboard the *Machias* have time to be.

McShane eggs him on further. "C'mon, you won't get your hands dirty. Where t'hell you think you're on, a yacht?"

Trent looks pale, uncertain. Maybe he's an M.D., but what does he know about surgery or about patching up shell holes and the like? Nothin'. Sick bay, yes. Band-aiding flesh wounds, yes. Pill-pushing, sure. He was too gentle for such reality, and McShane, who knew enough about incompetent officers, decides to let go. Boats are finally making their way to PC 1124.

On my way to the fantail, I bump into sonar striker De Rosa. He's pointing toward the smoking patrol craft. "Didja see the 1124 get hit?"

"Yeah, that bomb hit the stack. They're still callin' for help."

"That bomb had their name on it, Buzz. Poor bastards."

"That's horsecrap superstition, Dee."

"O.K. Call it what you want, Buzz. But you know what day it is? November 24. Friday to boot. Eleven twenty-four. That's their number, 1124. You figure that's a coincidence?"

I'm trying to dismiss it. Not many ships have four numbers. Our "53" isn't on the calendar, even. But I feel strangely comfortable touching the cloth-sealed Latin prayer my father gave me, which is in my thin wallet.

Bo LaBeau taps me on the shoulder. "Buzz, somebody up there is looking out for us. We were supposed to be refueling there. That PC musta' had an emergency and they bumped us out. Poor bastards. She's still smoking."

I turn to some of my gun crew. "Keep your eyes peeled," I say. "You saw what happened to that PC over there."

Smoke from the PC was beginning to reach us.

Patron Saint Pop Bryan

"Listen up, lads. D'ya wanna hear the story of Pool-shootin' Roy, a true American hero o' the last war? Listen close, you too, Bill Barney."

Nobody could recite the poem like Benjamin "Pop" Bryan. It's his hallmark. Poem reciting from a bosun mate first class? Well, if you knew Pop you knew he was the patron saint, if not the guardian angel, of the men aboard the frigate USS *Machias.* Maybe for the commissioned officers, too.

Funny thing was, he didn't have to serve. Didn't have to be out in the Pacific, escorting convoys, running patrols, firing on kamikazes, chasing Jap subs and keeping a salt-water ship in sea-going shape, not to mention enduring all the dull unpleasantries of shipboard life. He is past fifty, almost twice the age of the captain. Pop had been turned down three times before the desk recruiter tired of him and told him, "Pass the physical and you're in."

Well, Pop showed him and then some. "I've got three sons who are in the Navy. They aren't gonna do it alone." He utterly convinced the recruiter, and he knew seamanship. Coming in, he was Ben Bryan, BM 1/c.

After shakedown training near Bermuda and a return to the East Coast, a number of the crew go AWOL, and many more grumble about the captain. At Norfolk, a hearing by a congressman airs out the complaints. It's Pop who ably and fairly represents his shipmates. Weeks later, when Captain R.T. Alexander solemnly declares, "We will serve at least two years in the Pacific," the replenished crew dutifully accepts it. We're ready to do our duty.

Pop hails from Lake Forest, Illinois, and probably was connected with the fine liberal arts college there. You guess that he knew just about everything worth knowing. Our crew is mainly in their early twenties; even the skipper is but thirty-four. More than any other man–commissioned officers included–he is our truest link to the civilized world that seems to be fast fading in the expediencies of a massive war.

Pop could pass as poet Robert Frost's double not only in voice but in presence. He looks like a gentleman farmer, one who has endured fifty New England seasons. His wavy, white hair rests on a gently strong face with fiery blue eyes anchored in a ruddy-red complexion. He is six foot plus with much suggestion of previous athleticism. Had he not worn the enlisted non-com garb, men would have come to attention in his presence.

He is class and charisma. His language shows it. Never raises his voice.

"Now lads, we've got to do this right. Let's make the deck look like it ought to be." That was his manner.

Some other bosun mate might have bellowed, "Alright you lazy bastards, grab them chipping hammers and turn to. What ya waitin' fer! You, 'Troop,' knock off the scuttlebutt and get your butt on the deck. Want liberty in New Yawk, don'tcha?"

But there's style, too. With a voice as disciplined as Frost's poetry, he seems to nurse each phrase into being, giving it a life of its own. Like soft cement, those words firm instantly and you know they can be backed up mysteriously. There is "Mentor" written all over him, the antithesis of the stereotype bosun.

Pop chafed under the orders that sent him below deck during general quarters. He wants to be where the shooting is, not below in charge of a repair party. He got his wish. His 3-inch fifty gun crew decorated the skies of San Pedro Bay, Leyte, on many a night dirtied by Washing-machine Charley.

On Christmas Eve 1944, Pop commandeers the sound-powered phones of the men on watch and sings a heart-tugging *Silent Night*.

"Men," he whispers, "If the Japanese knew Jesus as their Lord instead of Hirohito, we wouldn't be out here." Almost out of the blue he said it. Pop was on the right side of everything.

In a way, he's everyone's ole' man. Like he'd represent you or listen to your problems though he had no authority to do so. Without lifting a finger, Pop kept any situation down to mere nuisance. He got straight to the bottom of any problem when asked for help.

It's funny to see how even chief petty officers and lieutenants respect him. It's as if he were experience personified and can know instantly the quality of their actions. "Carry on and quit your kicking," that's his motto. Every ship needs such a man, if only to keep the ugly business of war as honest as possible.

Some day he'll just disappear. No good-byes, just do a guardian angel disappearance. His work is already complete.

You Never Know

Pacific, my eye! Peaceful? Hardly. Deceptive? Yes. The only thing I'm sure about is nothing's for sure. Reminds me of the romantic ballad, "You'll Never Know." The last words are "if you don't know now." It's either irony or paradox, and only God knows the truth. If we were smarter, nothing would be ironic or paradoxical to us. If, if... The smallest big word in the language. Anyway, we're narrowing the gap. The paradoxical Pacific is teeming with seeming contradictions. Nature seems peaceful and yet danger lurks everywhere: below, above, and on the surface. If you jump to a wrong conclusion, it might be your own. The Pacific looks unbelievably peaceful on the surface, but it's also good at covering up its casualties and those that are man-made.

For at least a week now, our *Machias* is anchored in San Pedro Bay, Leyte Gulf, in the Philippines. Our crew and those of hundreds of ships are playing host to renegade air attacks, over a hundred of them, at all hours under all conditions. Washing-machine Charleys come in at ungodly hours, usually making a midnight call. Whatever they're flying sound like rattle-traps, like Model T Fords. Monsoon-like rains drive the general quarters gun crews under their gun canvasses. It's as if we've found some canvas shelter from a sudden rain at a picnic, but this is no picnic. One of us keeps a lookout should our radar not pick up low-flying aircraft.

Cooks see to it that sandwich-like concoctions are distributed around to all hands. More than one guy has said the sandwiches are better than the typical meals. I can explain this little irony, but there are bigger and better ones. Why would a twin-engine Betty bomber come in low, at twilight, and the Charleys, choose midnight sky-high? One is just a nuisance, like a mosquito, and the other means business, kaput! The Betty ought to be flying high with its bomb load and Charley ought to sneak in and get out fast after dropping some light stuff. Maybe we should ask the Japanese high command about this goofy strategy. You'd think the Betty would be more successful, but it's Charley who pains us by stealing needed sleep.

As if this isn't enough to test our patience, sonar thinks it's got a sub contact.

"There's some Jap midget subs loose in the gulf. We're goin' after 'em." Sounds like Blake Wilson, SoM 1/c. This one ought to be fun. The last midget sub chase left plenty of dead fish in the gulf, but no confirmed sinking. Midgets are dangerous and slippery, and there are hundreds of supply ships in the gulf, almost unprotected.

Probably a false alarm this time. The gulf waters are calm, but not for long. A strangely crimson sun is now sinking into San Pedro Bay. War-cruising watch at the depth charge racks will be lively for awhile. An Aussie frigate, the HMS *Hawkesbury*, might get in on the chase. They've been with us on a convoy run to New Guinea. They're a veteran ship and have been at it since way back in '39. They work well with us.

San Pedro Bay isn't deep, and a midget sub can lie on the bottom for awhile. Maybe we'll be allowed a film on the fantail tonight. John Wayne is showing us how to win the war. Hollywood is good at this sort of thing. A John Wayne show and a couple of slim, black Filipino cigars can go a long way. We saw *Air Force* at Morotai and six hours later at dawn shot down a Jap fighter. No thanks to Wayne, though. One cigar is equal to two cans of warm beer. Beer? So far we've guzzled about six cans of a nameless brew. Three shore parties in all. The limeys have their daily grog, but our guys have all the cigs they want. Mine I give to Herrala. The sub chase is called off, finally.

The exec is letting down anchor again. Nobody does it as well as the Moose. His is a performance, not a show.

Army artillery at Tacloban airstrip has given us damned good shows just about every night here in San Pedro Bay. A midnight Washing-machine Charley show is better than any Hollywood stuff. It's cat and mouse stuff, and the mouse keeps getting away. Searchlights try to converge on him and the shore batteries throw everything they have to get him off the stage. It's almost like a carnival, except that he disturbs our sleep. Not mine, since I don't hit the sack 'til about 00:30 after my eight-to-midnight watch, so it doesn't affect me too much. But we're at general quarters for about the hundredth time in the past week. The Charleys must be coming from the island of Mindanao, which has been by-passed and, like Halmahera, probably has a few airstrips and some leftover planes.

Last night at about 20:00 the film was pre-empted. It is the real thing. A Betty twin-engine bomber runs the gauntlet of our two mile-long rows of ships. She is heading toward shore to drop eggs on the airfield. She's no more than 150 feet above us, engines, wings, and fuselage flaming as tracers converge in geometric parabolas and some disappear into her long, cigar-shaped body. The Betty is a flaming inferno, but nobody ceases fire, not even the port side guns of the *Machias*. She is unforgettable, center stage all the way, a perfect symbol of Japan's inevitable destruction and defeat. A barrage of bullets follows her down the gauntlet until she bellies into the bay. This action lasts less than a minute. The orgy of firing lights up the dark sky, and after the Betty is downed, there are no cheers, just a sense of relief. How the Betty maintains a straight line is amazing, too, for the pilot could not have had all of the controls working. Even if he somehow were alive. What a way to go.

This close-up reminds me of an overly zealous base runner who has over-run third base, and the cut-off man is waiting to finish him off near third base. Surprisingly, "Betty" charges home plate and three swift infielders run her down just short of the airstrip, home plate. It's the last of the eighth and their home team is too many runs behind to make any difference. Seems like a show of bravado with nothing to gain.

The final game is scheduled to be played at Japan, I think. We lost the first one in Hawaii, but it was an eye-opener and it woke us up. Bet the boys from Japan would smile at my baseball analogy. It would please them to know that we know they know something about our national pastime. They've forgotten that we're good at winning wars, too.

We've had about a hundred wake-up GQs in the past week, and their toothpick hitter, Washing-machine Charley, will step up to the plate again around midnight. He'll pop-up as usual. We'll shoot the hell out of the atmosphere as usual. The pyrotechnics are awesome. Even the searchlights, with their mile-high tunnels of vision, are fine theater. Each Washing-machine Charley must feel like a batting-practice pitcher who's ducking line drives through the box but somehow manages to survive. Not once does a Charley flame downward. The flaming Betty put on a fine show. We'd like to see a Charley or two light up the sky like a Roman candle, but the odds are against it. They've cost us a lot more than what they're worth. It's like taking batting practice and not getting into the game.

A rumor that a Monday morning liberty will be granted is good listening. Getting ashore anywhere in the Pacific is fine; anything to get one's feet off scorching metal decks is welcome.

It's already been a month since Biak. It doesn't matter that there are no bright lights, no dames, no music, no nothing. Just put two feet on dry land for a change. Well, maybe throw in a couple of cans of beer. Even warm beer.

Fact of the matter is, there's nothing, no place to go in the Pacific. After Bora Bora, the ideal idyllic paradise of the Pacific, nothing stands out, at least on our routes. It would be fine to see Honolulu, but Manila is likely to be a wreck. Japan? Unthinkable. It would be nice to thank Tokyo Rose for providing the latest American music over short-wave radio. " Near You" is the latest hit. "It's like heaven to be near you" is how the song goes. Just fine for guys with sweethearts or wives. She plays the faithful and lonesome cards to the hilt.

"Hey Buzz, let's hit Tacloban tomorrow." Herrala is always for a shore party, ready or not. "Kerber's got the liberty list posted. We're in the first wave." Werner is a raw-boned Upper Peninsula Finlander who would have been a perfect pagan fifteen hundred years ago, and even now civilization has its hands full moderating him. I'm his anchor. But there is plenty of sail in both of us.

Once a month it's "Gimme your cigarette ration chit, Buzz." Sometimes I come back with, "Anything else, you good-for-nothin' hooligan?"

"Naw. You keep your two cans of beer. We'll get some in town."

"What if the town's off limits?"

He already has the answer. "We'll put it back on limits." It's the U.P. in us.

"You know I've been on shore patrol. These guys don't like trouble. They'll give you double, toil and trouble." I know that my Macbeth is bouncing off his ears, but at least he finds it a bit funny. You had to hunt for humor sometimes, though all you had to do usually is just show up in the mess hall or watch the deck force scatter when that shrill bosun pipe calls 'em to "sweep down, fore and aft."

You could watch Deck Officer Barstad, too. But don't be on his leeward side. He has a curious speech defect which allows him to send sprays of saliva, swiftly, windward to leeward, whenever certain consonants are uttered or stuttered. More than one petty officer walks away wiping his face after briefly encountering him. It's rumored that he avoids bars, not because of beer, but because somehow he unconsciously invites brawls. He's put two and two together, but has never found a dentist who could correct the condition. Now and then—and this is pure scuttlebutt—fellow officers might address him as "Saliva Sap." But since he holds a lieutenant's commission, none dare dishonor him to his face. Thank God Barstad was deck force and not my gunnery officer.

It's Sunday and it's liberty ashore. No Japoni invited. They're catching hell now.

"Now hear this. Now hear this. First section liberty party leaves at 11:00."

Then another familiar voice chimes in. "If you're going ashore, it's undress whites, uniform of the day. And stay the hell outta trouble. We're shovin' off tomorrow." Toby Switzer, the toughest bosun in Leyte Gulf and maybe the world, delivers these heedless words to a whaleboat load of thirsty, bored, tired but enterprising sailors. All we know is that the village of Tacloban is there. Church is unthinkable. Heaven can wait.

"C'mon Finn, let's take this road," I say. "We better not hit town with that bunch." The road is a recently worn trail probably used to haul military equipment in last month's invasion. Probably the same pathway General Douglas MacArthur took into town after wetting his ankles coming ashore for his "I have returned" shore party.

The roadway swings left to the west and into tall grasses almost shoulder high. A strange, chirruping cacophony drifts our way.

"What's that? Get down, Buzz."

Here we are, two guys in clean undress whites, groveling to a foreign sound near a friendly town? A bevy of local belles, laundering clothes in the creek while singing their rendition of American hit songs, spot us. Not bad at all.

"Look at 'em Buzz. Sight for sore eyes, ain't they? Geez, let's get 'em."

"Get 'em what? Our two cans of beer? Hell no. Sit right here and we'll polish off the beer now." He thinks I'm crazy. A couple of them look interested.

Warm beer, even unlabeled stuff, goes down fast. It also hits an unaccustomed drinker three times as fast and hard. Out of the tall grass a creek appears. A log crosses the creek, its topside planed down for surer footing. The washerwomen have quieted, seeing us sailors. My buddy mounts the log and motions me to follow. My fifth step doesn't touch anything but clusters of laughter.

Something slippery gets me. Maybe the beer. My entrance into Tacloban Creek is as smooth and wet as a baptismal dunking. Werner rescues me a little. The water is chin-high and my footing is uncertain. I stagger out, dripping like a seadog. The women hush and then the giggles ripen. Nobody can resist laughing at two soaked sailors, water dripping from pockets and everywhere. I'm beginning to feel a little like Don Quixote but not as safe.

"O.K. Let's head for town," I say. The younger women point the way; the older ones cast uncertain glances. "Town that way," they say, and keep pointing as if anxious not to welcome us liberators.

Still soaking wet and chafing and no town in sight, we climb a pine slope for a view of the bay. A boy ambles up and sings out in practiced English, "GI want to buy picture of Japoni? Cheap. Only two dolla."

"What you mean cheap two dolla? Give one dolla. Picture no good." My tightwad pal is out for a bargain again. "All light, one dolla." The boy takes the money and runs. Then a little girl bumps him and grabs at his two by three souvenir snapshot.

"You buy bad picture," she says. Almost crying, she wails, "Bad Japoni. Gimme picture." Werner holds on to his souvenir.

"Japoni hurt sister," she cries. "My picture!"

"No, my picture." He brushes her aside. "I think these two got a racket goin'," he tells me.

"Let's head for the Red Cross shack over there. Maybe they've got some ice cream or doughnuts. Maybe we can get out of these wet clothes."

Things aren't going so good. Warm beer, falling into a deep creek, a little girl crying, and an opportunistic boy, and now maybe surrendering our last pesos to the Red Cross. Back in Hollandia, the Red Cross prices were steeper than the shoreline. If this is Filipino liberty, then I shall not return. That's a promise. Maybe I'm all wet. Maybe this isn't a romantic war like McShane was telling us.

"You'll never know if you don't know now." Not too bad a line even if I'm talking to myself. Werner can't wait to get to the Red Cross shack. I think he smells womanhood or something. I smell irony all over the place. Like yesterday. McShane is trying to get Lt. Kemp aboard a plane to Frisco, where his wife is deathly sick. Caesarian went wrong. The pilot won't let him board even after five minutes of arguing, and McShane even threatens him. Can you believe it, a Jap plane swoops low and drops a couple of bombs and the plane is blown to hell. Must have killed them all. Kemp caught the next plane out.

I guess you never know. Sometimes the paper prayer comforts me. Maybe faith has a hand in it. My three brothers are still alive. Why do I still feel indestructible?

Monkey-Shines

When and where Mookie the monkey came aboard is known to only a few, the person or persons who traded for him down on the New Guinea coast. He was smuggled aboard in early October, somebody says. Scuttlebutt also says that his hangout is below deck aft in Kippy's gunnery storeroom, but he's invisible and remains a mystery to us. Of course we've got more than Mookie on our minds.

Well, I'm on the mid-morning watch and the little mystery is about to turn into a mere puzzle. The Conn speakers are humming.

"Now hear this. Now hear this. Monkey overboard. Somebody go in after him." The loudspeaker voice is that of Lt. (jg) McShane, who doesn't ask approval of the skipper to make such a flippant announcement. He stops our *Machias* dead in the water. We're two days south of Leyte Gulf convoying some empty transports to Hollandia, New Guinea. It's a warm December 20 and we've just outrun a nasty typhoon, but now a measly monkey is turning the ship around? Maybe this is why we're destined to finish off the enemy. We appreciate "monkey business."

"McAllister!" Kippy yells. "You're the best swimmer here. Go get that little bastard." Kippy isn't commanding. A second-class petty officer can't pull rank on a first class. He's imploring. Kippy is good with a tommy gun but hardly is the rescuer type at 200 pounds plus wrapped around 5 feet seven. This will be a nice wake-up scene, maybe even a dicey drama.

The USS *Machias* veers off its convoy-protecting station. This is unbelievable! Head-scratching and even belly-laughing infect the score or so of us who hear another solemn pronouncement: "Now hear this, now hear this." McShane can act. But maybe he'll get court-marshaled. The rescue is bound to be a good show.

The bridge spots Mookie; he's riding a slight swell ungracefully. He knows less about swimming than I do. I'm O.K. under water.

McAllister jumps into the eternal Pacific, diving a good ten feet from the hull. Will Mookie resist a rescue? No bets are offered. We want him rescued, pain-in-the-butt and all. It's just the first time I've seen him; nobody's seen him. The old man's been after him in a sort of haphazard way. He knows that a mascot is more valuable to our morale as a sort of lightning rod piece of resistance and defiance. He's our symbolic soup of sympathy.

The swells are fairly low, about one fathom. McAllister is cutting through the water like a shark after chow. Mookie seems to be accepting his fate as a landlubber monkey. He can't swim a lick, but he is upright. Salt water has a buoyancy and even a slip of a 10-pound monkey will float awhile. Mookie's out about 50 yards and he's no more than a dot on the top of a swell. Mac is closing in on him fast. He can swim with the best. In ten minutes our *Machias* has completed the about-turn. Might even overrun McAllister. An orange dye-marker is clearly visible, and now McAllister grabs Mookie. He holds him high; puts him on his shoulder.

Mookie does not like such a life-saving grip even if it's by a certified Red Cross life-saver. He's totally suspicious of all human-kind. Mookie slips through the hold, sits on Mac's head, grabs him by the throat, rests his feet on Mac's shoulders, and is enthroned. He's on his throne like a court jester mocking his lord beneath. This satisfies McAllister, for this is a brilliant life-saving feat. Plenty to write home about, and it'll convince the folks that he's not in serious danger doing such duties. Mac dutifully splashes onto the Jacob's ladder, sheds the monkey, and drags himself aboard with no more than a dribble of blood trickling down his right shoulder.

"Nice goin', Mac," Kippy growls. Gently, of course. His cigar follows his words.

"Thought he was gonna scratch my eyes out. Why did he go overboard, Kippy?"

"I chased him. He jumped on the rail and was swinging on it, but the grease was on his hands and the little bugger slipped. The old man isn't topside, is he?"

Mookie then gives the reception committee the slip. Only Kippy knows how slippery he is. Mookie is the archetypal grease monkey. That's it. He's a damn grease monkey.

"We're blood brothers, Mac. They know grease, we do grease. Got his hair slicked down, lips slicked, even eats the purple graphite stuff. I'm always cleanin' up after that little bastard. I don't think he likes sea duty. Remember that mascot mongrel we had goin' down to the Panama Canal? He didn't like it either. Staggered all over the deck. Never got his sea legs. One day nobody saw him. Must've fell over the side. Guess somebody done him a favor."

Mookie leaves a trail of water, and it leads below deck. We're relieved and can't believe McShane or any of the j.g.s aboard has the crust to stop the engines and rescue a monkey. I doubt a Jap captain would do it. That's why we're beating up on 'em. We favor living above ground, even water, and even a pipsqueak monkey has a right to it.

Kippy carries coffee around, usually with a wry grin, and

torpedo juice is suspected. Maybe Mookie has access, too. Lots of maybes here. Convoying ships is dull routine work; we must and can adjust to it. Mookie is good at making the best of his disoriented existence. Maybe he's discovered a still; Mac says he smelled alcohol. No jungle monkey can walk a sun-scorched deck without shoes. He is definitely a below decks, nocturnal creature. Small wonder his presence is damn near a military secret.

But some of the commissioned officers know. The skipper knows, and Kippy knows that the skipper knows. Of course, Mookie does not know. He has yet to get his bearings. The mast maybe is a jungle tree for him. Bet he's been up on the revolving radar, rotating, surveying the sea world for more miles than us topside ants.

Perhaps some primal intelligence warns him not to "grease-up" before his climb. Perhaps it wears off after the first 15 feet of mast. I can imagine a little scenario with Tennessee Whitehead. "Ya'll git a captain's mast if ya don't git down heah rot awaya." Mookie slides down faster'n a fireman and disappears into an air duct. I'd like to see that one.

Who can explain Mookie's climbing the highest peak? Almost as inexplicable as our climbing a mountain. Maybe it foreshadows his last action aboard this strange metallic world that threatens to be his permanent home.

Mookie gets more sociable. Every now and then someone spots him. At gunnery practice he scampers below decks for shelter. His passageways are the air ducts that connect some of the compartments and give him entrance. He knows the murky bilges at the ship's keel as well as the foul odors of the paint locker. Mookie knows the ship's geography better than most of us and travels it expertly. His 20 inches by 10 inches of size easily fits through the air-conditioning ducts. But how he survives without attending mess call is top secret. No doubt he makes post-midnight raids on galley scraps the cooks dare not offer the crew.

'Til now, Mookie still is in the good graces of the captain, partly thanks to Kippy's carefully scripted apologies and cleanups. Of course, the generally jovial gunner's mate occasionally spouts complaints about the little bastard, but the intimate crowd knows "he protesteth too much." Sort of a smokescreen for hiding one's true feelings. Kippy is not asocial, but he rarely expresses a huge desire for companionship. Seems to like the lonely life in the below decks gunnery storeroom. So he easily tolerates Mookie's monkeyshines. Mookie applies graphite grease to his lips, wipes his hands anywhere and on anything. He's been called everything but "grease monkey," even if he pretends to be Kippy's assistant.

Mookie's dunking is followed the next morning by some fiery expletives from the captain's cabin. By his own account, Lt. (jg) McShane knocks on the skipper's door and judiciously inquires, "Captain, sir. Is something wrong? Sir?"

"Goddam that monkey! I'll kill him, I'll kill him!"

"Sir?" McShane already senses that some nefarious trick has been administered on his royal skippership, so he probes further.

"May I come in, sir?" He respectfully cracks the door open, and seeing the captain with hands cradling his head, dutifully asks, "Are you all right, Captain?"

McShane then slides into the stateroom and almost trips on the captain's cap, which contains a yellow, circular cargo of crap. The odor is inhuman; it is the epitome of monkey business.

"I'll get a steward mate quick." The skipper's celebrated "scrambled-eggs" cap might no longer be the "heavy, heavy lies the crown." McShane chuckles at the foreshadowing idea.

Maybe the skipper is due for a transfer.

But now Mookie is on the skipper's shit list, literally. Our mascot is now a rated Celebrity, first class. He's upgraded from a ho-hum mystery to a scuttlebutt reality. In short, he's now the talk of the ship.

Nobody could get away with this crap, not aboard our *Machias* with its sometimes heavy-handed executor, Moose Hanna. Somehow, Mookie's favorite target is the head area and headgear. McShane carries the story back to the wardroom, where several of his compatriots feel that their commander's comeuppance at the hands of an unformidable foe sort of balances things out for them.

The story soon reaches all quarters, but few believe it. It makes Kippy nervous and defensive. Two snap inspections, probably in hopes of snaring Mookie, fall short of the mark. No inquiries about Mookie are asked at the inspections, but the skipper's searching eyes are tell-tale.

"He's *personna non grata*," McShane tells Kippy. "His fate is sealed, Kippy. O.K.? Who brought him aboard, where and when? C'mon, spill it."

"Damned if I know, sir. Argo told me he guessed he was swapped for in the Russells for torpedo juice. We got the juice and him. We gave 'em 100 gallons of fresh water. Peden might have been in on that deal. The black gang, maybe. Maybe he was getting into their gunners mate's torpedo juice. Stuff is pure alcohol, ya know. A drunken monkey aboard a swift PT boat ain't no picnic. Bet they fished him out more'n once."

"Well, I guess that's an academic question now. They say Carl Peterson swapped some civie shirts for him in Hollandia. Well, no matter. It's too late."

"How's that sir?"

"It doesn't matter. Mookie is *finit*, finished." There's a touch of sadness in the eyes of the enlisted men's favorite officer. He represents us; he supports our grievances at the deck court-martials for petty offenses. Probably would even defend Mookie if given half a chance.

"Kippy, you been hiding him?"

"Nah, sir. He just hangs out here. Can't get rid of him. True grease monkey. Breaks the monotony 'round here. Skipper's pissed off, huh?"

Mookie, instinctively perhaps, disappears for awhile. Maybe instructively, via Kippy. Locks him up, perhaps. Maybe smuggles some chow in for him, too. Kippy has a pull with the cooks. He seems to coffee-up at unusual hours. Not having to stand watch, there is ample opportunity to get in some late-night galley raids. Maybe there's a torpedo juice or a still connection.

A lot of water has passed under our keel since then—more'n two months. A lot of the Mookie stuff has died down. Haven't seen him since his first dunking. Almost lost Trupiano over the side, chipping, early last November near Mios Woendi. Not too far from there now.

Hollandia, New Guinea, here we come. It's the milk run from Leyte in the Philippines down past the equator with empty Liberty ships. Our division of four frigates adds an Aussie frigate, the HMS *Hawkesbury*, but Mookie couldn't care less. It's late December, almost Christmas, but later than he thinks. Our *Machias* is the wrong kind of jungle, totally unfit for a non-swimming monkey. He's been the only fun thing relieving us from the endless hours of convoying and anti-submarine patrolling. Our in-port visits by midnight Charleys are mere trivia in comparison. We crave comedy, if only to re-establish our sense of sanity.

The sea is angry. Swells are rolling 15 feet; the deck is

deserted. Only the ablest sea legs navigate it. All of the sane sailors are in their sacks. I see Kippy struggling to close the hatch. Mookie is headed toward the K guns at the rail. A darkened moon doesn't help. Our corpulent gunner's mate falls, wham, on his rear. Mookie's grease trail finally caught up with his benefactor. This is farce. Then quickly, pathos.

"Grab him!" he yells. Mookie pauses, then swings on the top rail, 4 feet above deck. Too late. Mookie is over the side; his greasy hands slip off the rail. Kippy and I watch his impish body dissolve into our wake.

"King Neptune's got him now, Buzz. Damn it. At least I got a snapshot of him."

"Well, there's some consolation, Kippy. The Japs won't get him."

Near Miss

It's all a matter of timing. Good timing. Lt. (jg) Kemp had it, missing death by a minute on the Tacloban airstrip. Lt. (jg) McShane couldn't convince the pilot of a DC 3 to cram Kemp into a states-bound plane. That squabble set a terrible karma in motion. A Jap fighter dropped its eggs near the transport, and the occupants had no time to call it luck, fate, or whatever.

I think we've been at the intersection of time and space a few times already. Everybody out here has. Bosun Toby's pipe alerts us. Exec. Hanna is on the P.A.

"Now hear this. Now hear this. Batten down all hatches. Prepare to hoist anchor. Prepare to hoist anchor."

The eastern sun looks troubled. Wind is kicking up and white caps are flecking San Pedro Bay. Ships in our column are getting underway. Something is up. I hail Monk Marshall on watch on the fantail.

"What's goin' on? Midget subs in the gulf?"

"Nah. There's a typhoon northeast by east of us, and it might change course. Gotta get out to deep water and get plenty of space between ships is what I hear on the bridge phones. This wind's already gale force in the gulf around Samaar. We got four, five hours leeway, maybe."

We've got company. Lots of convoy company. Most of them Liberty ships. At least the Fifth Fleet is nearby, somewhere off Samaar, north of us. Liberty ships are none too seaworthy. We're triple-welded and ride well, but a typhoon? I have two pneumatic life jackets and a kapok, and the water's warm. This will be tougher than the swells off Bermuda during our shakedown cruise.

Heavy seas meet us as we leave San Pedro Bay and reach Leyte Gulf. The Allentown disappears suddenly under a swell, and just as suddenly she's mast-high above us. I decide to go below deck and maybe hit the sack. Only the watch is topside. The O.D. on the bridge is ordering all men on watch to find secure posts amidships at the quad forties. Wind is whipping furiously, and I can barely make out what he's saying.

Spray is already hitting the bridge. I'm due on watch in a couple of hours. Opening the leeward starboard hatch is a minor skirmish and I'm rolling side-to-side down the passageway, heading toward my bunk in the bow. It takes good rhythm and timing. It also takes cooperation with the ship's moves, like a bronc rider staying with a lively bull. Thank God I've got good sea legs.

Bet the guys down in the engine room are having a slippery time of it. No non-machinist will dare set foot on the grated walks during the rough weather. Bet the head has plenty of visitors; the bunk brigade won't be policed by Red Strom or Toby. It's almost each man for himself. This is a mean, ironic trick that the otherwise peaceful Pacific is playing.

Wind is coming from the port stern at about 50 knots. We're rolling a bit but nothing serious. Now and then we drop fast, sort of sinking-like. The falling feeling can make a guy lose a few ounces and gain some very light hair. It's little comfort to know that if we're lucky and the typhoon doesn't recognize us for bait, we might only feel her outer band.

Down in the mess hall where a few of us are playing a quarter-a-game pinochle before hitting the eight-to-twelve watch, we can hear the painful cacophony of puking at the head urinal trough. Many a tough sailor has realized his precarious mortality there. In a short hour this will be a quiet ghost ship. In another four or five we may escape the clutches of the typhoon. But this is the season for them.

Time, tide, and typhoon wait for no man, or men, someone said, so I'm doing the waiting instead. Typhoons run counter-clockwise and you've got to aim the bow into its teeth. We're getting shoved around a bit, but that's all.

I find Monk Marshall near the port 40mm.

"You're relieved, Monk. What's the word?"

"We're O.K.," he says. Conn says our timing is perfect. We're on the outer band. We'll be out of it in about three hours.

We're all relieved. Especially the guys we just relieved.

Kamikaze Kiss

After nights of stargazing on watch, telling directions is easy for me. This time it's east, but this means little without a geographic memory of the island groups. Gone is Leyte Gulf, days of pesky single plane air alerts, and sneak bombing at dusk of the Tacloban airstrip by Jap fighters who trail incoming planes that cannot find their carriers. Perpetual midnight Washing-machine Charley visitations have already become mere memories in a strange world decorated with novel experiences.

Fourth of July-like nights pierced by mile-high searchlights and heavy firing are now deadly still. All that remains is a five Liberty ship convoy quietly being escorted east by southeast, according to the Cross. This is not the route to New Guinea, our usual convoy destination. But there is no cause for alarm. The Pacific is sprinkled with islands. I have no map. I do have a hunch that this time fate will have the upper hand over destiny. It's March 12 and Luzon and Manilla are well in hand. There really isn't much to worry about out here now except a wayward sub or two. Even the Ides of March do not matter. Well... Maybe.

The wake is lively, very lively. It glows as if the atoms in the water are dancing on its moon-lit trail. It's a comforting combination of man's turbulent machine and nature's power to embellish.

Our daily news sheet declares that MacArthur's army is still cleaning up Leyte but is well into southern Luzon. Manilla has been plundered. We convoyed up the Luzon coast last week and saw artillery fire all the way into Linguyan Gulf. They're bound to find plenty of our guys who were taken prisoners at Corregidor. This is the first big clash with the Japanese army. There's a lot of payback, overdue.

The Ides of March is fast approaching, but that's just Julius Caesar stuff. Superstition is only superstition. This is nearly a separate peace. Not Hemingway's, but maybe it'll be good for a few days. The stars are blameless and all's well with the chaotic world right now.

Just as days are wont to melt into one another, and usually with no distinction, our eight-to-twelve morning watch is still shepherding empty Libertys and mustering a modest 12 knots. When I take the phones from Marshall, the deck is already hot and the sky clear. Chipping hammers are rattling the deck; an ironic reward for sleepless nights in Leyte Gulf. Yet there is something therapeutic about deck hands chipping away and painting. Makes it looks like there isn't a war on. Just doing normal, everyday clean-up stuff. Nice to hear Bosun 2/C Bo LaBeau getting after his deck hands, about a dozen in all.

"Dammit, get those hammers goin.' You heard Hanna."

Hanna, the exec, is an executioner. He execs and exacts. Moose Hanna is bullish always, and in the no-B.S. sense.

"Ya, Bo. Tell us what he said, Bo." Seaman Trupiano is pulling Bo's leg again. Troop has celebrity status, almost immunity, after making his infamous protest dive over the side. At least now he's tackling the deck and not the hull.

"You got a short memory, Troop. Remember when we shot down that Jap Oscar at Halmahera? First Jap fighter we see and we nail it. Easy as pie; nothin' to it. Big cheer."

"O.K., O.K. What did the Moose say? Tell it again, Bo."

Just as if Bo is waiting for this cue, he puffs up, musters his deep New England twang, and spews the near-immortal lines, poker-faced, almost Shakespearean. He doesn't even look at Troop. It's as if he's borrowing the lines to motivate the crew.

"O.K. You f---ing heroes, get back to work. There's plenty more where they came from."

In fact, the cheer soars into a roar when the Oscar trails smoke a half-mile off the starboard stern, swings to the starboard, and slowly heads for Jap-held Halmahera, where it smashes into a puff of smoke against the shore bluff. Bo captained the starboard quad 40mm, and you almost get the notion that he is playing Hanna and the scene. About an hour later he has to content himself with giving a mundane order to knock off the chipping and painting.

"O.K. you guys, take a break and stow away your gear."

Deck hands can disappear faster than five bucks at a craps game. Especially when the deck is hot and it's close to the noon hour.

Our *Machias* is zigzagging on the convoy's port side, about a thousand yards from the closest Liberty. It is customarily routine and dull. The sky is also dull: not a lively cloud in sight. The salty Pacific is flat, calm to a fault. It is endless, infernally endless. To a careful captain, the suspicion of an ambush might grow, but this is not the right time of day for it. Nor the right kind of convoy. It's serenely dull, the kind of welcome boredom after a tiring exposure to danger from the air. Another two hours and my watch will be over, and then up to the flying bridge, where the air is one hundred percent pure. Stuart Whitehead and I will stand, breathe, say nothing, and ride the *Machias* for a half hour or so.

The sound-powered phone, onerously tight over my ears, hums ominously. Radar men open the line to the entire watch when something is brewing.

"Con, we've got no IFFs bearing 358, position angle 5

degrees, range 21 miles."

This gets my attention quick. No IFF means the contact has not given the correct identity or has given none at all. On the con, Seaman 1/C Leon Baham responds matter-of-factly, "Conn, aye aye," and reports it to "Ralph" Peterson, Lt. (jg), the officer of the watch. In another thirty seconds the radar man delivers a second report.

"Con, three aircraft bearing 356, position angle 12 degrees, range 17 miles and closing."

"Con, aye aye." Baham's poker-faced voice is none too calming. Nothing like getting IFFs unexpectedly. True, U.S. pilots often turn off their IFF signal until necessary. But it is untypical for them to stay low, especially in friendly waters where we are. Ulithi, the Fifth Fleet headquarters, is less than an hour south. So far they're bogies, but that means not a damn thing to the O.D. on the bridge. But why are they flying so low? Pete better be alive up there on the bridge. He's regular academy and a go-by-the-book man if there ever was one. Out here that ain't good, not good at all.

"Con, range 10 miles, position angle 4 degrees. No IFF."

They're hugging the water. Why? C'mon Pete. Call GQ. Let the old man know.

"Con, aye aye." Dead silence.

A sweaty-faced fireman is headed for the rail and some cooling off. For Chrissake Pete, call GQ. Seconds are marching by in slow motion. The illusion of safety

"Hey Rocky, let's get this 20 ready." The three fantail 20mms are enclosed in a triangular gun shield and elevated about 4 feet above deck. Another black gang guy shows up and I show him how to hoist the 20 pound magazine drum in place should there be time or need for a second drum. Fifteen seconds of firing is an eternity, and eight rounds per second go fast.

They're real bogies! My aircraft recognition training in Philly helps. In single file, barely above water and headed in a straight line, parallel to us and just yards off on our port side! A Betty bomber is the lead plane. Cigar-shaped, twin engines. Next is an army fighter. Third is a rinky-dink seaplane, probably a reconnaissance plane. These planes don't belong together; they're odd ducklings. They're about a mile out. Dammit, Pete, call GQ.

They're coming in low and slow. Con is silent. The decks are deathly quiet. Never mind GQ. It's too late for that. They're sitting ducks, dead ducks. Crazy bastards. They're still flying parallel to us, out about 50 yards and barely off the water. I'm transfixed. They're coming, dammit! Well, come on.

"Con, permission to fire." I've got ten seconds, maybe.

They're asking for it. Right into my fire. I'll just lead the Betty. Any hits will set her blazing: they're made of wood and cardboard. I'm in favor of living, and these bastards are too damn close for comfort.

"Do not fire! Repeat, do not fire!"

Fear and anger are locked into my senses. They're only seconds away now, just off our port stern. They're in slow motion. Everything is racing in slow motion.

"Con, permission to fire!" This is what I'm here for, trained for.

"Do not fire. Repeat, do not fire!"

The lead pilot's face in the nose of the big Betty is all I can see. He's almost staring, sort of daring the danger. Maybe daring me to fire. I'm numb. But if he swings in, nothing's stopping me. I want to live and I know I can still take all three down. I'm broadside. They're crazy to ask for it. They're going straight on!

It's a frozen moment. The rag-tag seaplane is dragging along and my 20mm is still pointing dead ahead. I have no feeling except that I know that I'm still alive. I don't know how long I've been in the 20mm shoulder harness.

Nobody is topside. Even the two below-decks men have disappeared. A sense of relief smothers the questions I almost ask of myself. I have a lot of understanding to catch up with. Being only twenty-one hardly helps, but I know that the years teach much more than the days ever will.

I am so stunned that I say nothing to the guys at chow. How can I say anything? No matter that all three planes were sure hits, how do I explain why I didn't fire? And why did I wait for the command to fire? I should have let them have it for coming at us. There's a helluva lot that's a mystery to me. I feel wrong about everything and so I am silent. Why did the pilot look my way? Was it a silent salute: "You're doing your duty as I am doing mine. No hard feelings, American, but I've got a more important task to do. It's nice that we can meet this way and not kill each other. You're not important enough."

"What'n hell was that, Buzz? How come—" the small water-tender 3/C asks me. I don't answer. Three airbirds right in the palm of my hand. Was it fated to end this way? Was fate more interested in the Japanese? Or, were they more willing to be the objects of fate?

Pete didn't call GQ. The old man's instructions, maybe. Three hours later, after clearing the submarine nets at the Fifth Fleet's Ulithi Navy Base, a PT boat crew volunteer an answer. I yell at them, "You guys see an Oscar, a Betty bomber?"

"Yah, there wuz three of 'em headin' fer that seaplane tender down yonder. Maybe dem destroyers shot 'em down. Fleet's gittin' ready, I reckon, to hit 'em good."

Academy Pete must have gone by the book. The navy's book or the skipper's book. Me too, the book of life. The right to live, stay alive. And suddenly a small brainstorm rains down on me: the Big Book is there, too, looking after me, so help me God. I touch the little prayer sealed in cloth in my wallet. O.K. Pa, I say. You've got the years of experience and you did attend that seminary in Capestrano, Italy. Anyway, who in hell wants to be a hero? I just want to get back home in one piece.

Funny thing, those kamikaze kisses probably were merely a polite courtesy call. A last call, so to speak. For them.

"To err is human... divine."

Sam Severson's wry humor can turn any piece of classical wisdom into a romantic truth. With the scarcity of information, let alone of truth, the pickings are lush. With so many moments of truth left hung out to dry, he could not resist the temptation to fully air things out.

Severson, Yeoman1/C, probably believes that forgiveness (and indeed vengeance) are exclusively the Lord's work and not to be entrusted to just any old mortal. And this is just as well, too, for he above any other man-jack on the *Machias* seems privy to the errors of man's ways, both civil and military. He might even have subscribed to the Light Brigade notion that ours is not to reason why, but to do and die. At any rate he's damned good at warehousing inside info and doesn't do any foolish telling.

But if you ask Sam, discreetly of course, he'd part with a tidbit or two that far exceeds mere scuttlebutt. Sure, half the ship knows that the skipper raked over a corner pier in Charleston, South Carolina, for they were eye-witnesses to the event. And a few were around in Finchaven, New Guinea, when he denied having said, "Let go the anchor," claiming to have said, "Let down the anchor" which, in fact, amounted to a difference of a few hundred fathoms. But the quiet and reticent yeoman is in the know of damn near everything of importance that transpires.

Sam could and did tell which commissioned officers never heard from their wives. The skipper, for one. As for the other, well... That's too delicate to mention. He might tell you that Ensign Logan was confined to quarters for "misusing" the mail, a trumped-up charge. Sam knew how far and fast he could carry his very own "mail," literally and figuratively.

A few have secured his confidence; no one could, after all, be expected to keep this juicy stuff under his skin. Take the time, for instance, when Officer of the Deck LT. (jg) Barstad actually snored while on his bridge watch and had to be wakened. That's a court martial offense. The awakener, another commissioned officer, judiciously disentangled him from detection. But Sam knew about it!

There was the time when newly assigned gunnery officer Lt. (jg) Spinks directed me to show him the switch box, which activated the hedgehog battery located behind the second three-inch fifty and just beneath the bridge. Spinks opened the switch box with a key.

"Now Buzz, how does this thing work?"

"I don't know, sir." Truth is, I didn't know.

I suggest that we ask CGM Zed, but he declines. Doesn't want to show his lack of knowledge to an enlisted man, I suppose. Even I know that ignorance compounded by ignorance is a sure-fire thing. Spinks, searching for some kind of visual rationale that might absolve his temporary ignorance, trips the wrong button. Instantly he discovers that the system works, verifying mankind's experience of trial-and-terror learning. However, the consequences of Spink's act has a rippling effect. First, twenty-four mini-torpedoes shoot over the 3-inch fifty gun shield sounding like a Browning 30 caliber machine gun. An arc of hedgehogs dissolves one by one into the calm sea about 50 yards out over the starboard bow. Fortunately, none of the seasick sailors are standing at the time; all are strewn horizontally in front of the gun shield munching soda crackers, their remedy for seasickness. They're totally unaware of the event.

The error seems done with. I blink, certain that I'm accomplice to unnecessary ordnance destruction, which is at least good for a deck court martial. Spinks is confined to quarters for a week. His sentence would have been harsher, but someone has to stand the O.D. watch. Sam doesn't parade this trivia around, but takes satisfaction in seeing the former U. of Mississippi professor of literature made null and void for awhile. Spinks, you see, sees the world via classifying, and Sam's niche is not high in this hierarchy. How Sam finds out is beyond my imagination and integrity.

No one—except those who know better—suspects that the trial dropping of a depth charge set at pattern Able, at a cruising speed of ten knots, constitutes an error. Except Sam and maybe the "con" guys. Pattern Able is the shallow setting, set to discharge at about 50 feet. It does discharge, and it blows the stern end of the *Machias* at least ten feet out of the water. It also flattens everyone in the mess hall, including everything that passes for chow. This makes for a surrealistic mixture of chow and men and a slippery deck. This is not mistaken by the victims as a taste of practiced warfare. The simple truth, Sam whispers, is that the skipper had a math mix-up or hiccup. The hiccup is volcanic and the secret matures into top-secret. We take it as a test to determine how much punishment the ship's rear can take.

The parade of errors is almost endless and almost seems natural. But of course they are unrecorded. To err is human, and to keep a screw-up secret is likewise human. In Morotai and Halmahara in the Dutch East Indies, a natural error erupts. Scene one: We shoot down a Jap Oscar fighter headed for a seaplane tender carrying high octane gasoline for the Fifth

Fleet's scouting planes. Scene two: Encouraged by the ship's enthusiastic audience, we're ready for a second helping. Then, flying to the most deadly of generalizations, which is that all airborne planes are the enemy's, our gun-happy crews send a hail of fire at an unsuspecting army Liberator, our four-engine bomber. Its pilot takes the bomber into a dangerous vertical climb to avoid becoming a statistic.

There is no forgiveness emanating from the air command on shore. And, while there is a handsome description of our gunnery prowess in scratching one Oscar, no mention is made of the Liberator's dance with death. Perhaps because he escaped with hide, crew, and airplane, the Liberator pilot might have forgiven the *Machias* or, even more, thanked God for the blown "ambush."

Sins, or errors, of commission are bad enough, but errors of omission are worse. Minutes before this baptism of fire, our first in the Pacific, a messenger scurries down from the bridge ladder and into the captain's quarters with the O.D.'s request to call general quarters. The messenger throws a strong stage whisper into the captain's quarters.

"Captain, sir. The O.D. requests permission to sound general quarters. Sir?" No immediate response. "Sir!"

"Yes, yes, yes! Call GQ!"

I can't believe what I'm seeing and hearing. I'm running to my battle station on the three stern 20s. Meanwhile, and for a five-second eternity, the first of three Jap fighter planes sweeps past our *Machias* and several other frigates en route to our seaplane tender a half mile down the way. The captain's first commandment, which evidently is set in stone, put it authoritatively: "Thou shalt not call general quarters without my consent." And there is no better true academy man than Lt. (jg) Peterson to carry out such dogma to the letter.

"For Chrissake, call general quarters!" Captain Alexander repeats as if somebody else has fouled-up. The ping... ping... ping... pounds my ears.

Perhaps a protocol exists among the four ships of the division. Perhaps the USS *Allentown* had first dibs on calling GQ, thus enhancing their chances to fire first at the intruders. Perhaps anything goes, all's fair in love and war. Perhaps my eye, too, I think. I pass all this on to Sam, who knows what to do with it. Maybe he'll write a book of our misadventures.

I recall we saw 40mm ammo directed at a hillside gun by a PT boat. It's a nice three-scene act, a nifty prelude for our expectations We line the rail, watching the scenario. Two of our shipmates are aboard the PT. Both are itching for action. One is Bo LaBeau. They just went along for the ride. Experience for the sake of experience.

I decide to sleep topside again, starboard amidships. Maybe I suspect more bad GQ calling. I like to be around the action. To err is human; to omit is humane.

Two pitch-black nights later, another disciplined O.D. notifies the skipper that a Japanese craft has just slipped past our bow within yards. The craft probably lands some infiltrators. When it's discovered nearly kissing our bow and the message is delivered to the captain, his reaction comes swift and sure and silly.

"Double the guard. Issue them shotguns. Tell them to be on the alert."

No Deck Log entry, either.

Sam might have put it a bit differently: "23:45. Unidentified craft crossing starboard bow bearing 090 true. Craft fled. No ammunition expended."

Perhaps discretion on both sides is the better part of valor. One never knows until it's too late. And where is that fine line between bravery and foolhardiness, duty and honor? Perhaps the wise thing for all is: if you don't fire, we won't. That would make for a boring war, but maybe that alone would be an honorable way out.

To err is a captain's prerogative. Somebody has to take credit or blame. But for all minuscule errors, none of which could have won or lost a battle, not even "for want of a nail a horse was lost, for want of a horse...," the epitome of all sophomoric errors is the refusal to change an order. Assembling a convoy is a formidable task. Escorting it through Leyte Gulf is no less easy. And in the darkest hours of the night, the chance for error multiplies.

There is an island dead ahead, obvious to the naked eye, to lookouts, and to Officer of the Deck, Lt. (jg) McShane. The course is preset: 067 true. The island is also pre-set: it won't move.

"King, tell the captain we must change course. Dinagat is dead ahead." The convoy, surprisingly showing an unmilitary but American mind of its own, veers to starboard in the absence of no course change.

Helmsman King raps on the captain's stateroom hatch and is stopped by the skipper's robotic words.

"Steady as you go, McShane. Steady as you go."

"Steady as you go? The captain must be asleep, King. King, didn't you wake him? We're gonna go aground!"

The island doubles in size. The rear escort ship does a right flank on a 185 degree true. It's now disobedience or prayer or worse.

"Go tell the captain I'm in unison with the division on 185 true." Jeezus, he can't get me on this. Not gonna let a goddam island sink us. Not after coming this far. The Old Man must be just talking in his sleep again."

The Last Romantic War

Maybe, just maybe after the debris of war settles, one could sort out the real from the imagined errors. As for forgiveness, just being alive is all that matters. Perhaps, also, if one could survive the mini errors, that collective experience would pull one through a major blunder. Perhaps, too, if the war ended in a month, I won't think about such foolishness again. Lots of ifs and perhapses. Perhaps too many. A damn loaded pair of dice.

The Deck Log will surely smooth out the unnecessary errors. Sins of omission, most of them. Other secret goofs, too. Only the skipper's personal log will know. After all, the skipper has a future to worry about. All I have to think about is staying alive.

On the lean, positive side, the skipper shows great compassion when he orders the ship's phantom mascot, Mookie the monkey, fished from the sea on December 10, 1944. The second most positive action is the skipper's ascendency to division commander and continued duty in the southwest Pacific. His ambition is made of stern stuff, for seasickness is his constant companion. Macbeth couldn't handle such stuff.

Not so very long ago, I had the once-in-a-lifetime experience of pointing a very loaded 20mm at three Japanese aircraft, each of whom could not have avoided being shot to pieces at 15 yards as they flew by skimming the water. I still think of it as my "kamikaze kiss." It's the ship's best kept secret.

Lt. Commander R.T. Alexander, ambition *et al.*, becomes a full division commander at Ulithi. And with no fanfare yet! What an omission. Only the news that we are unexpectedly states-bound prevents covert celebration. One piece of good fortune a month is all we can handle. After a year in the Pacific, we can use a few weeks states-side.

What a book it would be, *Sins of Omission: Tales of World War II*. Plenty of guys could write it.

One of a Kind

It hasn't taken me forever to learn that even a war can't curtail human nature. Lack of living space affects us: tight quarters increase tensions, so we need relief. We're vulnerable to amateur comedians and con artists. And the two are often joint ventures. Such a soul is "Boots" Capitani, seaman second class. The moniker is fictional, but it sounds like he's at least the captain of his soul and his name suits him just fine. He sees everything as comical and turns the lousiest realities into a good laugh. Maybe years later I'll see him in a different light and thank him for providing us with a likeable, even believable character. There are more than enough sour faces aboard.

He'll grab anybody and do a jitterbug, tossing his partner around, accompanied by a not bad *a cappella* voice. Give him a five-man audience on the fantail after evening chow and he'll deliver every time. His joke bag is deep, very deep, deeper than his voice.

Boots can make any of us laugh with his one-liners or a malapropism. They're all originals and only he could have said it. Maybe they were spontaneous, maybe not. Smart-dumb cracks like, "If you wuzn't so alive, you'd be dead by now." Just thinking of his vocal monstrosities makes my heart chuckle. Not only was he adept at crap-shooting, both with dice and the gift of gab, but he rarely ruined his standing with his victims. Nobody held a grudge against him; Lt. McShane has to stop the flow of his crap earnings now and then, but the losers didn't complain. Shooting craps isn't my dish, but I'm tempted to watch the dozen or so guys surrendering paycheck money his way.

He can survive anywhere. Take the time at Pearl when Boots is trying to smuggle a pint of booze past a Marine guard. Getting it aboard ship would be fairly easy, especially if he behaves halfways sober. But Marine guards at Pearl are cynical and untrusting. They seem to think that the island should never again be entrusted to the US Navy. Some of them think they're always at war. I have a hunch they believe that they, the United States Marines, invented war. And now that they've built up a bureaucracy of control, they act as if they own Oahu. They probably would like it for a rest camp.

I heard the story sort of second-hand like, but here's the gist of it. I'll put in my two cents, too. Marines aren't super-human: they're slightly flawed like the rest of us. They're opportunistic and just as slippery and polished as Boots at his best. But they're supposed to go by the book. A slippery Marine guard can either be a dull pain in the buttocks or a con artist if he has capitalistic instincts. Boots, of course, is an opportunistic capitalist. He had shelled out some bona fide crap money on his last liberty for a pint of Southern Comfort to take back to buddies who hadn't been granted liberty. Oh, he knew the power of generosity! He had taped it just above his right ankle under his bell-bottom tailor-mades. Well, some smart-ass Marine frisked him and relieved him of it and threw in a few disparaging remarks to boot. Boots sorrowfully watches the guard wave the pint to his buddy, who promptly relieves him. Faking that he's reluctantly accepting the loss, Boots keeps his eyes peeled on the itinerary of the booze. Sure enough, the Marine consigns it to a private place on his person.

Knowing the ways of the world, Boots comes to a quick conclusion: How do the Marines really dispense with confiscated booze? Who better than he to deal with that matter? Presto, a practical joke. All in the line of duty, of course, and in the interest of justice.

He suspects that the Marine guard contingent has an affinity for good old Southern Comfort. So, on the next liberty escapade, Boots enjoys and downs a pint with buddies and with just a little shine on, prepares his assault on the Marine guards, all of whom, he deeply believes, should be out there taking more islands and not taking liberties at Pearl. After all, a reputation should be earned day after day. He urinates into the bottle and tapes it to his leg. He feigns a staggering entrance at the pier. The typically diligent Marine, suspecting nothing other than a slob-gob, braces his rifle at port arms.

"Hold it, swabbie, right where you are," he commands. Boots wobbles a bit, cracks his goofiest grin, and salutes him with an "aye aye, sir." This further convinces the Marine that Boots might be bluffing his way through and that he's carrying contraband.

Acting tough, the Marine snarls, "Stand still, you swabbie. Got any booze on you?" His buddy begins the slapping inspection. In a second or two he rips the pint off the leg and barks, "We can slap you in the brig for this. What ship you from?"

"*Minn... Minn... Minneapolis.* That cruiser d-d-down d-d-dere." It's less than a half truth, and his stutter is convincing.

"O.K. Get your ass d-d-down there." Fondling the bottle, he turns to his buddy, laughingly. "I think we picked up a bottle from him a couple of nights ago. Good stuff, too."

Just what ole Boots wants to hear. He even has his pint looking like a couple of swigs has been drunk from it. Now to distance himself and make a run for it.

The pint bottle crashes on the pier at least 30 yards behind the high-tailing Boots.

It's one story that Boots won't let go of. One thing nice about it. though: Boots doesn't stretch it. And he never tells it near a Marine. Let it suffice to say that sailors cannot live by or on water alone, and they must have more than warm beer to keep up their morale.

Perhaps because Boots has convinced the authorities that advancement in rating is not his idea of fighting a war, he's held on to his meager rate of seaman 2/C. He's not a seaman and never would become one. But, because he's never second when a race is run, his shipmates suspect that he has unusual class and therefore respect him as being first class in the art of survival. He will surely become a politician later, or even an attorney. Boots simply has know-how in manipulating the means to gain an end. He seems to be there, wherever the action is, at whenever the time. And, like a clown, he'll entertain you in the process. And like a clown he's a damn good judge of reality. And, like a good clown, he'll win out or get what he wants in the end.

His nose for news leads him to the ship's stills. At least four stills are undetected, probably because the benefactors value their product and thus guard it well. Some, like a moderately corpulent gunner's mate, openly walk topside with "coffee" in hand, keeping any overly zealous chatterer at bay. Kippy is king of his gunnery warehouse, and entrance is by invitation only. But Boots somehow infiltrates the black gang's stills and keeps quiet about them. The shrinking of bona fide alcohol supplies is generally attributed to "evaporation." This explanation of shrinking supplies by storekeeper Hargat is surprisingly accepted. Boots, however, assists in the process.

Come to think of it, maybe Boots and Mookie, our monkey ex-mascot, have plenty in common. Both monkied around plenty and both are gifted with natural talent. Of course, Boots knows what he's doing. Mookie didn't. You can't go overboard all slicked-up in grease.

Sadly, Mookie is no longer aboard. *Homo sapiens* is. Boots continues to play the clown but never the fool like Mookie. There's a helluva big difference, you know. Two of a kind is one thing, but Boots, he's one-of-a-kind.

Unsungers

Among the variety of words spewed forth by the hearty crew of the *Machias*, discounting profanity, one is never spoken: hero. Who hasn't heard that heroes are made, not born? But no one talks about heroism; that's somehow taboo, a sort of unwritten law. Our *Machias'* ship's company, like any other normal bunch of young men, just want to get it over with, victoriously, and go home where living is in their own hands.

There's a straight line between what is brave and what is foolhardy. Above this line is the idea of courage. The moveable factor is fear. The brave overcome their fear; the cowardly do not. The foolhardy are ignorant of it, too numb and dumb to realize what they are doing. Of course, no one talks of this distinction and, for that matter, no one wants to be thrown into such a testing situation. But when such an occasion arises, an "unsunger" will rise to the occasion.

There have been a hundred or more calls to general quarters in Leyte gulf alone and many more along the way, and our *Machias*, along with sister ships Charlottesville, Sandusky, and Allentown, are settling down to convoy a dozen Liberty supply ships. Leyte air alerts were scattered around the clock, and it's with relief that the open sea is again beneath us. Routines are more than welcome; chipping hammers pound the deck with an angry fury, and the odor of paint somehow overcomes a 12 knot wind. Ocean swells increase and are troubling. Troughs of 15 feet or more generate heavy rolls, a testy condition even for our seaworthy frigate. It's not a carefree deck; good sea legs are called for.

Suddenly, the rattling chipping hammers stop.

"O.K. Troop, no bitching. You heard Lt. Barstad. Get your kapok jacket on. I got this bosun chair secure. It'll hold." Bo LaBeau is still second class bosun. Troop is still seaman second. Not that he isn't capable, but a few deck courts for minor infractions never sit well with the gold braid. Even though he finished every boxing match on his feet and victorious, coming late off liberty and being too independent a guy doesn't win influence. His mouth is as big as his heart, and if he's in the right, look out.

"Hold it, Bo. Dammit, I don't like this shit, paintin' over the side. I never signed up for doing this crap. In port, ya, but geezus, we're at sea."

"None of us signed up for this crap, Troop. C'mon, over the side."

Troop struggles into the chair, right leg first, hanging onto the rail cable and then lowering his left leg into the rope chair. His feet search for balance against the hull. Bo dangles the 5-inch paint brush in Troop's face and then the paint bucket.

"Goddammit Troop, be careful. These swells ain't no joke."

"No joke, huh? You gotta be jokin', Bo."

Gunner's Mate 3/C "Blarney" Barney is greasing the quad 40mm just above the tip-toeing and swaying Troop. He leans over and barks, "Hey Troop. What 'n hell you doin' over the side? Extra duty, huh? I know you're a damn good swimmer, Troop, but you won't last five minutes out there!"

"F--- you, Barney. I'll show that goddam Barstad."

"Watcha gonna show him—You jumpin'? You ain't got the guts."

The *Machias* then zigs to port abruptly and crashes through a cresting swell. Black, sooty smoke is pouring from the stack amidships, forcing me to duck for cover into the ammo clip shack. This smoke reminds me of the foul breath of the monstrous freight train engine back in my hometown. I had to walk alongside it as it crossed the two blocks of water-filled mine pits in mid-town. It often caught us kids walking home from school.

"Man overboard!"

I sense what's happened and without asking anyone, grab an orange dye-marker from the depth charge deck locker and heave it like a football as far as I can in the direction Troop might be. Almost foolishly, I throw everything into it as if another 20 yards matter. Our *Machias* stops, full engines astern, and swings to starboard. GQ is pinging away; the ship turns into a teeming anthill. The *Machias* is at 23 knots, flank speed, cutting through the towering swells. In six minutes Troop is spotted and hauled in.

LaBeau looks about as relieved as Troop. "What gives, Troop? Soon as my back is turned you're in the drink."

"Tell that S.O.B. Barstad I didn't fall. I jumped! Tell Barney, too."

Paint chipping ceases. Barstad himself is temporarily made null and void. He's confined to quarters. Troop becomes a sickbay celebrity for an hour, having downed two shots of medicinal whiskey. He rates the Unsung Hero citation for his winning a labor dispute over the forces of inept command.

But did he fall or jump? Troop claims he jumped and admits that he thought he was a goner. "Hero? Hell no! I was just plain pissed-off. Damn fool? Yup. Those swells damn near got me. Another fifteen minutes, maybe. I could barely see the mast."

From then on, painting over the side at sea is a lost art, thanks to Troop. As far as I'm concerned, he's at least a small "h" hero. It'll never get into naval history books, but I'll never forget "Troop's Leap!" Maybe it'll make an appearance in the Deck Log. It stopped a dozen-ship convoy!

Water Tender 3/C Warren Wilson is the generic unsung hero. Right size, right place, right time, right guy. Rightfully doing his duty. Several tubes in number one boiler had blown out. Japanese-held islands were nearby, perhaps 20 miles away. As Chief Water Tender Robert Clevenger told it, "We secured number-one boiler and started cooling it with sea water. There was no doubt which tubes were gone: the fire box was cherry red and gave enough light to count the tubes that were pouring steam. When the pressure was off the boiler, the manholes in the end were opened and the balance of the steaming water was dumped into the bilges and pumped over the side. About this time it became clear that we intended to lash somebody wrapped in burlap on a paint stage, wet him down, and push him into that still steaming boiler with instructions to count so many tubes up and so many tubes over and drive in the steel plugs. This was to be accomplished in total darkness." The Chief stopped, drew a deep breath, and relit his cigarette.

"Just looking at the situation you could figure that whoever went in on that paint stage would be subject to live steam longer than most of the lobsters you eat, or to put it another way, he would spend more time closer to that red-hot brick than steak on charcoal. Also, most of us could never make it through the manhole on a stage. What we needed was a small man with a big heart. Small in size, but big in courage. It would be quite a feat to lie there lashed on that stage, cooking on one side and steaming on the other and keep your cool to count to the proper tube holes and drive in the plugs. When we asked who would like to be the first, Wilson said, 'Aw hell, I'll try it.' He did it on his first crack at it."

"Engineering Officer Bill Nix had said we'd be out of

commission for seven, eight days. We're ready in eight hours. Wilson just done his duty, is all." Chief Water Tender Clevenger said it sort of proudly, but in low key.

The Department of War could easily run out of medals at this rate. All a guy has to do is his duty. Thousands of guys just did it. No big deal. He's "unsung" in my book.

Take Chief Electrician Mate Ed Brush, for instance. Climbed the 52 foot mast and installed the radar motor. It's easy enough in ordinary conditions or in port, but when the ship is in a trough and rotating so that nothing but water is beneath you, it takes strength and guts to get the job done. My hat's off to the guys who weathered seasickness for months. It's off to the guys who always overcome natural fear and hold on. Nobody mentions the word hero. Doing one's duty is heroic enough.

I never had much time to think about the the kamikaze who "saluted" the *Machias* near Ulithi and flew into his fate breaching the Fifth Fleet's vanguard. His escorts had time enough to be polite, paying their respects to the last "friendly" enemies they would have. They did everything but wave. They went even beyond the call of duty.

The Betty bomber pilot who ran the gauntlet of at least fifty ships in San Pedro Bay is another unsung hero. Probably unknown, too. Red-hot tracers by the thousands penetrated his blazing Betty bomber as he kept on a line heading to the airstrip. He seemed bent on dropping its eggs on Tacloban's airstrip. I doubt if his commanding officer ever will learn how he and his crew went down in flames.

Unsung heroes, yes. If the tradition of war continues, a song for unsung heroes ought to be written. If there's a perpetually guarded Tomb of the Unknown Soldier, the "Unsungs" deserve at least a song. My two brothers now fighting in Germany deserve it. Fiore is a signal corps cryptographer with three others and a jeep, climbing trees and setting up switchboards, constantly in and out of the front lines. Knows too much to be allowed anything more than a private's single stripe. Staff sergeant John has weathered Africa, Sicily, and malaria and is facing a pretty hot future. I hope he's got my father's prayer. Not sure about Johnny. He's worse than I am about beating all odds. Yet he was always trying to protect me. They'll have some great stories to tell.

Duty, thy name is not yet written. Your last name is hero and middle, honor. I just want to get home "almost unsung."

The Pearl

Like an aloof Gibraltar without a twin and without any seeming purpose, Diamond Head, Oahu, pierces the peaceful Pacific. Simply there, its furrowed ridges and unpretentious peak pretend to point into waters that are everywhere and go nowhere. It is nature's lighthouse where none is needed. And even for the best of sea legs and liberty-starved sailors who have perused the Pacific for months, the reality seems almost a mirage.

Trade winds which blow relentlessly, mercilessly for six days from Eniwetok are now subsiding. Twenty-foot swells, avalanche-like, have pounded the hull of our *Machias*, each threatening to sink her and us. Her gracefully-flared bow would plunge deep into the troughs, slicing the lunging swells and sending a shooting spray over the flying bridge. Stu Whitehead and I often stand there, ducking the spray while beneath us lies a deserted deck but for the six men on watch. This ride is simple and predictable now that the triple-welded seams have stood this ultimate test. For five almost sleepless nights I endure the buckling groans of the bow plates as our good ship rises through an onrushing swell. The bow sleeping quarters seem like a derelict ship still inhabited by dead bodies, and through the perilous nights I count ships rather than sheep, which requires of me the epitome of faith. It's as if the Pacific does not intend to let us go.

On the seventh day the trade winds subside to 20 knots, almost coincidentally with a peeking, curious sun. A vague horizon off the port beam suggests a land mass much longer than the typical island of the South Seas, seeming to strain into an identity. Above, on the bridge, I hear the order to helmsman Bill King.

"Steer 355 true."

"Aye aye, sir. Three hundred fifty-five true, sir."

The port rudder softens the sea. Now the *Machias* is rolling gently, and in minutes deck hands stream topside. This newfound peace is written on the faces of bosun Pop Bryan and John Hobson. The buckling of the bow plates and the terrible pulse-like pounding has robbed the old bosun of much needed sleep. Pop, white-haired and fifty-two, both looks and behaves in a meditative manner.

"Thank God she's triple-welded at the seams. Don't know how she could have taken such a battering. Thought we'd never come up through some of the big swells. Thanks for this frigate. She's well-made." Pop was smiling faintly and did not wait for an acknowledgment from Hobson. It was always good to see Pop topside, though I never talked with him, just listened or listened in.

"You topside guys have it easy, Buzz. We been hanging on to something every step. There's more puke in the bilges coming here than we had in that typhoon near Leyte. Everybody's sacked in. Gotta have a cast-iron stomach for this stuff. Damn glad we didn't draw North Atlantic duty. Hey, they got Pearl on radar." Hobson is acting as if he really can't believe it.

"This shindig's almost over, son. You re-enlisting?" Pop is always patriotic, everybody's guardian angel, everybody's ear. If you have a complaint, you take it to him. If you'd gotten a Dear John letter, it's Pop's bailiwick. He's in charge of ship damage below decks. Could recite "Pool Shootin' Roy" and even "Stopping by Woods." Gave the impression that he, too, "had miles to go before I sleep."

Pop had a knack of making everything connect. Had three sons in service and met his Navy Lieutenant son aboard a supply ship in Leyte gulf in November. Full of insights, always took a positive look at the world. He was sharp, alright. Hobson suspects Pop would be waxing philosophical any minute now. The swells were softening and the air on the flying bridge made up for the oily smells by the bearings, the twin shafts, and other sundry machinery.

Maybe the late trade winds were bringing in the fragrances of Hawaii. Before long the crew would be chased out by Eric Strom with an assist from Toby. The two were one hell of a one-two punch. Master at Arms Eric would enter politely and pontificate. "C'mon you guys. Wanna die in bed? Up and out. Chow in fifteen minutes."

"Call that chow? You jokin'? Ain't no such thing as chow around here. Cripes, that dog robber's chow ain't fit to be et. Navy's got all the good chow. Hell, ole' Kelly hisself don't eat none of it. Took us reserves to come in and fight this god-damn war." Strom was ready as always with a firm rebuttal, even if it didn't back up our chief commissary guy. "Up in five minutes or you're on report. O.K.?" We like Eric the Red anyway. He doesn't like being out here anymore than we do. He'd end the war sooner than any of the reservists would.

Then there's Toby. He's always around. Nobody 'cept Pop Bryan looks him in the eye and backs him down. Pop still has the look of a college prof about him and Toby respects intelligence, for he's slightly short on certain categories of it. Toby's college experience had exposed him to such stuff when he was not knocking the hell out of tackles and ends as a blocking back at Hardin Simmons. Played at Drake, too. Gave them their money's worth. Our *Machias* has been getting their money's worth, too.

Pop gave his money's worth, too. All of it. In spades after the big "Diamond" attack. His ideas are as pure as gems. "Remember those cats' paws that those Bora Bora natives dove for us in Fauni Bay? No more than half an inch with color patterns built in. They were complete in themselves and truly exotic."

"Yeah they were, Pop. Got some in my locker. What about them?" Hobson swung his gaze northward. "Diamond Head is showing up clear now."

"That's a colossal diamond, son. Nothin' like it anywhere. But let me tell you a little about pearls. You know, we didn't pay anything for Bora Bora; it's French. Just a fuel base. Not many beautiful islands like it in the world. Untouched, almost innocent. Nobody died there. Now Pearl, that's different. More'n a thousand were killed. The Arizona, for one."

"What'cha getting' at, Pop?"

"O.K. now. Think of Oahu as an oyster and Pearl Harbor as a pearl. The island itself is natural as an oyster, but the harbor is artificial, man-made mostly. It's like good and evil: evil is parasitic on good, but independently real. Follow me?"

"So where does this evil come in?" Hobson looks like a willing student and pleased that Pop is unloading an idea on him.

"Well, that's almost it, Johnny. There's another pair in this equation: means and ends. The means—*how* you choose to do something—always affects your goal, or ends. In fact, how you do something will become the what. It's like the parasite becomes the body it leaches on. How we travel becomes the destination itself. We become what we eat, you see."

"Tell that to the guys inside the Arizona, Pop. They'd damn well be pissed-off."

The Last Romantic War

Pop didn't ask me, but I agree. Those sailors are part of the Arizona alright. Diamonds are desirable. It's O.K. to make them but not take them. The analogy seemed clever if you let it stop there. I think this analogy is the key one in our lives. What's more important than good and evil or the relationship of the individual to the group, as in government. I know McShane has plenty to say about that.

Diamond Head is indeed impressive. Hardly as quietly exotic as Bora Bora, but it looks symbolic. Sort of a jewel. As the crew pours topside, they too are caught up in the memorable names of Diamond Head and Pearl Harbor. And in less than an hour we were in their midst.

Perhaps Pop's good-evil scenario might be too deep for us. As for me, I'll settle for its being the alpha/omega of this colossal war. Let evil take care of itself. No, that's the trouble maker! Good has held its own so far. The creation is good; man, not God, has "created" evil. My birth has been good, thanks to many factors. Evil is a persistent parasite. If the how is corrupt, any idealism will fail. Can there be an ideal idealism? I wonder "how" I'll rank Oahu...

Some day after it's over I'll read that prayer and ask my father to translate the Latin. Then the shoe will be on the other foot.

When the War is Over

It's of Honolulu, not Pearl Harbor that we're thinking. As the swell-tossed USS *Machias* dutifully and respectfully enters the bowels of that ill-fated harbor, our crew, unordered, looks on the mess of battleship row much like the way a high school student might look on a history book by the ancient historian Pliny. We are already forgetting the past; bring on the present!

We're tired and worn thin. But even this make-believe, Dorothy Lamour–Hedy Lamar Hollywood version of Honolulu seems a prize ready to be enjoyed. It's as if to the winner belong the spoils. And we've re-won the Hawaiian Islands. And if ever a ship at sea were ready for liberty *a la carte*, it would be our *Machias*. But we have definitely matured.

After sailing from Eniwetok, through days and nights that felt like they would never end as we hoped that the ship's vaunted triple-seam welding would hold firm, the sight of Oahu is like finding an oasis in desert. The incessant buckling of the bow plates has been worse than Poe's pounding heart. And now all this seems a sort of romantic, Gothic history.

Finger-pointing at capsized battleships cease and thoughts of dress blues, salty tailor-mades, of course, run rampant from stem to stern. Some few on the fantail are rounding up a game of craps to fortify their liberty money. And, as always, the best bluffer and most monied man of the game, whose snake-eye skills assure a pot, is Joe Contini. Joe, who never let a ring opponent last any longer than need be, used the money-bluff to put his craps opponents away fast. Had plenty of loot to back it up. In the ring it was different. His uppercut did it.

To me, any adieu to the Southern Cross left a sentimental shellac on my memory. Of the dozen or so who stayed on their sea legs through the battering swells, I not only bested the smashing pitches but, like a bronc buster, I exalted, gratefully, in the marvelous climb from seasickness to rider of the flying bridge. There's about a 45 degree swing when the swells are rough. While many munched on crackers, I and the flying bridge were companions. Now, on the flying bridge above it all, the war and its "times are out-of-joint" circumstances can be looked down upon. The *Machias*, like myself, is a survivor. My cheese cloth prayer and me. Unbeatable team. I had jokingly chided my father, "Pa, this paper won't stop bullets." It wasn't said in disrespect; in fact, I was deeply pleased that my father had thought of me in this way. I sometimes remembered it when there was no occasion to. I never told any of my shipmates about it. You just have to have faith in faith. Almost another paradox.

Up on the flying bridge the sea seems spectacularly dangerous. Oh, how the bow sinks into the sea! Our *Machias* is like a lover in ecstatic agony, moving somehow towards an almost imaginary, unreachable destination. The ride, both manner and style, is our destination. Maybe there is no destination, just a stopping-off place. For a moment the ship seems suspended, and indeed it is. It's as if she's preparing to lunge free and then, thinking the better of it, dives back into the sea. The way of all flesh.

Now, once past the submarine nets and into the safety of Pearl, our home-coming has begun. Dice are rattling against the 20mm clip shack and festivities are underway. Port and starboard liberty. Somebody has to mind the ship. The Marines won't. The unlucky assemble on the fantail.

"They're looking for petty officers to apply for the Coast

Guard Academy. They're already thinking post-war. Maybe getting ready for the Ruskies. Anybody interested?" The messenger of these marvelous tidings, Bo LaBeau, confesses to no interest at all. "Hell, if I couldn't get first class bosun aboard ship and now they want some officer candidates, nuts to them."

"Bo, we thought you wuz gonna sign over. Thought you wuz a twenty-year man." "Ding" Davis says it with eyes twinkling and tongue in cheek.

"You guys talking like it's over. We just took Okinawa. The Japs ain't quitting. These kamikaze pilots ain't quittin'—just committin' suicide." Bo paused. "Hell no. They promised me bosun first, but stopped all promotions. They must think the war's over."

Felix Magrone, a newly anointed gunner's mate, chimes in with his customary mild cynicism. "They won't get me to re-enlist. I won't eat any more soda crackers once I'm outa here."

My world is of a different order. Get the hell out of bell bottoms: yes. Into the newly proposed GI Bill for discharged veterans of the war: yes. Take another try at pro baseball? Maybe. Bemoan the loss of seventy-eight bucks each month and room'n board in the service? No! It's not that the future is visible and clear; it's more like, "let's let the past go." It's been on my mind ever since Hitler's "drive to the East" back in '39. I was sure even then that the rippling effect would reach America's shores. It turned out to be a tidal wave.

Our rendezvous thickens with crap game dropouts and also the usual victors. Colone and Capitani do a mock jitterbug. "Over-the-side" Frank Trupiano breaks out *a cappella* and the clownsters break into song. Any song will do now. They find just the right one:

When the war is over

The Last Romantic War

We will all enlist again.
Oh, when the war is over
We will all enlist again.
When the war is over
We will all enlist again.
In a pig's ------- we will!

Maybe it's a bit premature to think it's all over. Yet somehow they looked like men who had done their duty and done it exceedingly well and felt good about having done it. Tomorrow, however, isn't a sure thing. No day on the USS *Machias* ever is. No day anywhere is.

Just the same, I sang louder than I have in a long, long time. It doesn't matter that having no listeners doesn't matter. I'm singing to me. That's what this war is all about. It'll be a wide-open world, a wide-open life one of these days.

Tonight I'll sample Honolulu, the dream liberty of every sailor who ever got this far! This time I'll see if Honolulu's hula hula is more eye-catching than Bora Bora's. Now if I can only squeeze my undisciplined feet into dress uniform shoes.

Anchors Aweigh!

At 07:42, the USS *Machias* un-moors, hoisting anchor out of Pearl Harbor. At 08:00, I am on watch, having relieved Monk Marshall. This morning's anchors aweigh and passing through the cosmetically clean battleship row is methodical and swift. The changing of the watch is equally so. The Pacific as we've known it is pure past tense. Future tense is on our minds. This first watch will mark the beginning of our new but temporary liberty. Honolulu has been a taxing celebration, but all hands survive. Some heads are still buzzing. Mine isn't. Now we can relax a bit.

Twilight scatters its shadows on deck as the smoking lamp is out. Our *Machias* seems like a relieved ship asking for a peaceful, starry night. The still South Pacific Ocean is solemn: only our wake is alive. It's too early for stars and too soon for reminiscing. Memorable moments will catch up months from now. But it's not possible to be on watch with an empty mind. Sound-powered phones press heavily on my ears; yet they, too, are quiet. Then, almost suddenly, darkness obliterates the phantom of time and the magic of memory seizes me.

There might not be any frigate like a book, as Emily Dickinson said, but life on a wartime frigate can almost fill one. It's only been a year since commissioning, but it seems like a lifetime. But my "book" is in the making, as are those of my shipmates.

Now, this is a pacific parting. It's not a Romeo and Juliet parting. For once, destiny will slap fate in the face. This is

The Last Romantic War

America's foundation-block: destiny. Each of us can experience and direct our own destiny to its limit. America and me: the destiny twins. We're both in and on the same boat, not ship, as Stuart Whitehead said. I know I'll do alright, but will America? Our ship's newsletter tells us of Eleanor Roosevelt's dream of our future: a brand new United Nations! The League of Nations, it seems, wasn't good enough for her. She *knows* history. Why repeat it! Maybe we need another bureaucratic empire. FDR's New Deal alphabet soup didn't satisfy her thirst for idealism. "ISM." That's the problem in a nutshell. Those fatalistic kamikaze kids are relying on the windbag of fate once too often.

I don't mind seeing our wake melting into the Pacific. Maybe I'm too optimistic, for we only have taken the threshold islands of Japan.

The fantail is quiet. Seas are calm and our present harmony makes up for the pounding it gave us from Eniwetok to Oahu. As usual, my depth charge seat sets me apart from the immediate world and joins me with the universe. Stars glitter like diamonds in the darkening sky. Maybe getting down to earth is better. Yes. Gals, here we come. In every port a gal. A glass of port with her. What's a name. A rose by any other name wouldn't taste as sweet. Rosa of New Orleans. Parting is such sweet sorrow. Chalk it up to experience. To love or not to love isn't the question. All's fair in love and war. Nothing's fair in love and war. The readiness is all. I am ready. *Semper paratus ready* for sure. I am just an insignificant, magnificent speck on this rare planet, somewhere going into nowhere. I'll kiss the first ground in the USA, first chance I get. Then maybe the first gal.

America the Beautiful. I've always liked it better than *The Star Spangled Banner*. Somehow it all comes down to love and war. Our flag sends tingles down my spine, but *The Beautiful* is far more than just a symbol.

I can't wait to get ashore to eat real food again and paint the town red, white, and blue! This is going to be one sweet homecoming!

Toby the Titan

Nobody aboard the USS *Machias* knew Toby other than, perhaps, Toby himself. This would require a peer, and he had none. So maybe it's guesswork. He is unforgettable. To me, Toby is one third Popeye, one third Atlas, one half enigma, but all Titan. To put it bluntly, not even the commissioned officers knew what made him tick. Nor did I for that matter. They were sure, however, that it was far better to know him than to understand him.

Toby didn't fraternize with anyone except Bo. Consequently, we knew him by what little we saw of him up close and by reputation, which eventually merged into legend. You could make up a story about Toby's antics and it would be believed. Much as Pop Bryan was the patron saint of the *Machias*, Toby earned the title of Titan.

It was believed, for example, that Toby grew up as an orphan and forged a living raiding garbage cans. Looking at Toby working out on the fantail, one would doubt that he had ever been under-fed or even mistreated. He's a full six feet, carries about 205 muscle-pounds, and is built like a football blocking back as close as one could imagine. Toby keeps his fine, blonde, straight hair short and close to his skull. Although his facial bones are prominent, his dark blue eyes stand out. He's always clean-shaven and ready for liberty. It doesn't matter that he's not handsome. And it is easy to imagine him as being the 97 pound weakling on the beach who, like the American Dream, grew into a powerful giant. In short, he was a Nordic Adonis, if not a Greek one.

When you think of Toby, you think of bosun Bo, a junior-sized version who is at his side constantly. Funny thing, Bo played a pulling guard in high school and Toby the Titan cleared the way at right half for at least three Midwest colleges, tramping it for four or five seasons. This was fact. He would be quick to tell you—if you were privileged to be with him—that "him and Ray 'Bulldog' Turner was good buddies." Turner was All-American center from Hardin-Simmons in the late thirties, he'd be sure to add.

There's so much story about Toby that it's hard to know where to begin. That and the stuff that might be just rumor. Bo was awfully tight-lipped about him even though they cavorted on liberty time and again. You saw his soft smile that would freeze if you crossed him. Nobody crossed him. Pop stood his ground with him, mainly because Pop was always in the right and Toby respected him. Nobody else challenged him. Toby cussed out the bridge from his station at number two 3-inch fifty just beneath the bridge. After being ordered to cease fire, he kept his gun crew firing at a disappearing Jap plane. He was not disciplined. We could have used a dozen like him.

Little stories were always surfacing about him. Trivia on how he would crunch light bulbs or how many times he would hoist 50-pound barbells. I often watched him on the fantail in mid-morning bringing the heavy iron above his head. This despite plenty of Pacific heat. Getting the barbells aboard ship attested to his influence and that he deemed muscle to be mighty important. Nobody had more shoulder nor heftier biceps. He was built like a "T" but not to a "T."

Toby was good natured but bad-tempered. They worked in tandem. Perhaps it was of necessity. His muscle energy was devastating and dangerous. His naiveté made him vulnerable.

After a liberty in Honolulu, a sailor who broke rank from a circle of liberty returnees handed him a pint bottle. The navy gob mentioned the Coast Guard in an unfavorable way, taking Toby off guard. Toby took a one-second swig, sniffed the bottle, and in two seconds the practical joker splashed into Pearl Harbor, liquifying himself.

He wasn't the last blue jacket to taste the salt water of Pearl. An enraged Toby tossed about ten white-uniformed sailors, two at a time, into the drink. It was a ten-pin sweep. The Navy shore patrol surrounded him and he did them a favor by being taken peacefully.

Moose Hanna, our exec, thought him important enough to bail out. Privately, the Moose asked Toby what happened for him to cause the second worst dunking of Navy personnel since December 7, and Toby answered, "Hanna, sir, ah kin tell the difference between piss and Southern Comfort. I got pissed-off."

"Sure 'bout that, huh Toby?"

"Ya sir. Defendin' ship's honor, sir. Gave 'em a taste of salt water, sir."

Toby's eyes were a dead giveaway. Honor? Yeah I guess it's honor, he thought, but shit, it was more a case of expediency. Once you fling a couple of semi-loaded sailors into the salty sea and a half dozen are still puzzled and standing, you'd better complete the job. Toby completed every job and this one too, with a laugh thrown in. Hanna suspected that Toby tossed in the pun knowingly.

The Moose snorted, "Toby, if you'd left them high and dry, I'd rip off a couple of your stripes. Gotta let them know we been around, too."

It was vintage Toby and vintage Hanna. It's always vintage with those two, the toughest twosome aboard the *Machias*. Other *Machias* shipmates bragged that these two had reshuffled the deck of a Honolulu bar and scrambled about twenty deck hands off the cruiser USS *Minneapolis*. Again, it's just a matter of duty. It would be goodbye to Pearl tomorrow.

Toby didn't know this, nor would it have mattered. You don't fool around with him on any day of the year. But he is most dangerous when alone, and he is alone most of the time. This is so because, being a Coast Guardsman, Navy gobs would fling their meanest barbs at their senior brothers. "Hooligan Navy" is the usual taunt. Alone and ready for fisticuffing at a drop of name-calling, Toby almost welcomes the exercise. Perhaps we avoid buddying with him because he's a magnet for trouble. This also accounts for too few eye-witness accounts of his feats. Further, this lack of hard evidence gives rise to some exaggerated tales. But every last sailor aboard the *Machias* knows you bet on Toby against huge odds and win. Such is his reputation among the tough crew of the *Machias*.

March 28 and Pearl hi-jinks are only memory now. The future is almost here. Not only Toby but the entire crew welcomes the cold, invigorating waters of Puget Sound. After unloading ammo, it's every man for liberty and then a ten-day leave. Few realize that in just a few short days the crew will disperse in groups of twenty or more and a few, like Toby, will be shipped out singly. It's Bo who passes the bitter news on to the deck hands.

"Toby's gone. In-patient at the Marine hospital in Seattle. We'll be outta here before he's back. Ship won't be the same without him. Pop Bryan's gone, too." Bo fondles a cuppa joe as if it contained the spiritual epitome of the *Machias*' bad and good guys. It's a one-two knockout of giants.

"You gonna miss him, Bo?" Troop knows the answer, but he can't admit to the sentimentality of it himself. Sure, Toby is tough and sometimes mean. But they know he'd stand up and fight for them, anytime, ashore. They saw the worst and best of him, for Toby often acted impulsively. But he remains a stranger to most of the deck hands. Flare-ups were swift and regrettable. Sometimes it cost him a stripe or two.

"Troop, there's not another like him in the whole damn Navy or Coast Guard." Bo sipped the lukewarm liquid as if it did not agree with him, but it was more likely that the breakup of the ship's crew didn't suit his taste.

"Hey you guys," he whispered, "we're headed for Cold Bay in the Aleutians. Gillam just told me. A bunch are getting off in Kodiak and a few more along the way. Yup, the old gang is breakin' up. Our orders just came."

"What we doin' in Cold Bay, Bo?"

"We're goin' with three, four frigates and we're giving them to the Ruskies. Looks like they're gonna give us a hand against Japan. This war ain't over by a long shot. You remember the kamikazes off Iwo and Okinawa? They ain't quittin'."

"Feel a helluva lot better if Toby and Pop wuz here, Bo. They kept us together."

Some of the guys nod and some seem far away in thought. It's like a high school commencement and getting diplomas and being told now the real battle for a good life is on. High school had not been a snap and here it is, the big leap into the school of hard knocks.

"Take it easy on liberty tonight. Save it for your leaves. If you're close to Newport News or Norfolk, check up on Toby. Pop is probably getting discharged in Cleveland. He's about 50, you know. If you're hittin' the bars, toast Toby for me. Pop don't drink, so toast him with the chaser."

It's like the end of the fourth act in a five act play. And it was sure to end in the Pacific Theater near Japan itself. Nobody could replace either Toby Switzer, our Titan, or his counterpart, Pop Bryan, our patron saint. Damn it!

Pacific Poetry

Names of places speak more to the heart than such abstract words like valor, glory, in vain. Guadalcanal resonated with action, what men did there. It filled my mind in August 1942. No history book description could do it justice like my imagination did, and that wasn't good enough. That was earthy prose; now the poetic spirit has settled in.

I remember a line written by a WWI English soldier, Rupert Brooke, that went something like this: "If I should die, think only this of me..." But I also recall another poet whose far less romantic poem poses a huge question: "Does it matter? Losing your legs..." Plenty of us know of Rudyard Kipling's "Gunga Din" and Alfred, Lord Tennyson's "The Charge of the Light Brigade." Maybe their romantic charm is enhanced by the passage of time, which often strengthens the imagination's influence. Karl Shapiro's "The Death of the Ball Turret Gunner" hardly elevates the romantic spirit. But the act of writing a poem itself touches the romantic spark in most of us, even if the poem itself doesn't ignite that spark into a small romantic fire.

Somebody said that romance is where we are not. The cartoon strip of Flash Gordon which I read nine years earlier, with its rocketry and inter-planetary wars, stirred our imagination. Our rockets are now ballistic missiles like our hedgehogs.

But this war is still our war, not a Flash Gordon escapade full of deadly spaceships. Men are still making personal decisions, even at a gut level, oftentimes hand-to-hand, ship-to-ship, plane-to-plane. Events often take on a personality rather than a logistic profile. Our poetry might soon be old-fashioned stuff, experienced mouth to ear, and not through some new-fangled spaceship equipment. Take bosun Pop Bryan, for instance. He can recite a stack of poems. "Pool-Shootin' Roy" is one of them. It's about a soldier who was a pool shark, and in the war he pocketed a whole bunch of German soldiers. There's still room for poetry out here. After the experience is digested, maybe we can put it into poetic form.

Our slow-motion war allows nature to be our silent partner. It's hard to forget the beauty of Bora Bora, an island about 100 miles northwest of Tahiti in the French Polynesian group. She is pristine, virgin, and a perfect composition in itself. To turn her into a metaphor, from map to metaphor, as it were, comes easily as I broke rank at roll call to explore the archipelago of islets with adventurous eyes. But my memory of it is mainly from offshore where I saw her whole and not from her foothills, and it still affords an ample if incomplete view.

Of all the islands I've seen since Bermuda, Bora Bora is of the purest composition—just as God intended her to be if He had played favorites. So I cannot help but deposit this imagery into my memory bank. Some day I'll complete it and do it poetic justice.

Bora Bora

Is she... Island that I see,
Godiva of a pagan sea—
Ah, but that was moons ago,
When Venus winked at me.

There she rose... In a waking sea

Anthony Gianunzio

The high tide running, rushing free,
Showering sunbows in her show—
Flaunting Eden's ecstasy.

Yet still I see her rainbow face!
I hear the pagan call to go
To that far-off island place
Whose siren song I know.

On an islet near Biak in late September of '44, our *Machias* crew, each of us armed with two cans of warm beer, take a liberty ashore. This islet is a pile of white sand with palms shading its shore. I try not to hear the tossing of beer cans which land on clusters of shell casings from a defunct Jap anti-aircraft battery. An angry swell over-runs the beach. My shoes and "dog-tag" passengers are swiftly sucked out to sea. I know enough to let the sea claim them, for these are shark-infested waters. Someday a fisherman might find my shoes and my I.D. bracelet and perhaps wonder how the unlucky sailor died. My shoes soon disappear from flotsam into the defunct status of past tense jetsam. I see a poem there, too. It too not quite ripe for writing. It seems fair that my dog-tags are a parting gift to an ocean anxious to devour any careless intruder, for we are in a sense pure foreigners to it. This imaginary poem I call "Shore Party," and I get a slight kick out of the pun. It's a modest, one-dimensional poem, but that's because, well, maybe because I am unschooled in the art of writing. I think it goes like this:

On the shell-strewn, disheveled shore at Biak,
My "shellback" sea legs peruse the land—
But I, accustomed to a more innocent sand,
Muse of another time, of beaches far more kind.

The Last Romantic War

Then, uninvited, the Pacific rushes over me,
Pirates my shoes and metal I.D.
Let the sharks eat them, I say—
(And left even more, unsaid).
No matter, I'm still me.

Up in Leyte Gulf I promise, casually, that the Betty bomber pilot deserves an epitaph or still more, a poem for having run our gauntlet of a hundred warships. A parabola of tracer bullets form geometric patterns never seen in textbooks. The currents of gunfire are spectacular. Its pilot aims his flaming bomber at Tacloban's airstrip as he skids into the gulf. Flames melt instantly in this watery grave. His crematorium has not been a lonely end. It's deserving of a poem. I doubt if I'll write it.

If the warring Pacific weren't so unexpectedly deadly it would be easy to think of poetry at sea and whenever an island enhances the horizon. Even the names seem to sing out poetically. All one has to do is line them up in phonetic harmony, mix in a dash of prose, and stir the imagination. Every name means something and some of them, everything. I'd sometimes try it on watch, but never put it on paper, which, incidentally, is hard to come by.

At school, Miss Hebert and Miss Overton whetted my appetite for the written word. Frost is my favorite. I love the poem "Birches," for I had done just that up in the Creek Woods Hill. I and a couple of buddies would be "swingers of birches," not suspecting what a prophetic metaphor of life it would be. And "The Road Not Taken" is another that sank into my subconscious. I can nearly recall the exact words from "Stopping By Woods." My classmates couldn't agree on the errand and why Frost had repeated the last line, "And miles to go before I sleep," but any half-awake student knows there's a double meaning to that last line. We're all on double journeys if we're truly alive. Metaphor and analogy are the stuff of meaning.

Not that a poem requires a meaning. Just the music of the sounds can be enough. For example, the brand-new vocabulary of Pacific places is poetry *a la carte*. A childhood poem begins, "Listen to the music of the Indian names... Pontiac, Michelamacinac, Washtenaw, Saginaw." Each word has to be enunciated carefully; each syllable needs an equal accent placed on it and a slight pause. Pon-ti-ac. The strange-sounding, romantic names of the Pacific I'd heard aboard ship or read about are a vocal potpourri of sounds loaded with vowels. Simple names like Pago Pago and Bora Bora fit in well. These names floated by as if being towed by an airplane, circling and leaving it as one huge ball of fire finally disappearing, almost spiritually, into a cloudy flotilla of feeling.

Once while on watch somewhere near Mindanao and momentarily hypnotized by the Southern Cross constellation, those almost magical names paraded slowly across the equatorial hemisphere as if being towed by a meteor. There they were, a lexicon of a war that was in its last chapters. HAWAII, GUADALCANAL, WAKE, SAVO, KISKA, TRUK, GUAM, and ESPERITO SANTO. And then the next stanza: TULAGI, BOUGAINVILLE, RABAUL, SAIPAN, TARAWA, ZAMBOANGA, MINDANAO, and PALAU. The skies then swarm with names, most of them still strange-sounding and barely recognizable:

MIOS WOENDI, BIAK, HALMAHERA, MOROTAI, MARCHESI, LEYTE, LINGAYEN, TACLOBAN, SURIGAO, MINDORO. And more, followed by a fleet of stars in battle line "T" formation: CORREGIDOR, LUZON, MANILA, BATAAN, TINIAN, OKINAWA, IWO JIMA, NAGASAKI, HIROSHIMA, and TOKYO.

The Last Romantic War

The never-mentioned names, bombing dots in the big picture, rate at least a stanza. Ever hear of Bunawan, Davao, and Kabacan? They felt and saw the rhythm of low bombing. They too belong in a poem, not merely transformed into prose sure to be written long after they are fact. Some of the names are soaked in blood, and they deserve to be washed clean by the poetic imagination of a soldier or sailor or pilot who has been there. Not that poetry and the poet are a sort of historical clean-up committee of one, but the somebody who does it should have a least experienced it first-hand.

Prose is well-suited for history; poetry reads better for life and the living. It's right-now stuff that awakens any time you look at it. To be alive... To live is all that matters. Maybe this plaything called war does some good. It gets your attention, makes you realize a few things, everything, before it's too late. What is a war but the shadows waiting in the wings to steal the show? That's what this big shindig did. It upstaged the lot of us. It was just a Saturday dance, that's all that it was, but oh what it means to me... If you couldn't see the poetry deep within the big show, well, how could you grow?

Too bad that the pedants got their hands on it. Stifled it with form. Then got fancy and fashionable. Seems we always louse up good ideas. They get rigged and turned into money-making ventures. True believers crowd in, grab the idea and squeeze it for all it's worth. I guess that's what romance is all about: the rescue from a straight-jacketed civilization. Romance the rescuer. Maybe by default. It needs rescuing too. What a helluva merry go aground.

A piece of poetry can put any ream of reality into its "proper" place. There is no proper place. Even here. History is always being rewritten and a novel can be dated, but a poem... Like love, it is eternal.

Dry-Docked

It's spring, but Puget Sound somehow seems chilly and lonely. I don't feel lonely; we're back in the good old U.S.A. at last! The Bremerton, Washington, shipyards are swollen with ships. The *Machias* is nestled in dry-dock, a sort of hammock where shipyard workers can penetrate her ailing body and ready her for sea again. Rumor has it that she'll be loaned to the Russians, who are bound to pounce on Japan and grab the northern islands lost in the war of 1904. The big boys met in Yalta and we were ordered states-side, so there's a deal on. The Commies are licking their chops even though Manchuria and Korea are teeming with Japanese troops.

Seems to me that we really don't want Russian help—only the threat of it. The Japanese probably will throw in the towel sooner. The Chinese communists must fear their Russian brethren, too, as they've skirmished on the Siberian border. As for me, I'm occupying Seattle after a hefty leave. The first leave section is already gone.

Heavy wisps of smoke from welders' torches foul the air. A soft staccato rat-a-tat-tat of air hammers, coupled with swinging arms of towering 100-foot cranes, need not remind me there's still a war on. Sailors with sea bags hurry past me as I stroll toward the USS *Machias* bedded in dry-dock. She needs alterations, repairs, rest, and we need LIBERTY. Lots of it. America is a giant store and our pockets are full of eternal youth.

For that matter, I need some alterations, too. They come

easy: a navy-blue serge tailor-made uniform takes care of the boot, GI uniform. For sixty-five dollars, a bit expensive, I can finally look like a bona fide sailor. There are ribbons, too, that I'm entitled to wear. Hell, everybody has ribbons here, and besides, what do they really count for, I respectfully ask myself. But if you're in tailor-mades, you should have earned them via sea duty. It's reward enough just to be on American soil again. Anything American is home, sweet home. And I did kiss the first kissable soil I stepped on. The girls, I reasoned, could wait.

The dock swarms with uniforms, uniform saluting uniform, but I avoid it by side-stepping or pretending not to see. This is true as much of the commissioned officers as all others. No offense on either part. Guys here have all been out there, and these salutes are almost a nuisance now that the tidying-up and final victory is nearly in sight. GI Joes are hell-bent for Berlin, and the Jap navy and air force are practically impotent. Of course, the kamikazes will raise hell. Here, near Seattle, ah, liberty is a certainty and I'm basking in it.

A bevy of Waves swim by me, almost provocatively. One, a curvaceous, auburn-haired petty officer, turns her head invitingly. Too late, I'm heading for the noon-to-four gangway watch. Damn it. She might have been the one with my name on it. So far, no bullet has found its mark, but Cupid aims for our spiritual heart.

One thing nice about this war: the variety of experience can't be matched. Sure, the routine stuff—gobs, lines, chow, scuttlebutt, drills—pain us to no end, but a nifty surprise here and there changes things. On Florida Island across the bay from Guadalcanal, I poked my head through a curtain of tangled vines simply out of curiosity. So near a placid shoreline, an unexpected jungle screeches at me, alive with screams of jungle warfare. No curriculum can teach this, only experience. And the tuition cost varies. Many pay with their lives on these exotic, remote islands. Many, many others drank it all in: a sort of "the drinks are on the house, Uncle Sam's house." Trouble with learning by experience, though, is that no two experiences are identical. One factor can rule it null and void, useless. A swift imagination is the surest road to learning and staying alive.

More Waves float by, almost casually. Where are they coming from? Where are they going, is a better question. And then another surprise, or rather a shock.

"EXTRA, EXTRA, the President is dead. Roosevelt dies. EXTRA! The president is dead. Roosevelt died this morning. EXTRA! READ ALL ABOUT IT!" The paperboy is waving a rolled-up newspaper and selling them like hotcakes.

What rotten luck! Our leader is down with victory practically in his hands, and he won't be around to enjoy it. Just like having a month at Wrigley field with the Cubs snatched away when Roosevelt signed the lowering of the draft age to nineteen. Damned ironies contaminate life. Like the irony of scrap iron that I gathered from the pit with Eddie Peterson and sold to the local junk dealer for five dollars a ton. He, in turn, sold it to a ship-building Japan. From there it was shipped to a surprise no-return address: Pearl Harbor. God's little ironies probably aren't that ironic after all. If we knew everything as God should, would, and does, these wouldn't be ironies at all. Our ignorance and inability to understand probably created the idea of irony in the first, second, and third place.

I pass right by the paperboy, whose business is more than brisk. Some Waves, all with handkerchiefs mopping their noses, are sobbing respectfully. Not a smiling face anywhere. Down the way, our *Machias* is propped in dry-dock, looking like a duck out of water, helpless. She seems unlike the glamorous beauty that sailed out of New York thirteen months earlier. Her flag is tattered and shredded, worn down to about 12 inches from the field of stars. It is sooted and seems to squirm where it droops amidships as if it were anxious to get out of the tangled mess of repairs. I salute the flag and then O.D. Lt. (jg) Barstad who, as was his wont, blinks and disappears. The petty officer of the watch, Bill Barney, throws out the usual crap at returnees.

"Just back in time, huh Buzz. Did you make out? What's goin' on down there?" My buddy Barney doesn't really give a hoot about answers, but only getting relieved of duty. He makes toward the mess hall on the double with high hopes now that the crew is reduced by half via their measly ten-day leaves.

Nobody has wavier hair than Boots Colone, not even Victor Mature of the Coast Guard. Nor was anyone more the rogue. But he's a smiling rogue, and most of his cracks are delivered with tongue in cheek. This time he looks as if he were ambushing an unsuspecting butt of a veiled joke. I'll lend him my semi-willing ear. The scarcity of personnel—at least ten deck hands are denied liberty because of goofing off—forces Boots to seek an ear outside of his usual society. He can't wait to unload on me and I can't wait to find out his latest flight of fancy.

"Hey Buzz, can you beat this bullshit. I'm restricted for five liberties just because that bastard Barstad said I was goofing off. I think he overheard me telling on him. All I did was repeat what the chief was saying about him."

"O.K., O.K. What did the chief say about Barstad?" Everyone aboard knew that it could hardly be something good; in fact, nothing that Barstad touched or looked at turned out good. Just the opposite of King Midas: everything he touched turned into pennies. Often it's burlesque or at best pathetic. On the other hand, Boots always is good for a laugh and he did nothing to be tossed into the brig for, in or out of ignorance. So I urge him to spill the beans.

"Well, I was telling a couple of my buddies that this chief was sayin' Barstad had to get close to a person's face to speak. Then, when he did speak, spittle would spray the victim's face. Yesterday, Barstad was speaking to chief motor-mack Swindeller. This other chief, and I can't mention his name, was in hearing range, and when Barstad got done telling Swindeller whatever he was telling, Swindeller stared at Barstad for a second or two, and then he wiped his face."

"He wiped Barstad's face?"

"Hell no. He wiped his own face and he kept looking at Barstad and said, 'Mr. Barstad, would you spray that again, please.' Barstad gulped, did an about red-face, and Swindeller damn near doubled-up laughing, he was so proud of the pun he had punished the bastard Barstad with."

Colone's impish grin, accented by his deep cheek dimples, flourishes briefly, then gives way to an inquisitive stare toward the fantail. "Do you know what those workers are doing down below by the canned goods storeroom?" It is an angry rhetorical question and he is swift to answer it. "Putting in an ice cream machine! Sonofabitch, we never got any until we got back to Pearl. Now the Ruskies, who don't even know what ice cream is, are probably gonna have it for side dishes. Next thing you know we'll ship 'em apple pies and they can have pie a la mode or something. Ice cream in Cold Bay, Aleutian Islands. They can sell it as Cold Bay ice cream to the Eskimos, that is if there are any of them still there."

"How do you know we're headed for the Aleutians?"

"I keep my ears tuned in, Buzz. The ICC shack has all the latest stuff."

"Remember when we hit Hollandia last September? The Red Cross had a kind of hospitality shack high on the bluff overlooking the harbor and they were offering doughnuts, coffee, and ice cream? For a fee, of course. Luckily I had some green money. Cash on the line, you know. I wondered where was the GI army. Even if we'd had ice cream aboard, we couldn't eat it. Ice cream would have confused our stomachs. At Pearl Harbor we took three days to get back to normal. Maybe the Commies could stand a little purging too." I felt proud of my pun. Colone takes it very differently.

"Well then, whose goddam idea is it. Barstad's? Nah, he ain't got that bad an imagination. Musta been some pork-barrel senator from this state. Gotta dole out contracts to the locals to outfit all these friggin' frigates we're giving to the Russians. Hah, that's a big laugh, ice cream pork-barreling. They'll keep the war goin' forever!"

"You got a point there, Boots. Churchy and Big Joe got this whole war stuff figured out just to stay in office. Roosevelt is dead or he'd get a fifth term. Stretch the Constitution."

"Hell, I didn't vote for him. Almost got an absentee ballot."

Just when the point seems dulled, lanky Barstad steps through officers' quarters hatch, stops, and aims a barrage at Colone: "You finished painting that bulkhead already, Colone? Speak up, what did you say?"

"No sir, I didn't spray nothin', sir."

Colone winks. Barstad keeps up his perpetual blink. "You weren't supposed to spray it on, Colone. Just brush it on. Let's get it squared away before cap'n comes aboard."

I read Colone's lips: "Not gonna get in sprayin' range."

Both head for the bow paint locker. It would be a dangerous mix. Colone and paint detail don't mix. He's been an expert at goldbricking his way out of paint details across the Pacific already, and Barstad isn't too good at nabbing anything or anybody gone astray.

I eavesdrop on their paint locker dialogue. It takes a damn

good interpreter to decipher Boots' gobbledegook. Wait 'til Colone and the Ruskies clash. That would be a comic war of words and worlds. I've an unshakeable faith in the champion of American ingenuity as represented by one Boots Colone. It would be one fine war of words.

The Russians will be damned glad to relieve us of our gallant *Machias*, if only to leave Colone in their wake.

Serenade Sublime

Our frigate *Machias* is at rest, high in dry-dock in Bremerton, Washington Navy Yard. Guys are on liberty or on leave. Me, I'm stuck with the eight-to-twelve watch. Lt. (jg) McShane's the O.D. The *Machias* needs to be Russianized before we deliver her to Cold Bay in the Aleutians. We're throwing in an ice cream-making machine so that the Russians fully appreciate our taste for capitalism. That's McShane's little joke. The Ruskies are tying down Japanese troops in Manchuria and Korea. We want them to move, but not into China. It means our service on the *Machias* is done.

The Andrews Sisters are *Drinking Rum and Coca-Cola*. I've done that in a few places. *My Dreams Are Getting Better All The Time* with the Pied Pipers can't be any truer. Must be the Hit Parade. They must be writing songs just for the guys and gals in service. Some of the guys have pin-up posters of Betty Grable, Rita Hayworth, an unnamed busty blonde riveter, or of their own wife or sweetheart. I've been on four ten-day leaves and the popular songs fit more than well back home. War memories go with you and even if you don't talk about them, they're a part of your disposition.

Guys and gals of the first world war had their songs, too, and I like them. But when you too are part of the scene itself, the songs get in your blood and stay there. Maybe thirty years later they become ambiance. They've become not just a memory, but a part of you. In England, *Bluebirds Over The White Cliffs of Dover* probably will last forever and they might feel it ten times as deeply over there. To us, it's another piece of charm out of the recent past. Almost all the songs these past three years dramatize the war situations. *Don't Sit Under The Apple Tree* and *You'd Be So Nice To Come Home To* are just two of dozens of our songs. I know the lyrics of dozens of these songs and can tell you some connecting experience.

It's easy to take music for granted. I've taken our good stuff for granted more than most guys in the military. I've never found any fault with it, and right now in these eerie, almost sterile surroundings, the Hit Parade on the radio rescues me from the acrid stink of welding rods and the occasional cacophony of shipyard slang. A shipyard is little more than a civilized junkyard. But it certainly gave us a huge advantage by 1944. Tonight it seems nostalgic, since we haven't heard any music for months. The music, the shipyard, the times strangely seem out of joint.

A river of Hit Parade songs is pouring out of a destroyer escort in the next repair unit. I'm at the gangway, and their sound is coming in clear. It's like I'm chained to my duty. I can blame, or thank, the music for this.

Many of us will forever remember names like Glenn Miller, Benny Goodman, Tommy and Jimmy Dorsey, Louie Armstrong and Prima, Duke Ellington, Les Brown, Kay Keyser, Woody Herman, and other big band guys and gals who are also artist-performers in their own right.

Maybe I'll get De Rosa and McShane to gab a bit about their music experience.

Dee taught dancing in Chicago and McShane's been around plenty, too. He loves to talk with the non-coms. He won't let a bar or two get in the way. A "JG" (junior grade) among commissioned officers is like seaman first for us. Besides, he's not in the Coast Guard regular category; he's just in for the duration-plus, like us.

It's pretty easy to carry on an inner monologue while on watch. Beats talking to the fish or to the stars. I tell myself that nobody can beat Harry James's trumpet in *I Had the Craziest Dream* and the way Helen Forrest or Keely Smith sing it. Nobody's around to dispute it. Bing Crosby's *White Christmas* is realistic sentiment, and Tex Beneke's *Chattanooga Choo-Choo* sounds good. I like the way Doris Day sings *Sentimental Journey*. The lyric of *Moonlight Serenade* is invisible, but Glenn Miller's rendition of the melody will outlast any of us. That song simply had to be written by someone, sometime, in America. It awakens everything. It's made for dancing, and if I ever find my dream girl, it will be a favorite.

I can reel off dozens of favorite songs. *It's Been A Long, Long Time* sums up what a lot of guys feel who haven't seen their sweetheart for a while. "Kiss me once and kiss me twice, it's been a long, long time. Haven't felt like this since can't remember when" says everything about the painful wartime separations. With a depression and then a colossal war, romantic music like this soaks up the emotional void just like religion can. That's what I tell DeRosa, who's just finished making the rounds on our watch, and he agrees. He's got that far-off look in his eyes and I know he's thinking about Jo from Plainwell, Michigan, that he met at the local USO and danced with. Writes to her all the time.

"Dee," I say, "you danced plenty in the Aragon ballroom on the north side of Chicago, right?"

"You got it, man," he says. "Ain't nothin' like it. Was dancing there every Saturday night since '39. The place was always jumpin'."

McShane chimes in. "You young bucks jitterbug and free-wheel it on the dance floor. Pick out a gal and let her improvise, too. We write and dance to our own script. Hirohito's got 'em dancing his tunes."

I suspect that Prof McShane is headed for a lecture, much as I agree with him. But he's got rank and ideas, so... He's not finished with his idea.

"Freedom to be is a romantic idea. We're almost born with it. It's in our politics, economy, choice of religion, even in our music. The Japs see it different. These kamikaze pilots aren't volunteers, exactly. They're flying dead weight with a load of dynamite. If one in twenty gets through, they succeed. This war isn't over yet. We'll be out there in a gunboat over in Japan in a couple of months. There's still hell to pay."

McShane looks a bit too perplexed to suit me. I don't cotton to the gunboat patrol idea. We've already put in about 50,000 miles at sea. I can tell that he too wants to change the subject. I want him to talk about the big bands, but before I can ask he asks me, "What are you gonna do after this is over?"

"Go to college. Back in '42 I was going to enroll at Lake Forest College. I was bussing at the Deerpath Inn, making dough and residing there, hoping to start college and maybe the V5 program. Now we've got the GI Bill. Maybe I'll go to Western Michigan College in Kalamazoo. Teach for awhile and maybe coach. You going to teach?"

"Getting a Ph.D. in English literature at Brown University. I guess I'll teach."

"Know anything about music? I don't mean that classical stuff, the opera and that. You know what? We never heard radio music aboard except that Tokyo Rose incident down at Halmahera."

"I played trombone in the high school band and I wasn't too good at it. Glenn Miller, Benny Goodman, and one of the Dorsey brothers were. Yeah, I like music. Never studied it though. How 'bout you?"

"I remember the words of songs back into the twenties. Older brothers were singing them around the house. How about you, sir?"

"Knock off with the sir, Buzz. Hell yes, I listened too. Enough Sousa to last a lifetime. Was asked to try out for the Coast Guard band. I saw Frank Sinatra at the Paramount and Radio City Music Hall. Just happened to be there. Not bad. Heard Crosby sing *White Christmas* in person. The Japs didn't count on jazz and the big swing bands and our popular songs. Songs a guy and a gal can dance to. Sometimes I think it's the songs that make this war bearable or we'd all crack up. Ever dance to *In the Mood*? Everybody's gonna git hitched as soon as the war's over. These romantic songs are doing it."

"I don't jitterbug, but I get by with the slower ones. Never danced to the *Beer Barrel Polka*. The last happy song before the war. The dancers raised the roof at the American Inn in my hometown. Lowdown, noisy place and rowdy. I like the slow stuff. Wonder if they'll forget these songs just like we forgot nearly all of the World War I songs."

I don't expect an answer, but I think I hear him say, "Not a chance."

Maybe he's thinking about Miller's *String of Pearls*. Maybe I'm thinking about some of my hometown musicians. Guys like Joe Billo and his band, Fritz Spera and Fra Corsi, Ray and Popee Amicangelo, and a lot of them whose names escape me. Ray took two accordions into the Marines with him. Lost one on Guadalcanal, I heard. The Hit Parade is still going good on the DE.

"Where's your hometown, Buzz?"

"Iron Mountain in the Upper Peninsula of Michigan. Great melting pot. Dance halls like the Nightingale, the Pine Gardens,

Anthony Gianunzio

Dreamy River, the Riverside Club, the Eagles Ballroom, and the Knights of Columbus Club brought us all together. I was a little too young, but I listened. A good classical school system, too. We invented the "melting pot" idea. Swedes, English, French, Italians, Polish, Finlanders, Germans, Norwegians, Jews, Palestinians... Everybody. Music and baseball and jobs brought us together. We believed in education. You know, in Europe, education is the mark of class. It's highly respected."

"Nice way to put it. Sounds like you had a good time growing up in them thar hills. I come from a coal-mining town in Pennsy. I know about that assimilating stuff first hand. Not all that good, but what t'hell. We're here together and not doing too bad."

I want to keep talking music. "Ever see Argo jitterbug? How about Capitani and Trupiano? Ever see him toss Troop over his back? *A cappella*, too. We listened to the Hit Parade every Saturday night at home. Did you?"

"Sure. Who didn't? You know I'm only about seven years older than you guys. They played the college circuit. I enlisted a couple of years after graduating college. Got to be another Ninety Day Wonder like just about every officer aboard. I know the big bands. Nobody played trumpet better than Harry James in 'You Made Me Love You.' I've seen and heard them all."

"The songs themselves have plenty of class," I say. "Tunes and lyrics seem to match. They're all believable and the feeling doesn't need a big or complicated story behind it. They haven't covered half of the possibilities, either, but the ones out there just had to be written. We needed a Christmas song. I remember coming out of the Michigan Theater in Kalamazoo in late November '42 and the leaves were ripened and I was humming White Christmas. I knew that I'd be home for Christmas. So is that song out of the film *Casablanca*, 'As Time Goes By,' where

Bogart lets his love fly away for the duration and the cause."

I thought I'd almost made a speech. McShane squinted into my face. "You're pretty good about analyzing this stuff, huh? Where'd you get these notions? Gonna teach in the high school, I suppose. Gonna make the world a better place to live in, hey. Make the world safe for democracy, huh. Well, don't get too friggin' idealistic. The road to hell is paved with good intentions."

I had to chuckle when he said that. My idealism has suffered a little in the past few years, but it's still alive. But I'm not out to set the world straight. Dictators are setting the world straight and on fire with their 'isms.' I remember a song by that name just about the time of Pearl Harbor. I was ready to set the Cubs on fire, though.

"Yeah, song writers know what's on our minds and what gals want to hear. They're buying the records, you know. All this romance in the air and on the airwaves is doing it. We're all pretty much ready for it. We've got a lot of catching up to do."

McShane has a dreamy look in his dark eyes. I have a hunch he's got a gal somewhere. I know he's got a lot more to say. He says it.

"I'm headed for Frisco when the first bunch on leave gets back. Got a gal waiting for me there. It's almost like a farewell to arms. Only I'm not running from; I'm going toward her. Maybe this whoop-de-do won't last much longer. We're smashing through Germany."

I recognized that "farewell" business, the allusion to *A Farewell To Arms*. I rather like talking with him. He's not much on small talk. Makes you think now and then.

"Frisco's a great place for romance, Buzz. It's got everything: the Golden Gate Bridge, even the Bay Bridge. The cable cars up Spy Glass Hill and down to Fisherman's Wharf, The Top of the

Mark, great restaurants, scenery fit for sore eyes. Everybody has a good time there. Almost as good as New York. It's got charm like New Orleans and the French Quarter. Plenty of brass bands, too."

The Hit Parade swells all of a sudden. De Rosa, who's listening all through this stuff as if he's disinterested, comes alive.

"That DE over there has its radio on full blast. Doesn't our C.I.C. Room have a radio, sir?"

"That's like asking me if Artie Shaw can play the clarinet. Yeah, go ahead, turn it on."

Wouldn't you know, "Gonna Take A Sentimental Journey" is on. Les Brown and his Band of Renown, with Doris Day singing it like she's the gal next door. Just like I was saying, there's a song for every occasion. The Hit Parade sounds just like back in '41, so long ago. There's a slew of light romantic numbers coming up, the announcer says, including "Candy," "I Call My Sugar," and "I'm Beginning to See the Light."

The pier is too well-lighted and seems all the more deserted because of it. This warm eeriness feels strangely comforting as the music sinks into my senses. We're alive even if stuck on the ship. It's the big bands, the best thing that happened in and to the war. Sometimes I think the songs saved us from the war and won the war as well. They're like poems, faster than frigates, transporting our memories anywhere, anytime.

McShane is wandering topside, checking the new ice-cream machine and other improvements that will end the war five seconds sooner. Some clusters of Waves swing by and wave. I'd like to join 'em. I think they hear the yearning of the music. This eight-to-twelve watch is better than the one at sea. At least you see a different kind of "Wave" every few minutes. They're the hometown kind of girl, looking to get into the act for fun and frolic. They have their liberty, too. All work and no play doesn't work. DeRosa's got the wardroom radio on almost full blast. It's "Accentuate The Positive," a brand-new song being sung by Johnny Mercer. Yup, you gotta accentuate the positive, eliminate the negative, don't mess with Mr. In-between, as the song says.

This Hit Parade is my serenade sublime. Only six months or so ago Tokyo Rose was accentuating the negative. "Near You" was being played and what we were feeling wasn't worry about the faithfulness of gals and wives. We were getting a kick out of being instant celebrities when "Rosie" mentioned our ship by name. Told us our location, said we were in for trouble while the *femmes* are having a good time state-side. Hell, any kind of recognition then was music to our ears. One of the guys jokingly said, "Tokyo Rose, it won't be too long and we'll be near you." That'll be the day. I mean it, not negatively.

Now that Iwo Jima and Okinawa are ours, what's left is Japan itself. When the first section of guys on leave gets back, it's our turn. I'll take the train, the Milwaukee Road's northern route, and be home in a couple of days. The train will be jammed with servicemen all the way.

We're in the eighth inning and we're leading, seven to one. Just want to finish the game, face the music, and dance. "You'd be so nice to come home to," I say to the gal I've yet to meet. "But who knows where or when?" Like I said, there's a song for every situation without being sticky sentimental.

A guy could write a book about the songs and it'd be even truer than what often passes for history. You know, facts all over the place. To me, facts are but the residue of truth. The inside story couldn't even be found between their lines. But if you ask any GI about any song, he'll give it real meaning in the context of his war and life. If a picture is worth a thousand words, then many a song can picture a thousand memories.

If I say all of this to McShane or DeRosa, they'll think I've gone goofy. Maybe not. But I know one thing for sure: music has gotten under America's skin in this occasionally unforgettably romantic war.

I hope the Hit Parade survives. I know it will. DeRosa keeps it turned on strong. I think it has won the war.

The Last Romantic War

There is nothing like a train. Even on this, my fifth and longest run: Iron Mountain to Green Bay to Milwaukee, and now somewhere following the scenic Snake River, Idaho perhaps, en route to Seattle, where the *Machias* is being readied for the Russians. The Chippewa Run into my hometown touched every emotional fiber imaginable. The world is my oyster and I'm almost certain a pearl is in it.

Nothing is left but the mopping up. Back in dry-dock before going on leave, I caught a piece of conversation that won't go away. Lt. (jg) McShane was telling Lt. (jg) Spinks something sounding too ominous for the beginning of our juicy fourteen-day leaves. "Spinks," he says. "You're a professor of literature down at Mississippi U., but I wonder if you figure that this is the last romantic war. My imagination tells me so. How about yours?"

Damn it, I wanted to hear the rest of it, and it's been off and on my mind ever since. I've got time to think about it now. My "sentimental journey" took me home alright, but the war, oh the war took me farther and further.

Cliffsides above the tethering shadows of the Snake River deflect some evils that the war has spawned, and yet this train just seems to keep rollin' along. I know that the statistics, the suffering are beyond the counting, but the good, the gains, the growth cannot be fully felt yet . We probably experienced ten hours of hot action, a few hundred in anticipation, and maybe eight thousand hours in a state of readiness. But this is only a fraction of our military time, and much of that has been spent in relatively safe adventures.

If romance is fulfillment via experience, then this world war has accelerated it a hundredfold, and in quality as well. Every hour has been new; every day another dimension. And thirst for adventure is never quenched no matter where it can be found, be it Broadway, Biak, or Bora Bora. We are not mere tourists, but even more than travelers, for we played the most dangerous of games: life vs. death. Encounters with people I'd ordinarily never see or meet and scenes nobody save the wealthy could ever look upon were "free." It's a universal education, maybe beyond that of a university. Where else could I have grown so swiftly, so necessarily? How else can I have realized the prices in the great unlimited store of life and the how of paying? It's all just as new as each bend in the river below, in each surprising scene just around that bend. For a few sailors doomed on a tiny rock in the Pacific, the battle against boredom might be endless. But for the rest of us, the liberty of experience in port or elsewhere challenged our imagination in the most romantic way. Since no two experiences are exactly the same, they did not become the stuff of logical conclusions; instead, they expanded our own personal universe of growth. Well, maybe.

How the swift, slender Snake River seems to dash toward its destiny so differently from the mighty, swollen Mississippi. There's a tiny paradox that I must mention. Of necessity, perhaps, our ship's crew, like that of most military units, trains as a group. Maybe because this control or discipline is imposed upon us, our individualism flames like brush fires on the prairie. Our *Machias* is loaded with it; personality and identity are expected of us. The variety among us would make the robot goose-steppers feel hopelessly inferior and dull.

The romance of freedom, ignited by the ancient flame of

Prometheus, burns bright among us, perhaps even more than that of the Minutemen at Bunker Hill, Concord and Lexington. It seems to be our eleventh commandment: We shall be free to become a nation just as each of us is free to develop a unique destiny. What's more romantic than creating one's destiny rather than staggering before the bullwhip of fate? This was is a war against totalitarianism. We want and need the right to become what we're capable of. What's more romantic than this?

Lewis and Clark traveled on the Snake River to fulfill America's expansive growth. It's very strange how much in harmony our train is with the will of the river below. And I'm on the same romantic ride by choice. McShane would agree with me, I know. He and I have chatted a few times about the nature of things. In non-academic language, mainly.

Let's imagine the kind of conversation McShane and Spinks had the day I left on leave. Spinks was a lit prof at a university in Mississippi, but the two were as unlike as *The Iliad* and *The Odyssey*. They were as different as a boxer and a slugger. Maybe their opening round would be a sort of sparring session. McShane might jab at Spinks with a "So you think war is little more than logistics and the winner is predetermined like fate?" And Spinks would counter wildly with "No such thing as a romantic war, and if you think so, you're ready for a Section Eight, Mac."

That's what he'd say; everything was either black or white, either-or. Nothing but absolutes. Might be good for arguments, but not for conversation.

Back somewhere around Bermuda, I remember I had a mild bout with romance myself. Said a lot of things about romance, most of which came from high school readings. Well, almost a year older now with a thousand new experiences and I can't say that I've changed my mind. When I laid eyes on Bora Bora, it was both a dream and an unfinished reality. Every place has its charm. Maybe it is all in the eyes of the beholder, like beauty. I saw a lot more than what the travelogues say, more than what National Geographic shows. In my romantic imagination I hear McShane bedevil Spinks:

"Spinks, what kind of war you gonna take back to the classroom? Those budding Einsteins will want to know all about it. Will it be a bunch of stats or the spirit you found in it? Gonna tell 'em what it's like to be on the flying bridge on a starry night under your Southern Cross?" I can see Spinks girding to throw his own right cross. "Romance? What do you know about romance, Mac?"

"Only what I know. What I know from experience."

"Well spill it, then. Let's hear it." Come to think of it, Spinks has plenty of curiosity, I remember. Triggered the hedgehogs by accidentally tripping a firing button. A pattern of twenty-four splashes on a flat ocean decorated it romantically for a few seconds. The classic side of the experience fell far short of the scene. He saw splashes and felt sunk. And was confined to quarters.

Now the Snake River seems to widen around its bends as if to recharge itself in its journey to the sea. Something like a rattler uncoiling and ready to strike. McShane has a touch of fire in his eyes that I've seen more than once. He was on the Rutgers boxing team and gave a good account of himself in '41.

McShane might have said this, or did I overhear it? But it sounds true enough.

"Remember when you'd bring the Encyclopedia Britannica to dinner and you'd read one entry, alphabetically, at coffee, and promised to take us through more knowledge at every meal? And I damn near... That what you think life is, a prescription? You're linear, if you get what I mean. You don't

have a romantic bone in your body." Says it matter-of-fact like, without any sarcasm or feeling of superiority. I almost see me telling Spinks to come alive. Maybe I'll kill another half hour with this inner monologue. I mean dialogue.

The Snake River springs a surprise a minute. Just like my three years so far. Every place I've been, every person I've met, something is retained. I enter service an green sapling, but now I'm a romantic "sophisticate." Not worldly, just more experienced. I feel more "inner monologue" coming.

"Spinks, it'd take me a week to expound on romance," McShane might say. "Even I know that the ideas about romance are changing or expanding, and growing into maturity necessary to fit the times. When there's a new set of living conditions, the romantic always seeks fulfillment, not mere adjustment. Romance isn't on the defense; it's always moving ahead, growing, like the majestic Mississippi River; or maybe it's the Snake River, untamed, rushing into its manifest destiny. Romance must overcome or we shall cease to be." This kind of talk would make my imaginary Spinks' persona edgy. But it's hard to harness a romantic imagination, and besides that, it's fun.

"Mac, I've got two hours to catch a plane at the airbase. Make it quick."

"Short and sweet? Nah, a formula would spoil it, Spinks. Besides, there's no formula. It's a matter of how over what, knowing how to live. This war has flooded us with experience. It's opened up so many lives. The sky's no longer the limit."

"Yeah, and killed too many, too."

"There you go, looking at the facts on the cynical side. The romantic's perspective, his modus operandi, is a genuine optimism. He's got faith, pure and simple. Live, live all you can. Take the road less traveled by. Life is not in the form, but in the *flame. Be careful how you see the world: it is just so. Do I need to quote more romantics?"*

"I get your point, Mac. Tell me, how do you figure that this one is the last romantic war. Make it quick."

(McShane, I'm taking this one myself, an outer monologue, so to speak.)

Can't think of a better place than to be on a swift train racing through Idaho while answering it. This train, with people engineering it and traveling in it, zipping full speed ahead through wild nature, is as romantic as you can get. Except, of course, you need the one you love beside you to complete the romantic scenario. The key thing is people, people who are actively, intimately in charge of their lives and truly experiencing it. But the way things are going, we're going to lose the personal quality of life, bit by bit, and the same will be true of war. The machine age is here, technology is everywhere on our doorstep, in our minds, and soon our hearts will be wrapped in wire. Jet planes are already in the skies, and who knows what's next. We're going to take a back seat; no, we won't even be in the vehicle. In an eerie sort of way, it was spectacular to watch P38s down Zeros in a Pacific dogfight. It's going to be far greater than Alexander Graham Bell's "What hath God wrought?" We're headed outside of ourselves into various orbits and into new selves. We'll be numbers like the I.D. dog tags we wear, like the one I carelessly lost on Biak's shore but do not miss.

Yes, this war is still a romance, more so than any other. Maybe because more of mankind got into it for good reasons. We at least know what we're against and what we're for, even if we haven't understood the selfish motives of power-mad neurotics. Hopefully, war itself might become too dangerous. And maybe, just maybe, it will be romance and romantics who will put it out of business. What a fitting irony: let a war be too romantic and it'll sew its own seeds of self-destruction!

There you are, Spinks. Be thankful that we don't have a Statue of Equality! You'll at least like that.

Twilight is descending slowly, certainly, following the gradual descent of the widening Snake River. Tomorrow my train seat will give way to my bunk in the bow. We're heading somewhere, always somewhere new. But always there's the "duration plus six months," one helluva contract.

Travelin' Light

"Get your sea bags ready, you lucky bastards. You guys are officially off the USS *Machias*. Kodiak's dead ahead. You'll bunk in a barracks there for a week or so, then head back to Bremerton. We're goin' to Cold Bay to freeze our asses off. Gotta show the Ruskies how to run this baby. Lt. Spinks is in charge of you, all forty-five of you. Soon as we tie up, you're gone. No ceremony. Count your blessings. The Aleutians never warm up." Communications officer Lt. Jennings threw the good news out and disappeared. Just like that.

It wasn't that the *Machias* was a lousy home, but a far-off island of the Aleutian chain was not exactly home, either. The chosen forty-five contained a helluva lot of good men. Perhaps we could be spared, or maybe we too were headed for even tougher, more demanding duty. Okinawa was taken; what else was there left but Japan itself? If anyone knew, anyone wasn't telling. After months of sea duty in the Pacific theater, why should I complain? Oh yeah!

Ah, that sea bag! Everything I own is tucked away in it with fewer than ten cubic inches to spare. Every piece of clothing is snugly rolled and packed neatly. I had long since discarded my pillow. I hadn't even saved the dozens of letters, not realizing that some day they might take on new or a more complete meaning. Always traveling light, always anticipating the whims of the military which would have me packing off to a service school, a Coast Guard outpost, or a ship.

I'd made ten growth transfers already prior to being a

gunner's mate aboard ship. In October of '42 I arrived at a receiving station called Gull Lake and was outfitted with mothball-smelling GI clothes. The station had been loaned to the Coast Guard by the Kellogg Cereal Company of Battle Creek, Michigan. Autumn in Michigan was near idyllic. There was only autumn; the war seemed distant. Only Fort Custer and the Augusta USO reminded us of it. Then off to Pine Lake near Plainwell, Michigan.

The training camps were fine and a good transition into Coast Guard life. Meanwhile, German subs were sinking American shipping by the megatons in the Atlantic. I'm then assigned to a math school at St. Mary's Lake, but needs changed quickly in those early days. No need for gunnery officers on merchant marine-manned ships when a gunner's mate would do. So, off to Chicago's Randolph Street station across from Navy Pier. After a month on frigid Lake Michigan, I'm off to Chicago's south side at the Jackson Park Station near 63rd street. Sometimes I feel like a hobo, travelin' light, in '42 and '43.

I keep my sea bag down to the bare necessities. In late February the lake gets larger, and the school a bona fide one: Great Lakes Gunnery School. Four months of it. I pack my sea bag once again, board a train to Norfolk, Virginia, where nobody stays for long. Within days I climb aboard the Dixie special, shooting it across the red clays of Georgia and on to New Orleans. I seem to have come full circle, having started near the upper Mississippi and now arriving at ole' Mississippi's mouth.

Yet my vagabond days have barely begun. Now, like any true sailor, my packing skills are fine-tuned. I probably have packed more efficiently than the average European, African, or Asian immigrant. After a brief stop in New Orleans, it's off again to the Galvez Hotel in Galveston, Texas. The food there is fit for kings, queens, princes, and princesses and not for future crewmen of the good ship *Machias*. Desserts beyond the imagination! I suspect we're being fattened up for some nefarious purpose. A ten-day leave is handed to us. This requires little or no packing. I'm off once again, for the third time to my hometown. Three leaves of a ten-day duration require efficient use of clothing. Now it's back to New Orleans and the famous pirate's prison of Jean Lafitte, where I await the *Machias*' appearance on the Mississippi. When it arrives, Algiers across the crescented Mississippi becomes my temporary home. That was it: temporariness, if there is such a word. But there definitely is such a feeling. And a taut sea bag is the proof of it.

Somehow, crossing the newly commissioned USS *Machias*' gangway was almost a relief. That good old sea bag could stay put, almost unattended. But when we've crossed the Pacific and criss-crossed it a few times, and when we're in sight of Kodiak, Alaska, the sailors' best friend is standing at attention once again. It was like a dutiful dog waiting to be of service. I should have named it Travelin' Light. It seemed to have a character and personality of its own. My bag is sturdy, a light, canvass-like material. Rivets line the top, through which a cord could be passed, sealing it. Our mat is wrapped around the bag.

Funny thing, a sailor's bag often seems a reflection of its keeper. One of my unnamed, corpulent shipmates sports a puffed-up bag that seems padded with pillows. Mine is lean and clean, minus any pillowing. In fact, it's minus anything less than the pragmatic stuff of life. Were it to sink at sea, it could easily be replaced, item for item. Those tailor-made blues which I've owned now for a month I would sorely miss. The broken-in white caps too, I suppose, in as much as they'd kept me company in interesting places. But letters that anchor me to yesterdays are gone; there is just today and tomorrow.

The Last Romantic War

Don't keep anything you cannot hold. Now that is a dictum I could live by. If you haven't really earned it, the chances are you can't keep it. If it isn't true, it ought to be. Honesty can last a lifetime, if anything can. And now this bunk about a girl in every port or any port in a storm. Not so true, at least not for me.

Sure there were gals in port and some out of port, and those memories would last a lifetime even if their faces were already dulled by time. But it was not a *modus operandi*. Love, I guess, is a work of art and is beyond craft; I was only out for stars, a far lower level than art. The mode is inclusive, not exclusive as love must be. So I am light-hearted; Cupid's arrows are easy to dodge. If I truly am traveling light, it's because I carry no emotional baggage. I remember carrying a too-heavy torch in high school. But Annlouise did enlighten me.

On leave, a tiny zippered bag is all I want, and no more than I need. It's the perfect companion next to, or course, an interesting girl. Must be a million sailors out there, travelin' light.

Ain't Misbehavin'

I doubt if many GIs ever expect to meet their dream girl while in the service even if it would have been a perfect antidote for all the other pains that the war might inflict upon us. Even the vulnerability of age seems hardly a big factor. So what's left? On the home front, the situation can't be much different. As the song goes, "They're either too young or too old, the best is in the army, the rest will never harm me..." As for the engaged, committed, and even married GIs, the warning is clear: "Don't sit under the apple tree with anyone else but me."

I'm sort of disengaged, but temptations, pitfalls, and everything else are always close at hand. There's no escaping curiosity, biology, and all else the world throws at you at the most inopportune times. *C'est le vie, c'est le guerre,* or maybe *c'est* just me. This burden of behavior rests upon an inexperienced conscience weighed down quite heavily by an overwhelming concentration of energies. So, my chance meetings perhaps contain only ten percent of pure chance. I seldom got out of chance's way, so to speak.

But let me tell you where I am and when. Yerba Buena, San Francisco. Some call it Goat Island. The Bay Bridge sits on it. Fig trees below where I am sitting are doing fine; the Axis prisoners of war farther on down are being guarded by Marines and are breaking rocks in what almost looks like a purposeful mission. The sun smiles through the heavy-leafed trees above me and I'm thankful for their shade. I'm also thankful that in just a few days I'll be taking that "Sentimental Journey," the final one to my hometown in Michigan. I'll be off to a GI Bill college of my choice in the fall.

This island has welcomed many a sailor and it seems a Gibraltar of a sort. It's almost devoid of humans, and quite unlike its companion, Treasure Island, which is overrun by Navy barracks. Peace and quiet reign here, augmented by an admiral's mansion, fig trees, flower gardens, and buoys near the shore. It's not quite the Garden of Eden, but it's not the Wailing Wall, either.

I said earlier that I ain't misbehavin', and that's true, mainly. And stop right here if you think this is a confessional. But let me tell you a few things that more than one guy can remember.

Galveston, Texas, in January of '43. Four of us gravitated to a place that advertised a complete chicken for just a buck seventy-five. We each devoured a chicken and several side dishes. Having satisfied this appetite easily, Denny says with a blank grin which surrounds his prophetic statement, "Let's get some dessert."

Three passive "O.K.'s" follow.

"I know a damn good place just around the corner. Best time to be there, too."

A wood stairway attached to the side of the building went up two floors, and that seemed innocent enough, considering we were not in Galveston's high rent district. A door opens as if someone is expecting us. There are people expecting us. They and three of us have great expectations. I have none except uncertainty. These girls are as young as we are. Two of us size up the group, another of us says, "Hi, Betty," and she quickly ushers him out of the reception-like room, which is furnished with large sofas, and these are loaded with girls who are giving us the once-over and smiling in curious ways. My two so-called buddies also disappear as if by some preliminary arrangement. I'm left alone, almost to my own devices, or in this case, vices. About three "scouts" head toward me. I'm still standing and pretending to mind my own business. An older woman says in a voice that is politely commanding, "Sailor, won't you sit down, please." Two girls make room for me and a third finds my lap before I realize this is a commercial.

"I'm just with my buddies," I blurt out.

A meaty blonde swings her thigh over the arm of the sofa and says, "How about it, sailor?"

"I'm just with my buddies," I insist.

Another enterprising *femme fatale* pretender, perhaps thinking that my preference lay with her, makes a beeline toward me. She says nothing, just stares, searching for my eyes as if daring me to be typical in this circumstance. After a few eternal seconds she giggles. I get up and try to walk in as respectful a manner as I can toward the door. It's a relief to meet three sailors there.

No longer do I go on a casual liberty with these whorehounds.

I'm much wiser in Seattle, April, '45. Our president has died at a health spa in Hot Springs, Arkansas. The "Hot" has nothing to do with our little unexpected sortie in a questionable hotel, our last desperate chance to get overnight sleeping quarters our first night in Seattle. I wander into Verner's and my room in late evening and hear a loud conversation. I open the door and am not too surprised at what I see. Nor what I hear.

"Five dollars," she says, firmly. She is a wisp of a girl, skinny as a rail, but her face is all business. His is a mixture of urgency and some consternation.

"Two bucks," he almost yells at her. I'm wiser now, also on the brink of a laugh.

The Last Romantic War

"Five dollars or nothing," she says.

"Nothing" seems to rankle Verner. I'm a bit rankled because his enterprise is a surprise. I'm also rankled because he's acting like a cheapskate. "Give her the five," I say. She looks run-down and over-worked. I was about to give her a fiver, gratis, just on those grounds alone.

Verner gives me an annoying look. "Two bucks," he grumbles.

"Give her the five," I insist.

"Gimme a one," he says, shoving a fiver into her willing hand.

I walk out thinking that there but for the grace of something go I. Well, maybe not. Don't think for a minute that I wouldn't rather see Verner spend his money in a different way. I don't even see prostitution as a necessary evil. I see it as a lousy joke on womanhood. I have sisters and a mother, all of whom I love and respect. I suppose that if we could scrape the money-sex out of our culture, there'd be a slightly better chance of curbing the war-mongers, too.

Back in late '43 at a Philly bar, I remember bristling at a Limey who was making some cracks about a girl pro soliciting business near us. He quickly reached my conclusion that we have a lot of mothers and sisters in England and America and that I have four. The war seems to have brought out the worst as well as the best in us. But we're under the obligation to make things better for everyone, which can only make things better for ourselves. I'll step down from the soapbox. Verner never told me if it was worth the five bucks. I didn't ask.

Don't think that this constitutes the essence of my experience. It's easy to dodge the pros of the back streets of love. It's the good gals and opportunistic babes who inevitably catch up with nearly all of us for one reason or another. And, further, the sexual hasn't always been the essential thing. At least, that's about as far as my imagination takes me, if not experience.

I recall the names and cities and moments, even the songs, and shall never forget some of them. The platonic and idyllic encounters even more than the sensual which, even now, are barely worth remembering. I see quality and know values more clearly now. I'm living life as genuinely as I can, and this has a good by-product: a memorable past.

At a mere twenty-one, I'm even now more sure that life is a romantic journey and that someday I'll meet that girl of my dreams. I'm just as convinced as I always have been that those three life jackets and my father's cloth prayer would get me home safely from any theater of war.

I'm almost convinced that the fourth "item" sewed it up. No pun intended, of course. I know too that just staying alive isn't the equivalent of being alive. We can make do and all that. Once this war slides off our backs, then we'll really go to town.

True Tales, Mainly

Like that of all ships, the deck log of the USS *Machias* carries the explicit and expedient events a la Remington or Smith-Corona. A heavy-handed Remington is great for one-finger yeoman typists. That a log is even being kept other than to record whether the weather contains alto cumulus clouds, whether the course changes from 071 gyro to 081 true, seems reasonable, but no seaman gives a damn. That two different typewriters, one a heavy-handed hunk of machinery and the other a more delicate, personal instrument, also would be of no concern.

In short, the *Machias'* log is short on information; even more, that information often errs on the side of authority or, more accurately, of ambition. The *modus operandi* mainly takes the form of sins of omission, and only El Capitan knows. Or rather, he and Yeoman Severson know. But as all the world knows, the truth will eventually out. That is, something closer to the truth. Where and when do not matter. Random tales surface unexpectedly, organically, like swiftly ripening tomatoes.

So it is in the Navy barracks in Alemeda, California, where five survivors of the loaned-out *Machias* gather for their morning coffee and reminiscences. Immune from the U.S. Navy while awaiting reassignment to a Coast Guard ship or installation, we finesse, side-step, and goldbrick through as many daytime hours as possible. Conversation is our order of the day, so any convenient mess hall fills the bill.

It's an utterly new world now. Only days before, it seems

forever; the whole world was screaming the news of peace, that a powerful new bomb had leveled Hiroshima and Nagasaki and that the Japanese militarists had finally yielded to an unconditional surrender. It changes everything. The freedom feeling is being felt in every conceivable way. Authority almost withers away: only the essential military manners remain. It's a fine time to talk openly, intimately. The mess hall tables are rectangular, but the talk is more suited to a round table. The *Machias* knights-errants have many tales to tell. It will be tough to throw much embellishment around us experienced warriors, but conversation is meant for more than advancement of learning. My ears are not closed. The untold tales begin.

Seaman 1/C Lorentz, at the helm on a blackish night while the *Machias* is anchored off Morotai's shore, overhears and oversees an incident that fails to make print in that piece of literature known as the deck log. Lt. (jg) McShane is on duty as Officer of the Deck, says Lorentz. The *Machias* has bedded down at Morotai. The O.D. and the two bow lookouts hear the strange engines of a surface craft rapidly approaching. At about 200 feet, the rising sun flag is faintly visible in the dark. Lookout Sicurella swiftly reports.

"Con, Jap patrol ship is off our starboard bow. Do you hear me, Conn?"

"Con, aye, aye."

Lorentz instantly relays the shock to McShane, who then orders him to alert the captain. McShane, not surprisingly, has no authority to call general quarters or to fire on the Jap ship. In the few seconds it takes to wake the captain, the ship crosses the *Machias'* bow, apparently equally surprised. Its mission, however, is obvious: to quietly land supplies for their observers and hold-outs on our watch-dog island, Morotai.

In a state of undress and as if in a deep nightmarish sleep, the captain could be heard clear up on the bridge.

"Double the guard! Issue them shotguns!" he bellows. And as an after-thought,

"Stay alert. They might return." This he says in a lower tone, maybe thinking that the Japanese crew might hear him.

McShane, hands tied but eyes alert, can do little but tell Lorentz that no doubt the skipper is half asleep and thank God the Jap ship is not in a fighting mood. The ship doesn't come near the *Machias* on its return to Halmahera, a giant island only 10 miles to the west, where about sixty thousand by-passed Japanese troops are languishing. Nor is an entry placed in the deck log about the strange incident. None of us have any inkling of that close call. One well-placed torpedo and Davy Jones would be secreting the story instead. Now, at the table, we come to realize how Tokyo Rose so quickly knew our identity and offered us her cozy, threatening welcome.

A few seconds of quiet follow before Argo offers his first-hand piece of hidden *Machias* lore.

"You guys hear about this one?" He knows we haven't. Even the ship's newsletter seldom has the complete stuff, only the preferred information.

"Well, this PT 105 tied alongside is begging for fresh water. 'Yeah, we'll give you 100 gallons,' Clevenger says. Then he says, 'Ten gallons of torpedo juice. OK?' Chief Water tender "Soup" Clevenger knows he has a deal. It's happened before on Mios Wendi Island, northwest of New Guinea, but of course on the QT."

Argo knows we like this story. We guess it'll lead to a stills aboard ship story. Must be a dozen of untold stories. But Argo goes off on a serious tangent.

"Me and LaBeau seize the moment. Bo asks, 'You guys doin'

a patrol? Can you take us aboard?' An ensign with a doubting smile says 'Sure, come on aboard. We're checkin' that island over there off the port bow. We think the Japs got a radio and a lookout there. We'll have you back by eight bells. O.K.?'"

"Never expected this good luck. A nice chance for action. We get ashore on this little island southwest o' here and there's a bunch'a army guys surroundin' somethin' and so we went close to see what they wuz up to. They had a Japanese officer right there in their midst, and he was neatly dressed in uniform, just standing there. He looks at us as if we could help him. One of the Army guys, I think he had sergeant stripes, says something like, 'We better make him strip. He could have a grenade on him.'"

"Well, this Jap took off his clothes, first putting his hat on the ground, respectful-like. Then he starts from the top and works his way down, eyeing the three or four guys who had their carbines pointed at him. He looks worried. So are the Army guys. Now he's naked and nothin' on him and the sergeant is standing there, not sure of what's next. It wuz kinda funny. About twenty Army guys and a bare-assed Jap, and you didn't know who is really in charge. Well, thank God, this Army "luey" (a new lieutenant) come along and motioned for the Jap to get his clothes back on. Best we could figure out is that he had brains enough to surrender to some harmless, inexperienced Army guys instead of to the Marines, who'd shoot first and then maybe ask questions. They had a lot of scores to settle for what happened to their buddies on the Canal from what I hear told. Maybe he was the guy who spotted ships coming in to the East Indies here and that's where ole' Tokyo Rose comes in. Just a couple of days before that she was on the short-wave radio and she gave us a spooky welcome. Remember how she started out with that spiel about we'll be sorry we came and how our gal friends and wives were steppin' out on us? Then she played the latest hit songs. 'Near You' is the latest. Line goes like this: 'There's just one place for me, near you. It's like heaven to be near you. Times when we're apart, I can't face my heart.' Not a bad tune. Hell, she was doin' us a big favor bringin' those songs near us. She was makin' my life worthwhile, as the lyric goes. Anyways, we had a damn good time aboard that plywood PT. Something like a 40mm opened up on us near Halamahera, but you know a PT can do 40 knots easy."

I remember Tokyo Rose's blurb too well and congratulate myself for not tying myself into a romantic knot. A war plus a sweetheart is too much baggage. Anyway, didn't Shakespeare say something like, the course of true love never does run smooth? I wasn't even on the path.

The seas, for that matter, were none too smooth either around the Indies. Before my inner monologue got going full speed ahead, Yeoman Severson avowed that he had a good fish story, albeit a whopper, that even he couldn't believe. It took him a good ten seconds to make a start. His forehead was furrowed fully across and then flattened as he began.

"Now I'm not too sure about this; maybe one of you know something. I think it was down in Hollandia after we dropped off the last British troop transport loaded with those GIs. Lt. Henning is like he's on a mission. Told me to keep awake for COMPAC material. Said he had some business ashore that would take an hour or so. Acted secretive and preoccupied. Ordered the whaleboat to take him ashore, alone. This is unusual. Logged back in about two hours later. Headed straight for the skipper's cabin with a three-inch manuscript." Then Severson acts like maybe he shouldn't tell his little gem.

"O.K. What in hell's so unusual about that? Go on, go on. What about the manuscript? Did we break the Japanese code or something?" Radarman Leon Baham thinks he's smelled something good. "What was it?"

"Like I said, all I know is what I think I heard. Lt. Jennings is telling Hanna something on the bridge, and I'm looking disinterested and jotting something down in the log book. Jennings said he'd been ashore to MacArthur's headquarters, walked into the building, found no one around, and scouted around, found a manuscript labeled "Philippine Invasion." Nobody around, so he didn't know what to do but relieve them of their "extra" copy. Got out of there fast as he could. Can you believe it? I never told anybody about it because they'd think I was going bugs. But come to think of it, all this happened just a few weeks before they landed at Leyte. It's so damn crazy it just could make sense."

Leon looks at Severson and smiles as if he, Severson, is dishing out another inside tale for which he held a mild reputation. Severson could invent a story even if not tell it well. "Why didn't ya log it in, Sevy? Write it up as a sort of footnote," Leon chides him.

"I knew you guys would think I was shittin' you. I got a better one for you. You guys don't know the half of what I hear. Betcha none of you know that we had an officer go off his rocker up in Bremerton dry-dock, didja?"

"Go ahead, we're suckers for a good story. Gotta tell 'em back home how we won the war with holy mackerel make-believe bait." Leon looks like he's got Severson on the hook. This one, Severson knows, had better be a lot better.

"Any of you guys hear that explosion on a Sunday morning up in Bremerton when we just pulled into dry-dock?" Severson sees our blank faces quickly changing into pure curiosity.

"Half was on leave and the others all got a seventy-two-hour pass. Some of the guys just got transfers or were shipped out.

Toby and Pop Bryan, for instance. Gillam went out to the east coast to a radio school. We were goin' to Cold Bay and the Russians were taking it over. Anyways, just a skeleton crew was around. Me, I stuck around. Inside among the officers there was somethin' goin' on. Just a few guys was around. That wasn't thanks to Captain Hanna. Thanks to Lt. Lucrette."

Severson couldn't tell a story but he knew how to build up some interest, even a touch of suspense. Wasn't only a few seconds and there was a "Yeah, go on. What about Lucrette? Never saw him for months. He ain't the only one who disappeared out there in the Pacific. Don't think I've seen more'n thirty guys out there for months. Yeah, what about him?"

"Well, ya know, I help him with the payroll and such. Just before most of the guys was coming back off their fourteen-day leave and payday was comin' up, Lucrette is actin' funny. Wouldn't check the money in the ship's safe. Couple of the officers got after him, and that's when they figured something was wrong, but they didn't know what. Maybe he was denied leave or something. He was the only guy who knew the combination. They had to haul him off somewhere for medical treatment. Heard they had to drag him off."

Leon came in quick with, "Bet that's one deck log entry that got wiped out. Section Eights don't get any publicity. Damn good thing the crew was gone or they'd 'a tossed him inta the Sound. Money's money, ya know."

"Hey, if you hada' live under the skipper, you'd a' cracked, too. McShane was tellin' me how he'd been on watch for seventy-two straight hours and they were tryin' to break him. This happened somewhere around the Panama Canal. McShane had his 45 by his bunk and waved it at Hanna, Nix, and R.T. who came into his room, stood by the door, and Hanna was telling him that he had to continue to stay on bridge watch. McShane grabbed his 45 and told them, all three, to get to hell out or he'd shoot 'em all. They left him alone after that. Even the skipper stayed clear of him. Don't think it was Hanna's doing, though. Hanna had just made exec; it was R.T.'s doing." Leverson looked kind of smug after that one, something like he was glad he'd gotten that one off his chest.

"By the way, Argo, what happened to your parrot?" Seaman first Bob Mildners knew, but he had to get a rise out of the radioman striker and erstwhile ship's barber.

"Glad ya asked. We both know who opened the cage and let it fly toward Halmahera. Wish I'd a' caught him in the act. There's no telling what I'd a' done to him even if he was second class radioman. We had it aboard for about five weeks. Ever since Bora Bora, I guess. The old man never found out. I guess that evened the score on me for scalping Lt. Spinks at the equator. You know, he had the guts to tell me that if I wanted to keep being the ship's barber and make extra money, maybe I should go easy on his hair if King Neptune threw the book at him. And Zed did just that. Spinks is from Mississippi, ya know, and I'm from good ole Jawja, and we don't have any love-lost twixt us."

"Thought all you Johnny Rebs was buddies."

"Stayed real clear of him from then on."

"Buzz, where'd you go on VJ night?"

It's hardly a memory for me; it's too fresh in my mind. Not only that, but what transpired is none too clear neither. This one I'd just as soon sit out, but Mildners insists. "Wuz you on shore patrol?"

Didn't tell the guys that I'd awakened to all that noise, horns blaring, sirens screaming, freight trains whistling, guys yelling, singing, and here I am lying in my bunk at the Alameda navy barracks, almost noon, and tears coming without thinking. Tears of joy, for sure. It was as if a dam had broken loose without any specific cause. It just did, that's all. It was one hell of a lump of joy. It settled everything quick. But there was a slightly sad side to it, too.

"I had a date with a teacher who was doing her masters degree at Berkely, University of California. Supposed to meet her at the Piedmont Cocktail Lounge in Piedmont. By the time I left the Navy base here, I got shanghied by some well-lit sailors who insisted I join 'em, which I foolishly did. By the time I got to the lounge a couple of hours later, it was deserted. No date around. She was more than just a date, and I could have kicked myself for lousing things up. Lost her phone number. Her last name could be spelled five different ways. I'm gonna find her back in Michigan." I went on with the meaningless and typical details of VJ night.

"So I hitched a ride from there, found myself in Chinatown, and I still don't remember how I got back here to Alemeda. Think I got down to Market Street and the Embarcadero, too. All I remember is people dancing, singing, and fireworks. Guys kissing gals, hugging, and more than that. Not giving a damn. Traded caps with a Navy officer. Had a couple too many, I guess. Glad I wasn't on shore patrol duty. It was a night to celebrate. A night to forget, but it was unforgettable." They all have foolish grins. Nobody talks. I don't pursue the question.

I have other stories too, but not the kind to pass around or even share. They'll be consigned to memory and never released. Not that they were bad; they're simply too personal. I can easily live with them and chalk them up to experience. The others are probably mulling over such reminiscences, too. There are hundreds of delightful and intriguing moments that would never be relived. All of it, of course, is too fresh; perhaps some day I'd fall back on them for pleasure as I had often done while sitting on those depth charges from eight until midnight, reliving so much of my boyhood and especially life on the baseball fields.

Mildners asks me for my home address. I take out my very thin wallet and am about to take a slip of paper from it and write it down. The "cloth" prayer falls to my lap.

"What's that?" he asks. "Gals' addresses and phone numbers, I bet."

"Nah," I say. I put it back carefully. My soft square of cloth hasn't changed in almost three years. I hadn't expected it to. That it was still lodged safely beneath a 1902 wedding photo of my parents was comforting.

While I'm writing my address, 203 Quinnesec St., Iron Mountain, Michigan, I see my house and hear my father respectfully saying, "Never mind son, this will keep you safe." It wasn't because I was off to war and just finishing my nineteenth year. I know now that it was the only manly way he could say I love you. Take care of this. It will take care of you, too. *Capish?* It was the softest command I'd ever heard from him. We were more than father and son; for a moment we were men.

Not that we ever had been equal. He had left Italy and the Capestrano seminary behind in favor of joining some *pisanos* in the iron ore mines of Michigan's Upper Peninsula. His religious spirit never left, nor did his longing for his sweetheart Isabella D'Alphonso. He'd make a living in the UP, saved enough money, made three trips to his hometown, and convinced her to marry him. She had kept her half of the walnut which had sealed his proposal and waited. They raised eleven children through the Great Depression and had surrendered four of them to Uncle Sam. He had risen from a respected miner ("John Jasper") to blaster to captain in a few short years and now to an elected office of Dickinson County Mining Inspector. As his seventh son, what had I done?

There in that US Navy barracks in Alemeda, California, one world seemed to have ended and another begun. It was not a time for sadness: a whole new world still lay before me just as it had for my father. And the horizons of this new world would easily rival those seen a hundred years ago. It would be an easy and exciting move from being a GI to a GI Bill. Just as I had given Glenn McQuillen "all I got," so had I given it all to Uncle Sam, and then some.

Still indestructible, I couldn't be any more beyond the war's school of hard knocks and ready for a civilized school. I wanted the world of a lasting education, not the short-lived cheers and modest money of the playing field. I wanted the top of the ladder, to climb out of ignorance into knowledge, understanding, and further: the ability to appreciate and, ultimately, to enjoy.

The Last Leave

There's nothing like a sailor on leave. Especially in tailor-made blues. Whites needn't be tailored; the blue stripes on white were color enough. I was fortunate: five ten-day leaves came my way. My first, after boot camp in the Kalamazoo, Michigan, area was followed by Chicago (Great Lakes), then Galveston, Texas, Philadelphia, and Seattle after months in the South Pacific and Philippine Theater.

The leaves were a combination of joy and sadness. The going home was fine: to see my parents and family was reassuring; the returning was merely discipline, especially in the spring of '45. Then VE and VJ lightened the weary load. But a far bigger one lay ahead.

Three years and the duration plus six is what Uncle Sam had asked. It seemed a lifetime call of duty. But now he was in the discharge mode. The millions he wanted answered the call one way or another, and he was not in too much hurry to shed us.

I had earned my Ruptured Duck, the symbol insignia of our pending discharge. Mine was scheduled to take me off into freedom from service in January, 1946. The base commander at Yerba Buena consented to my request for a late March discharge. I wanted to avoid the Michigan winter and be home in time to play semi-pro baseball and work through the summer before enrolling at Western Michigan College. Southern California was the perfect unwinding place from the year and a half of sea duty. San Francisco left nothing to be desired. But in just a few short months my easy-going respite from things military came to an alarming halt.

December, 1945, the letter was short and unsweet.

"Come home quickly. Your mother is dying." My sister Mary had kept the knowledge of my mother's serious illness a secret. The Red Cross verified my need for an emergency leave.

Isabella was a casualty of the war, of worry, of diabetes and painful gangrene. My three older brothers—Rudy, Johnny, and Fiore—were already home, safe and sound. I was merely biding my time. And now this terrible price we had to pay. She was only sixty-five and we were losing her. She was the fairest girl, my father said, in the village of Capestrano. "Sabella," (his term of endearment) was the main reason he had left his seminary schooling and sought a promising living in America. Having borne eleven children certainly is evidence enough that she believed in family.

"She is in a peaceful coma," Dr. Huron told me. I pressed my cheek firmly but gently to hers and felt a response. Perhaps it was my pulse which was racing. I tried to tell her everything in one unspoken word. The next day, Sunday, at six o'clock in the afternoon, the telephone rang.

Swirling snow that enveloped the graveside service only firmed my appreciation of life and her sacrifices. We had won the war alright, but I had lost much more than my mother. Isabella D'Alphonso was the ideal mother and person. Even more than my father, she had set the moral standards for our family. She had faith and knew how to direct it. It was ironclad, unblemished, beyond scripture, and unknowingly, it became second nature within me. It was almost as if she died so that we might live. She had faithfully given me an excellent start in life.

I was her tenth child and she named me Idolo, even after the priest's protest. After bearing ten others and still feeling reverent about life speaks loudly of her regard for it. The church insisted on Anthony for my middle name as its assurance of good faith.

Faith, yes faith. Sooner or later it all comes down to that. It is the ultimate idea; it is the link between God and man and the greatest gift we have. I had plenty of confidence in my person and the exceptional crew and those three life jackets, but these did not measure up to the hallmark of my unseen, cloth-covered, faithful prayer.

I know that life is not in the form but in the flame, as E.W. Howe wrote. Surely the spirit of the unspoken prayer is its reality, and it will remain with me forever. Material is fragile, but spirit is not. And I like to think that memory is its companion.

Perhaps this is why, the why of faith, that will keep me in touch with these times in surprising ways long decades from now.

After Words

My mind's-eye vision of history—or what I knew of history—may soon be little more than a mirage if our modernist-progressives write it, or *rewrite* it. If, as Henry Ford said, "History is bunk," it is probably so because "to the victor belong the spoils," and every succeeding generation is tempted to put their own enlightened view in place. Of course, time will tell, but I want to get some words in, "edgewise." What follows shall be more an explanation than an expression of their vision.

My concept of the world, that is, *the workings of the world*, rests with *how we see* the world. *The Last Romantic War* contains a limited, conversational description of the romantic view. To further complicate or perhaps oversimplify my analysis, the remaining views—classical, modernist, and pagan—have only been lightly touched upon.

Without my attempting to describe what is classicism and romanticism, which requires a book, allow me to simply outline the dynamics of the classical-romantic relationship and how it plays out. Simply recall the romance within this book and relate it to the lack of quality this "administration" continually foists upon us. Even worse, their respect for and understanding of equality itself is little more than a pathetic farce.

Let us assume that mankind, over the millennia, finally has become a social entity, has organized family, village, city, state, law, religion, government, and a culture rich in forms and tradition, and now has a civilization. Essentially, this is classical. This promotes our survival, and we are here because of this accomplishment. A civilization must grow, not just change, lest it decay morally and become slothful, less energetic and productive. Remember, it is *SPIRIT* that keeps us alive, not a false sense of it.

The dynamic needed is provided by the romantic spirit. The history of thriving nations is rampant with great names, so numerous, and they live in our annals today. They grew our civilizations. They rose when leadership was needed to reclaim absolute values, not merely convenient, transient, relativistic ones. Simply put, the romantic spirit re-enlivens the values that make a national culture flourish.

Now along comes the villain-culprit. Every drama must have a villain. Every generation has plenty of them: the modernist. They have their new magazines, newspapers, newcomers to the political field. They're far more concerned about fashion and fads, not style, putting their trust in groups, not individualism, the ends, not the means. They are not innovative, only full of gimmickry; they have no past or future, only what today will bring them; they are egoists, not truly concerned for others. They ask not what they can do for their country, but what their country can do for them. I remember what your "greatest generation" did for America. Ask any modernist about this and you will see them smirk. The modernist, bluntly, is everything a true American is more than ashamed of!

Problems are given temporary band-aids. We unleash the Federal Reserve money-dispensing machine, a temporary fix. Bureaucratic czars' rules sidestep laws; anything goes and is gone with the wind.

Your fathers, uncles, grandfathers, and their female counterparts really fought one hell of a war, a war that perhaps too many know too little about. And, more importantly, we were disappointed that so much talent and energy were sapped unproductively in its aftermath. But we still know, understand, and believe that the American ideal is worth fighting for, one way or another.

Our destiny began with courageous people—only a strong minority—of the thirteen colonies. Their spirit and persistence prevailed. The idea wasn't simply opposing taxation without representation: it was grounded in the idea that we held the god-given right to govern ourselves as free individuals and not be ruled by a king or another nation.

We soon realized that we must grow, just as each person must. We had to create our identity, not knowing the outcome. But the means—Manifest Destiny—were natural to our humanity. We have never stopped growing; we have our character, our personality, and the natural need to continue this still uncompleted, wonderful growth.

We cannot turn back. We cannot turn our backs on yesterday as we are doing today. the quiet, sometimes subtle perversions, sometimes audacious manipulations are multiplying but can be stopped, stopped by a courageous America. Most of us know Santayana's warning, "A nation that does not know history is fated to repeat it." We know it; that is, enough of us know it. We saw the quiet, swift Nazi capture of Germany and defeat of the Weimar Republic.

Demosthenes told his fellow Athenians that "if you deprive them of their liberty, [they] will die." History speaks for itself. Historian and educator Edith Hamilton, honored by the Greek government in 1956, issued a surprisingly visionary caution: "We have a great civilization to save—or to lose." Can there be a wiser, clearer, more heartfelt statement?

We've had our Washington, Lincoln, Madison, Franklin, Jefferson, and a host of great Americans in every field imaginable—even our John Hancock. We have never had to worry about decay from within. But "these truly are the times that try men's souls" (Thomas Paine, c. 1776).

We raised the Boomer Generation and maybe spoiled them just a little. We wanted a better life for you, that impossible dream only possible in America. Your fathers didn't talk much of their war experience; perhaps the movie news made them feel that their experience was little more than trifling compared with the big military stuff. That indeed was something of how I felt... until some boomers asked for the "inside story," the ambiance and romance of the personal scenes. They were as certain as I that those days carried much that the years had forgotten. the morbid military facts were already in texts and histories.

The Last Romantic War was never intended to be a memoir, which it is not. It belongs to no genre. It is a wide-eyed view of America, an original, natural, "built from scratch" romantic country which stayed on course until now. The last romantic, "good" war is gone but not forgotten. Its off-spring echo, this growing internal thunder, is its vital reaffirmation.

America, *My Sweetheart*, this is not gush. This book is a labor of love dedicated to you, the country of my parents, my family, and you, *dear reader*.

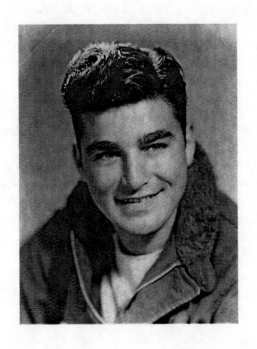

About the Author

Born in 1922, the seventh son of Isabella and Nunzio Gianunzio, immigrants from Capestrano, Italy, the author grew up in the ideal "melting pot" city of Iron Mountain, Michigan. He experienced the jazz age through a child's impressionable eyes, as well as America itself via ten long years of the Great Depression, which taught him as much as did the fine, classical public school system. A professional baseball career with the Chicago Cubs evaded him in 1942, when wartime service postponed baseball.

Tony Gianunzio

Anthony served as a gunner's mate aboard the USS *Machias* in the South Pacific and Philippines campaigns, 1944-5, earning two battle stars. BA and MA degrees from Western Michigan University followed. He taught composition and creative writing in the Sundance, Wyoming, Mattawan, and Portage public schools (1950-2003) and writing at Kalamazoo Valley Community College in Michigan (1987-2003). His interest in writing carried over into part-time writing of sports, features, and editorials for the Metro News and the Portage Herald.

More writing is on his agenda: Worldviews on romance, classicism, paganism, and modernism; a book of aphorisms, *1,001 One-liners*; *A Cat's Cradle of Faith*; *Hucklaberra's Yogisms*; a thirty-two-minute video of creativist behavior entitled "Creativity a la Carte;" and his next book, *Of One Mind*. (Their completion is all based on faith, optimism, talent, and HARD WORK.)

CPSIA information can be obtained at www.ICGtesting.com
Printed in the USA
LVOW13s1809041213

363880LV00003B/547/P